PEACE IN DIALOGUE: UNIVERSALS & SPECIFICS

(Reflections on Northeast India)

PEACE IN DIALOGUE: UNIVERSALS & SPECIFICS

(Reflections on Northeast India)

Edited by

Sujata Dutta Hazarika

AKANSHA PUBLISHING HOUSE

4649-B/21, ANSARI ROAD, DARYA GANJ

NEW DELHI-110002 (INDIA)

AKANSHA PUBLISHING HOUSE
4649-B, Ansari Road
Daryaganj, New Delhi-110002
Phones: 23268193, 9811582579, 09435116718
Email: ektabooks@yahoo.com

Peace in Dialogue: Universals & Specifics (Reflections on NE India)

First Published 2008
ISBN 978-81-8370-144-0

PRINTED IN INDIA

Published by Akansha Publishing House, New Delhi-11002 and Printed at Capital Offset Press, Delhi.

Contents

Section IV: Peace in Texts and Discourses

Foreword

The North Eastern Regional Centre of the Indian Council of Social Science Research (ICSSR-NERC), Shillong, as a part of its academic activity has initiated a series of dialogue in different parts of Northeast India by inviting scholars both from within and outside Northeastern region to discuss issues related to peace and peace process in Northeast. Three such dialogue proceedings were published by the Centre in book form under the rubric *Peace in India's Northeast– Meaning Metaphor and Method: Essays on Concern and Commitment, The Guwahati Declaration and the Road to Peace in Assam* and *Coming Out of Violence– Essays on Ethnicity, Conflict Resolution and Peace Process in Northeast India.*

Now we are pleased to present the fourth series in this direction on *Peace in Dialogue: Universals and Specifics: Reflections on North East India.* The various articles carefully put together in this volume by Sujata Dutta Hazarika under four different sections such as *Democracy and Peace, Redefining Peace: Issues of Governance, Peace: Issues and Strategies in Northeast India* and *Peace in Texts and Discourses* raise different issues with an aim to contain the various ethnic conflicts and to bring an emotional integration of the entire region.

Although the book contains a great deal on the discourse of peace, however, one missing link in this volume is the contribution of Christianity and Church towards peace process particularly in the states of Mizoram, Nagaland and Meghalaya which perhaps we will address in our next volume.

C. Joshua Thomas

Preface

The main aim of this volume is to bring to light the different shades of opinion and research on Peace without any claim to have explored all possible dimensions and implications of Peace and its probable negations. But it does make a modest claim to provide a structure with the participatory concern of further engagement with issues that come up in course of this intervention. An important point in understanding Peace is to override the assumption that because conflicts share some general patterns, the framework used to analyze and resolve them ought to be universal and applicable across culture and context. The arrogance of this approach notwithstanding, we have ample evidence now that universal models not only fail but also tend to trigger resentment among communities, especially at the grassroots level. As a result, in recent years, several scholars have begun to address questions of identity and difference in conflict, conflict resolution and peace-building. This includes exploring the roles of culture, history and disparities in power and privilege and new understandings of identity and community, which are emerging in the context of particular struggles. These struggles often involve challenges to and attempts to transform different structures of inequality and oppression along the lines of gender, ethnicity, race, class, sexuality, and nationality among other things. Our endeavour claims this as the point of departure.

The present volume brings together essays with diverse methodologies and multiple interpretations of the very discourse of Peace, both through lens of universals in the peace discourse as much as the dynamics of its specifics in the context of North East India. This volume aims to take the 'peace in dialogue' programme a step forward by responding to the needs of the political context offered by India-North-east relations to address diverse issues and urge the need to sustain such engagement while identifying new approaches to peace building and introducing new ways of thinking about conflict through a critical reflection on contemporary understandings of democracy, diplomacy, mediation and dialogue.

A mark of distinction in this book on peace and its realization is its display of a sensitivity towards understanding Peace not just in its intrinsic individual form but also through its structural dimensions of integration with a collectivity. Through wider worldviews like Buddhism, Vaishnavism, Bhakti cult and Sufism one encounters an embodied dialogue of Peace that interlinks individual to society. In discussing aspects of peace with respect to the different actors, issues and strategies such as women, insurgents, ethnicity, subnationalism, displacement etc., in the context of the Northeast, we have tried to explore the different ramifications and approaches to peace building that can contribute to a holistic understanding of conflict and its resolution in Northeast without limiting its scope to this region alone.

IIT-G, Guwahati **Sujata Dutta Hazarika**
April 2008

Acknowledgements

This edited volume, *Peace in Dialogue: Universals and Specifics (Reflections on North-East India)*, owes its primary impetus to a group of academicians, thinkers, policymakers and social activists, who have dedicated their lives to the cause of Peace. Their concerted peace efforts were the original encouragement for the organization of a National Seminar on *Peace in Dialogue: Reflections on North East India* at the Indian Institute of Technology, Guwahati (IITG) on 1st and 2nd February 2007. Incidentally, at this time Assam was facing one of its worst encounters with insurgency in the form of an impending threat to the forthcoming National Games in Guwahati. With a national debate and a political discourse of insurgency and national security going on, the wisdom of holding the National Games in a state which could not be declared peaceful was questioned. In this situation, it became imperative on the part of civil society to reduce the operating sphere of conflict and claim those spaces for democratic dialogue and reflections.

We are particularly grateful to Professor Gautam Baruah, Director, IITG, Dr Saundarjya Borbora, Head, Department of Humanities and Social Sciences (HSS) and Professor Sanjib Baruah, visiting professor at IITG for their unflinching support for the Seminar. Our special thanks to Professor Amalendu Guha, Mr B G Verghese, Professor B P Mishra and Professor Sanjib Baruah. They delivered a series of Special Lectures during the Seminar, which were indispensable for charting a clear territory within the nebulous ambiguity that any discourse on Peace entails. We are grateful to all the resource persons for taking the pain to travel to Guwahati and personally presenting their research papers and also revising their papers and sending them for publication on time.

We acknowledge IITG which provided a highly professional

environment, both academically and administratively, for sustaining such an interactive platform.

We are grateful to Dr C Joshua Thomas, Director, ICSSR North Eastern Regional Centre and the team of their young staff members particularly, Ms Fiasta, Ms Christine and Mr R M Pasi, who worked diligently throughout, deserve special appreciation. It is also our privilege to warmly remember here everyone at HSS Department, IITG for the wonderful cooperation during the Seminar, both academic and managerial.

We appreciate Dr Rangita Bali Waikhom for her valuable assistance in the Seminar as the rapporteur and Dr Siby George, Department of Humanities and Social Sciences, IIT Bombay for being the copy editor of this volume.

The Seminar was sponsored by the Ministry of Development of North Eastern Region (DoNER), Government of India and jointly organized by the ICSSR-NERC, Shillong and IITG at the IITG campus. We acknowledge these three organizations with profound gratitude for the logistic support to the making of this Seminar event. Lastly, we appreciate Mr M P Misra, M/S Akansha Publishing House, New Delhi, for his keen interest in the publication of this volume.

Sujata Dutta Hazarika

Contributors

Barua, Archana is Associate Professor of Philosophy in the Department of Humanities and Social Sciences, Indian Institute of Technology, Guwahati. Her areas of interests include Cognitive Science and Phenomenology, Philosophy of Religion, Applied Ethics and Indian Philosophy.

Barua, Krishna is Associate Professor in the Department of Humanities and Social Sciences at the Indian Institute of Technology, Guwahati. Her areas of interest include Comparative Literature, Cultural Studies and Translation.

Baruah, Sanjib is Professor and Chair in Political Studies at Bard College, USA. Currently he is Visiting Professor at the Department of Humanities and Social Sciences, Indian Institute of Technology, Guwahati. His important publications include *Durable Disorder: Understanding the Politics of Northeast India (2005)* and *India Against Itself (1999).*

Bharali, Gita is Research Associate, North East Social Research Centre, Guwahati..

Bhasin, Madhavi a doctoral candidate at Jadavpur University, is working on international conflict resolution and cooperation in Global India Foundation.

Brara, N. Vijaylakshmi is a Gender and NGO Coordinator at NERCORMP/IFAD, Shillong. She works on areas related to gender and has several publications in this field.

Chaudhuri, Mousumi Research Scholar, Department of Political Science, Gauhati University, Guwahati.

Das, Gurudas is Assistant Professor and Head, Department of

Humanities and Social Sciences, National Institute of Technology, Silchar, Assam. Earlier, he was Reader in the Department of Economics, North Eastern Hill University, Shillong.

Das, Samir Kumar is a Professor, Department of Political Science, University of Calcutta. He is author of *Ethnicity, Nation and Security: Essays on North-Eastern India* (2003), *Regionalism in Power: The Case of Asom Gana Parishad* (1998), and *ULFA: A Political Analysis* (1994). Besides, he is a regular contributor to a number of national and international journals on issues such as ethnicity, security, migration, forced displacement etc. He was a member of the editorial board of *The Calcutta Journal of Political Studies* and is presently a member of the editorial board of *The West Bengal Political Science Review*.

Das, Tania is a Research Associate at the Global India Foundation, where she coordinates research programmes on India's Global Relations and she had written a book on *Beyond Cold War: Security Council and International Politics*.

Dutta, Anuradha is Head of the Peace Center in the Omeo Kumar Das Institute of Social Change and Development. She is also the retired Professor of Department of Political Science, Gauhati University.

Fernandes, Walter formerly Director, Indian Social Institute, New Delhi and Editor, *Social Action*, is at present Director of the North Eastern Social Research Centre, Guwahati. Most of his work has been on tribal and gender issues and for two decades he has been working on development-induced displacement. His research work, "Development-Induced Displacement in Assam, 1947-2000" is currently under publication.

Guha, Amalendu was Professor of Economics at Gokhale Institute of Economic Research, Pune. He retired as the Professor from Center of Studies in Social Science, Kolkata. He was also associated with the Delhi School of Economics. He is the renowned author of *Planter Raj to Swaraj* and *Medieval and Early Colonial Assam: Society, Polity and Economy*.

Hazarika, Sujata Dutta is a Faculty member in the Department of Humanities and Social Sciences, Indian Institute of Technology, Guwahati.

Hussain, Monirul is a Professor, Department of Political Science, Gauhati University, Guwahati. Has done extensive work on displacement in Northeast India.

Jain, Rahul is Editor, *The North East Computer Today*. He has also been sub-editor with *The Sentinel* and Executive Editor of *The Eclectic*, a monthly international news and views magazine.

Misra, B P is former Professor of Economics and former Director of the Center for Himalayan Studies at North Bengal University, Siliguri.

Majumdar, Chandrika Basu is Reader and Head, Department of Political Science, Tripura University, Agartala.

Prabhu, V. is Senior Lecturer in Philosophy at the Indian Institute of Technology, Guwahati. His areas of interest include Philosophy of Technology, Applied Philosophy, Peace Studies, Critical Thinking, Applied Ethics and Philosophy of Education.

Shankar, Deepthi is a faculty member in the Department of Humanities and Social Sciences, IITG, Guwahati.

Sengupta, Dipankar is Post-Graduate Fellow in Economics at the Department of Economics, University of Jammu.

Sinha, A C is former Dean, School of Social Sciences, North Eastern Hill University, (NEHU) Shillong. He has written extensively on the cultural history and diversity of the North-East including *Text and Context: Studies in the Himalayan Communities*, 1982. His recent publications include *Himalayan Kingdom Bhutan: Tradition, Transition and Transformation* (2001). Dr. Sinha was awarded Smut Scholarship and invited as visiting Professor in the Department of Social Anthopology, University of Cambridge, U. K. for Lent term, 1983. He was also selected as a Senior Fulbright Professor to visit Universities in U.S.A., and spent one term, March to June, 1989 at University of California, Santa Cruz, USA.

Thoibisana, Akoijam is a Research Scholar at the Department of Humanities and Social Sciences, Indian Institute of Technology, Guwahati. Her area of research interest include contemporary western philosophy, specially the role of the body in science and phenomenology. She is also interested in religious studies, feminism, medicine and bioethics.

Introduction

Sujata Dutta Hazarika

"There is no way to peace. Peace is the way." (A. J. Muste)*

The twenty-first century is faced with many new challenges as we continue to grapple with the origins of violent conflicts and explore ways to prevent their eruption and their devastating effects. How can we seriously address and try to effectively stop the rise in violence all around us: from our homes, neighborhoods, nations to the international arena? Peace is thus one of the major concerns of our social and political existence. Right to a peaceful life is the urgent call of the hour, a rare conformity placed between political, cultural and social discourses. One of the paradoxes of modern life is that while innumerable benefits emanate out of leading a peaceful life, modern life somehow seems to accumulate an equal number of conflict sources. While the 'common person' has a very high stake in Peace, because of her natural aversion to violence, 'common citizen' has no power to negotiate peace, which lies with the State. What a common citizen can do is to reduce the operating sphere of conflict and claim those spaces for democratic institutions.

Most conceptual understandings of Peace explicitly or implicitly stress the destructive nature of violence, and focus on nonviolent solutions to problems and conflicts. At the same time, there is also a consensus among scholars and practitioners that Conflict is an integral part of life. Current debates in the field involve the most effective ways to prevent the escalation of conflicts and to successfully intervene when they erupt into violence through a critical examination of the definitions of concepts of peace and conflict resolution. In principle,

* As quoted in the Editorial of the *New York Times,* November 16, 1967. A. J. Muste was a renowned American non-violent activist.

most studies of Peace conceptualize it as more than the sheer absence of war or physical violence, making a clear distinction between negative and positive peace. Hakan Wiberg (1987) defines negative peace as "the absence of organized, personal violence that is approximately the same as non-war" and positive peace as "requiring the absence of structural violence".

This definition of Peace entails a broadening of the scope of enquiry by addressing structural violence and emphasizing 'Justice' and 'Equality' as necessary preconditions for positive peace to prevail. Thus peace cannot prevail without participation of everyone in decision making and enjoyment of human rights and equality.

An important point in understanding Peace is to override the assumption that because conflicts share some general patterns, the framework used to analyze and resolve them ought to be universal and applicable across culture and context. The arrogance of this approach notwithstanding, we have ample evidence now that universal models not only fail but also tend to trigger resentment among communities, especially at the grassroots level. As a result, in recent years, several scholars have begun to address questions of identity and difference in conflict, conflict resolution and peace-building. This includes exploring the roles of culture, history and disparities in power and privilege and new understandings of identity and community, which are emerging in the context of particular struggles. These struggles often involve challenges to and attempts to transform different structures of inequality and oppression along the lines of gender, ethnicity, race, class, sexuality, and nationality among other things. Our endeavour claims this as our primary point of departure and ultimately materialize into the making of this volume.

This volume brings together essays with diverse methodologies and multiple interpretations of the very discourse of Peace, both through the workings of its universals as much as the dynamics of its specifics in the context of North East India. It aims to take the peace in dialogue program a step forward by responding to the needs of the political context offered by India-Northeast relations to address diverse issues and urge the need to sustain such engagement while identifying new approaches to peace building and introducing new ways of thinking about conflict through a critical reflection on contemporary understandings of diplomacy, mediation and dialogue.

The Northeast has been an area of great and continuous civilisational intercourse throughout history, and has been thought of as "a gateway of commerce and culture that linked India overland to east and Southeast Asia", a "complex transition zone of linguistic, racial and religious streams." The 'indigenous tribes' of the Northeast represent successive waves of migrants, both from East and West, with many entering the region as late as the nineteenth century. The cultural mosaic was made more complex as a result of the British policy of 'importing' large numbers of administrators, plantation workers and cultivators from other parts of India. However, this historical 'connectedness' was systematically undermined by the British policies of progressive segregation of tribal populations into virtual 'reservations' called 'non-regulated', 'backward' or 'excluded' areas that were administered under a succession of unique provisions between the years 1874 and 1935. These provisions excluded the tribal areas from the pattern of administration that prevailed in the rest of British India, from the operation of the codes of civil and criminal procedures and from a wide range of laws that were thought to be unsuitable to the 'stage of development' of the populations of the hill areas of the Northeast, but at the same time allowed a gradual 'democratisation' that was taking place through the nationalist and eventually the Independence movement. An 'Inner Line' system that prohibited access to these areas to all 'outsiders', except those who obtained special permission from the government, created 'a frontier within a frontier', accentuating the political and cultural schism between the tribal areas and the plains and also between itself and the rest of India.

Regrettably, such isolationist policies persisted in the post-Independence period under the mistaken motives of 'protecting' the tribal population against exploitation by 'outsiders'. The cumulative impact of these policies was a deepening of fissures between tribal and non-tribal populations, as well as a contrived and unsustainable exclusion of these regions from the processes of modernisation and democratisation. Inevitably, with the progressive and natural erosion of these artificial barriers, the local populations were brought into increasing friction with migrant populations that were far better adapted to the institutions and processes of the modern world, giving rise to a proliferation of conflicts throughout the region. The dichotomous administrative system both in the pre- and the post-Independence era, produced wide variations between the pace of development in the hills and the plains, with the latter dominating the economic profile of the region, and the tribal areas lagging far behind. It is the wide swathe of the Brahmaputra Valley – comprising nearly 22 per cent of the region – that has long been the most economically active, with substantial plantation and industrial estates and reasonable infrastructure.

Moreover, the region with its critical strategic significance and, as is often remarked, remains tenuously connected with the rest of India through a narrow corridor, the 'chicken's neck' or 'Siliguri Corridor', in North Bengal, with an approximate width of 33 kilometres on the eastern side and 21 kilometres on the western side. This constitutes barely one per cent of the boundaries of the region, while the remaining over 99 per cent of its borders are international – with China to the North; Bangladesh to the South West; Bhutan to the North West; and Myanmar to the East. Illegal migration of Bangladeshi nationals into India and the use of Bangladeshi and Bhutanese territory by insurgents operating in India's North East are a grave security concern for the region. Circumstances in the theatres of conflict in India's Northeast go against the general presumption of a direct and self-evident conflict of interests between the government and its various agencies, on the one hand, and the terrorist groupings on the other. A complex collusive arrangement between various legitimate power elites and terrorist groupings exists in every single terrorism-affected State, and this arrangement facilitates a continuous transfer of resources into the 'underground economy of terrorism'. In contrast to the common perception of terrorist activity as violent confrontation with the government, there is a more insidious subversion of the established order through a consensual regime against a backdrop of widespread breakdown of law and order, and terrorist groupings have demonstrated their preference towards 'systemic corruption', rather than the dismantling or destruction of the prevailing political order. Thus looking at the pattern of conflict in the region, which has been in the grip of separatist insurgencies since India's independence, and ethnic strife thereafter, we can broadly classify the following categories of dissent:

- Movements for secession from the Indian nation-state
- Movements for full-fledged states within the Indian Union

- Movements for autonomy within Indian states
- Movements for reservation or special protection within the autonomous structures
- Strife between tribal population/ groups for control over land or territorial supremacy
- Movement against 'outsiders', foreign nationals etc.

Peace building in North East India, taking into consideration its background of multiple histories and voices in the intersection of innumerable ethno-cultural communities that make up its economic ambit, will have to be seen as a process in transition. Adjusting these diverse sub-nationalities and unique socio-cultural and subsistence economies within the wider Indian sovereign nation state has been a grueling experience for both sides. Although a majority of the communities in this region seem to have reconciled with their common destiny within the Indian union, the psychological problem of adjusting with a so-called ethnic mainstream gives rise to a feeling of insecurity, neglect and discrimination among the tribes which are of the mongoloid origin. This fact is further aggravated by the policies of cultural homogenizatrion undertaken by the policies of Indian Government. Media in the Northeast also reflects this chasm and in fact sometimes aggravates the tension and confusion in the polity. The national and local newspapers which have influence over a large readership most of the time focus on events of violence instead of analyzing the patterns or the process of violence. Moreover, a growing alienation of the civil society from participating in arbitration and peacemaking is leading to the reduction of the operating spaces for democratic institutions and dialogue.

According to the nineteenth century Sociologist, Emile Durkheim, conflict and change are universal features of contemporary societies and may be considered normal, within limits and even conducive to their well-being. Thus, while it is almost normal for every society to exhibit certain degree of deviance, conflict and security threats, both at individual and collective levels, in the case of the Northeast what one sees as a problem is, the increasing dominance of issues, like, insurgency and national security in political discourses which has gradually displaced and reduced those spaces that should ideally be occupied by more positive and peaceful concerns of a democratic civil society. While India's democratic ideals can be redesigned to accommodate the aspirations of the people, one needs to accept democratic space as the only holistic philosophy in its contemporary structure which includes human rights, gender equity etc. Thus all issues of democracy could be achieved through the democratic process and the revival of the idea of integration. The real challenge is to elevate the character of democracy to bring peace in Northeast.

Coming specifically to the contents of this volume it has four different sections dealing four diverse issues related to peace in the region. The first section deals on Democracy, Dialogue and Peace and in this section there are three articles and they explore issues of Indian national policy, diplomatic policy and democratic dialogue – all of which have had far reaching consequences for deciding Peace in this region. In the *Post-Frontier Blues: Deficits of Democracy, Development and Peace in Northeast India*, Sanjib Baruah delves into the region's history as a frontier and the fallout of such a policy, manifested as resistance to the frontier model of development. Introducing the idea of a 'post-frontier Northeast', Baruah draws attention to policy challenges that are attentive to the legacy of Northeast India as an erstwhile frontier. He elaborates on the transformation of non-state spaces into state spaces in the Northeast and shows that different parameters are used by the government for frontier and non-frontier societies. Pinpointing the challenges facing post-frontier Northeast, like massive changes in property rights, intensification of mobility as among the *Char* settlers and demographic transformation in Assam, he compares the situation of the Northeast with that in Malaysia and Fiji. If these challenges are addressed through appropriate policy making for the 'post-frontier society', Baruah sees radical reorientation of Indian policy towards the region and indeed the arising of a new paradigm for the future of Northeast.

B P Misra in his article on *Democracy and Dialogue: Lessons For and Lessons From India's North-East* begins by saying that a modern state is only notionally associational but it remains culture and community specific. He asserted that the modern state have often failed to articulate their particular situation due to their imitative approach. According to Misra India's Northeast is in itself home to a large number of communities and their respective status claims of nativity with one another leads to conflict and strife. Therefore, he is of the view that classical Marxism and modern Liberalism which is both formulated in the tradition of enlightenment is hopeful of rapprochement among all the people despite their differences which will then be the source of unity in a multination state.

Amalendu Guha's piece, *Sino-Indian Peace Process: Background of the Conflict and Its Resolution,* throws up many revelations on threats to peace which are not always external in origin. Speaking mainly to the younger generation of scholars who are not aware of facts leading to the Sino-Indian war of 1962, he attempts to bring forth the trajectory of the chilly experience before the war, the war itself, about half century of cold war that followed and finally the ray of hope now gleaming due to the current dialoguing taking place. The unresolved Sino-Indian boundary question was neglected in the 1950s and gradually disputes that occurred on the border led to the outbreak of the war in which India suffered a humiliating defeat. Conflicting claims over borders along today's Arunachal Pradesh led to an entirely avoidable war, if only the Indian political parties had not created a mass frenzy about the border question and allowed dialogue between the two countries to reach its desired goal. Guha ends in a positive note optimistically hoping that an amicable solution to the Sino-Indian border dispute, which is now in the offing, may give the momentum for solving the more vicious Indo-Pak conflict in a constructive manner.

The second section of essays entitled *Redefining Peace: Issues in Governance* tries to redefine the prevailing discourse of Peace within the wider body of governance, through an analysis of concepts like democracy, dialogue, negotiations, gender and extortion economy. Samir Kumar Das in his paper *Dialogues for Peace or Dialogues for Justice? Towards an Understanding of Peace Dialogues in India's Northeast,* highlights the variegated ways of conducting dialogues and takes cue from Ronald Dworkin's views on taking rights seriously in the light of policy making. The language for dialogue with the state can be either a language of right or one of the collective. The present system of peace dialogue subordinates the rights that are making the collective to thrive. Therefore, Das argues that the importance of the language with which we conduct our dialogues determines the democratic process. His paper also shows how we are living in an age of policies and how such a language of the collective, has appropriated the dialogues for justice.

On Identity and Underdevelopment: On Conflict and Peace in Assam, Gurudas Das says that the idea of making a nation state by the ethnic Assamese cannot be fulfilled due to many complications and one of the reasons was identity. Further he explains the history of Assam based on identity, politics, ethnic conflicts, insurgency and its economy which ultimately led to the reorganization of Assam in 1972. Das also raised the question on the identity of an Assamese and said that there is no particular concept to term a person as an Assamese. He further discusses the issues which led to the Assam movement and Assam accord which he says was due to the fear and insecurity on the identity of the ethnic Assamese populace. Identity and Underdevelopment therefore resulted to political instability and economic stagnation. Das also emphasizes that insurgency was a by-product of identity movements in Assam. He concludes by suggesting that the residents of Assam should be taken into confidence for restoration of socio-political stability and economic development of the State.

Vijayalakshmi Brara's paper *Women in Peace: But Are They in Dialogue? A Case Study of Manipur* gives insight into how the Manipuri women's movement and organizations are extolled for their participation in peace promotion but marginalized in times of peace negotiations. She makes an attempt to map women's immense participation, role and efforts in public sphere, exemplifying the case of Manipuri women. Questioning the mere agitationist nature of Meira Paibis today, Brara seeks to project an alternative paradigm of women actually brokering peace and other concerns of their day to day life. Deepthi Shankar's paper *Are the Voices Unheared? Women in Peace Process* primarily focuses on the neglected gender issues which have surfaced as a consequence of armed conflict. Victimization of women in armed conflict, the very politics of women's exclusion, women's voices, role of UN in championing the gender issue and international campaign on women and peace etc., are the highlights of the paper. The central aim of the paper is to demonstrate the role women can play in development and peace. Tania Das and Madhavi Bhasin's paper on *Structuring Negotiations for Durable Peace – The NAN Approach* analyses peace making and peace processes. The paper clearly brings to light the importance of negotiations in engendering peace. They have identified the threat to peace like inter-ethnic and inter-communal conflicts, structural violence etc. The approach to peace suggested is the Negotiation About Negotiation (NAN) approach, which is a quest for lasting and mutually benefiting peace.

Dipankar Sengupta's *Policy Making in a Terrorist Economy* draws up a state of affairs where terrorist organizations lay stress on extortion rather than their supposedly primary issue of secession. He argues that this shift is not conducive to economic growth as economic packages of the state in a terrorist economy will actually help to fill the coffers of the terrorists. Sengupta suggests a participatory and decentralized approach with the village panchayat as the nucleus because such an approach will alienate the sympathizers of the terrorists. Basing himself on Ajay Shani's contribution in this area, Sengupta explores further to explain how terrorist economy sustains itself.

The third section entitled *Peace: Issues and Strategies in Northeast India* explores the concept of Peace, locating it in the specific context of Northeast India. It is felt that the mosaic of complex diversity and culture in this region and its impending shadow of conflict cannot be completely comprehended without touching the sphere of displacement and dispossession, which in itself leads to further conflict and violence. As a result we have also incorporated certain contributions on this aspect of conflict in Northeast, without which Peace Building would be impossible, because in Northeast the main cause of displacement has been *closely linked with inter-tribal conflict arising out of growing identity politics centred around disputes over land and autonomy*. These Papers have contributed to the understanding of displacement in Northeast India due to ethnic conflict, development projects and environmental calamities.

A C Sinha's paper in this section *State Formation, Nation Building and Aspects of Peace in Northeast India* throws light on how the states in the region were formed. He points out that the present violence in the region is an uneven process of consensus building for a regional civil society. Indicating that India started with a paternalistic attitude towards this region and it still continues this approach, he argues that at certain level space was also provided as far as the question of

Northeast in the nation building process is concerned. Peace can be assured only if consensus building among the regional communities is generated. Civil society must create a space beyond the formal structure, work relentlessly, and must assert itself in a civic way. He concludes that one should use democracy to our advantage. Walter Fernandez, in his paper, *The Imperative of a Peace Process in Assam* reflects on what is happening in Assam and how to move ahead. Recalling the positive step of an ULFA manifesto a couple of years ago and the subsequent spurt of disappointing violence, he narrates the difficulties that have been there for peace in Assam to come true. He calls upon civil society to play its role by raising the cultural, social and economic autonomy issues rather than seeing the whole issue as merely political. One needs to avoid polarization and bring people to negotiating table and civil society needs to play a great task in shaping a vibrant Northeast.

Anuradha Dutta's paper *From Victims to Actors in Peace Building,* makes an attempt to analyze the role of the Bodo women as non-state actors and became actively involved in the movement with the initiative made by the Bodo students' movement. Though succeeded in asserting as key players in settling the conflict the paper also focuses on how women organization are excluded from the negotiating table in conflict resolution etc. This paper clearly defines the trajectory of women as victims of conflict, then actors and finally without any power in the specific context of Bodoland.

Chandrika Basu Mazumdar's paper on *Peace in a Dialogue: Tripura Perspective,* begins with the optimistic statement that militancy is on the decline in Tripura. Delving into the problems and prospects of peace there, she hails the new initiatives of attractive package of rehabilitation which is drawing a large number of militants to surrender. Mousumi Chaudhuri's paper *Genesis of ethnic conflict in the context of Karbi-Anglong district* reiterates the historical background of the ethnic violence in the Kokrajhar district of Assam. She reiterates how historically Karbi-Anglong formed a part of hill districts of Assam which was placed under the category of either "excluded" or "partially excluded territory", this categorization more than being a simple administrative division had significant implications for their socio economic growth. The relative isolation and negligence from the mainstream society and its own multiethnic paradigm paved the way for insurgency and unrest. The demand for autonomous state generated a number of armed groups who compete with each other for supremacy and protection of culture and identity due to threat from other communities. She discusses how transition from their traditional agricultural economy, alien development policies, settling of immigrants encroachment of land, led to a serious onslaught on their socioeconomic structure leading to large scale identity crisis and violence.

Gita Bharali in her paper *Development-Induced Displacement, Deprivation and Rehabilitation in Assam: Critique of NPRR 2003* discusses how development projects such as dams, factories, mines etc have been initiated and implemented in the last five and a half decades resulting in eviction of 50 to 60 million people, out of whom 40% are tribals. Only about 33% have had some sort of resettlement, the quality of which is far from satisfactory. The paper discusses the extent of land acquisition, displacement and deprivation caused by the development projects in Assam and also discusses the rehabilitation scenario in the State and make a critique of the rehabilitation policy from that point of view. Monirul Hussain's paper entitled *IDP's in India's North-East: Waiting for Elusive Resettlement and Rehabilitation* specially emphasizes the issue of ethnic violence in the Karbi-Anglong Hill District, in Assam during the month of October to December 2005. He considered the status of the IDP's in India and called them 'refugees in his/her own country'. Hussain also points out that in the Northeast, all the three categories of Internally Displaced Persons namely; those induced by environmental causes, conflicts and developmental projects together augment the general situation of conflict and violence among groups trying to secure their exclusive access and rights to limited resources.

The last section entitled *Peace in Texts and Discourses* explore the universals of Peace by reflecting on the notion of Peace in the works of Shankardeva, Ajan Fakir, Ibn Rushd, Wittgenstein and Nichiren Daishonin. These papers bring out the concept of Peace as understood by both science and religion as the universal truth transcending mundane questions of application and thus provokes a contagious hope to seek solution. Krishna Barua's paper *Bhakti as the Essence of Peace: Srimanta Sankardeva's Aesthetics of Prayer* brings out how Sankardeva's aesthetics of prayer, initiated in the turmoil torn fifteenth century Assam, restructured the indigenous and traditional aesthetics and infused a new spirit of peace in the lives of the people. She also shows how Sankardeva's teaching can bring peace in the households and act as a link between people in conflicts. *Crossing the Border: Inter-religious Dialogue in Medieval Assam* by Archana Barua is an interesting discussion on the pre-colonial medieval Assam's *Bhakti* movement, which paved the way for a healthy dialogue with Islam in Assam. The key players of this dialogue between two faiths were Sankardeva and Ajan Fakir. Barua bemoans the absence of such inter-religious interactions in contemporary Assam, while pointing out its potential and relevance to bring harmony in the current conflict-ridden society. The point that Akiojam Thoibisana and V Prabhu bring to attention in their *Negotiating Religious Discourse towards Peace* is the paradox of the inherently peaceful message of the religions and their actual propensity to trigger vicious conflicts, due to the tendency among people to look upon 'religious events' with a scientific, historical eye. The two authors propose a way out of this impasse by taking a Wittgensteinian stance towards religious events. They propose that if religious events are taken truly for their religious value, and reserve the scientific and historical criterion for matters of facts, violence in the name of religion could be avoided. Such a view perhaps broadens the base for negotiating the discourses related to religion to ensure peace and how we can bring peace through proper religious interpretation. Rahul Jain's paper in this section, *Rissho Ankoku Ron* draws a parallel between thirteenth century Japan and present day Northeast. The paper speaks about Nichurian Dishonin, a thirteenth century Buddhist sage and philosopher, and his treatise, *Rissho Ankoku Ron*, on politics, philosophy and religion. Jain tries to draw the parallel between the two situations and pleads for replicating the successful practices which worked in one situation in the other. We will be much pleased if the twenty articles authored by scholars from diverse backgrounds in this volume on the theme peace could lead to a meaningful dialogue to find lasting peace in the trouble-torn region of Northeast India.

Section I:

Democracy, Dialogue and Peace

1

Post-Frontier Blues: Deficits of Democracy, Development and Peace in Northeast India*

Sanjib Baruah

The Northeast Indian story is a far cry from the dominant national narratives of 'India Shining' – the slogan that celebrates India's democracy, high economic growth rates and its new-found prestige in the global arena. Today our policy towards the region seems to be at a crossroads. The debate on the Armed Forces Special Powers Act (AFSPA) underscores a policy impasse. The Reddy Committee recognizes that the law has become "a symbol of oppression, an object of hate and an instrument of discrimination and highhandedness" and it recommends repealing the law. But it also wants key elements of AFSPA to remain. So it recommends that some of its provisions be incorporated into a pan-Indian counter-terrorism law, in effect proposing a significant reform with one hand and taking it away with the other (Government of India 2005: 75, 77).

New Delhi's thinking on the region has of late zeroed in on closing the development gap as a magic bullet. Funds transferred annually from the coffers of the Government of India to Northeastern states, according to the Reserve Bank of India's Deputy Governor, now add up to more than what India gets from the World Bank, Asian Development Bank and other multilateral institutions put together. The amounts are higher

* The argument presented here is further developed in my *Postfrontier Blues: Toward a New Policy Framework for Northeast India* (Washington D.C.: East-West Center, 2007). The publication is available on-line: http://www.eastwestcenter.org/publications/

than the total foreign aid that Bangladesh receives (Mohan 2003). In the context of this analogy, it may be useful to recall some of the debates on international development assistance. Influential critics were skeptical of aid because in its single-minded attention to bridging "gaps", it ignored the qualitative factors that might inhibit growth.

A recent World Bank report on Northeast India sees institutional arrangements – one of the qualitative factors that critics of international development assistance had in mind – as the major obstacle to utilizing the region's vast water resources for sustainable development. It finds a highly centralized approach that suffers from "the paternalism of central-level bureaucrats, coercive top-down planning, and little support or feedback from locals." There is widespread distrust of these centralized structures among local stakeholders, who believe that most developmental initiatives would bring no benefits to them. The institutional arrangements are so dysfunctional that even an embankment project designed to benefit the people of an area, may be opposed by the very people it is supposed to benefit (World Bank 2006: 13-14). This provides further testimony to the impasse in our Northeast policy.

The commitment to spend more money to bridge what officials see as a developmental gap is unlikely to get the region out of what the World Bank calls its present "low-level equilibrium" of poverty, non-development, civil conflict and lack of faith in political leadership (World Bank 2006: 30).

Surely, it is time to recognize errors in old habits of thinking, ask some hard questions about how we have come to this point, critically examine prevailing policy frames, and envision a strategic course reversal.

Here I introduce the new term, 'post-frontier', to draw attention to policy challenges that are attentive to the legacies of Northeast India as a frontier. During British colonial rule much of the region was treated as a frontier – an area with vast tracts of 'wastelands' that needs to be settled with population from outside. But what outsiders saw as 'wastelands' had alternative uses for the locals – whether shifting cultivators or hunter-gatherers. It is hardly surprising that tensions between 'outsiders' and those with claims to being indigenous have been a perennial source of conflict in Northeast India. I try to identify a number of policy challenges that can be understood in terms of the region's history as a frontier, and the intended and unintended consequences of policies adopted in response to resistance to the frontier model of development.

Development policy and conflict management tools, which were blind to these contextual factors, have had serious un-intended adverse consequences, including fuelling old conflicts and generating fresh new ones. Directly addressing these challenges – policy-making for a post-frontier – could be the foundation for a radical reorientation of Indian policy towards the Northeast. The term is not meant to describe an actual condition. It is more a tool for imagining an alternative vision of change. This paper is meant as an initiative towards a debate that one hopes, would lead to a new paradigm for Northeast India's future.

Northeast India through the Lenses of Comparative History

In order to place Northeast India's predicament in a historical and comparative context, the region's extraordinary diversity and the in-between space it occupies as a cultural borderland, is a good place to start. All standard accounts of Northeast India refer to its linguistic and ethnic diversity.

Languages in Northeast India "live so close to each other," says Mrinal Miri, that "in many cases, one gets inducted into the life of the community not just through one language but several languages, so people grow up as naturally multilingual beings." When one switches from one language to another and mixes different languages in a conversation, "one doesn't move from one vision of the world to another in a kind of schizophrenic frenzy; but one is, as it were, a native citizen of a multi-visionary world" (Miri 2005: 55).

But what accounts for the region's extraordinarily large number of languages, dialects and ethnic groups? James C. Scott's distinction between state spaces and non-state spaces might give us a handle on the phenomenon. One of the world's "largest, if not *the* largest remaining non-state space" according to Scott is

> *the vast expanse of uplands ranging from northeastern India and eastern Bangladesh through northern Burma, northern Thailand, three provinces of southwestern China, most of*

> *Laos, and much of upland Vietnam all the way to the Central Highlands– more than two million square kilometers. Lying at altitudes from 500 meters above sea level to more than 4,000 meters, it could be thought of as a Southeast Asian Appalachia, were it not for the fact that it sprawls across seven nation states (Scott 2007).*

Historically this region's ethnic landscape has had "bewildering... 'gradients' of cultural traits." A person speaking three languages, for instance, was, and in many places still is, fairly common. If language was a poor clue to identity, so were rituals, clothing, food habits, or body decoration. This often frustrated ethnographers of an earlier era, looking for neat boundary lines (Scott, 2000: 21-22). Thus in the case of the Nagas, ethnographers and missionaries engaged in a struggle "to make sense of the ethnographic chaos they perceived around them: hundreds, if not thousands, of small villages seemed to be somewhat similar to each other but also very different, by no means always sharing the same customs, political system, art or even language" (Jacobs *et al.* 1990: 23).

Scott suggests that such a confusing ethnic landscape has something to do with swidden agriculture – the common mode of livelihood in the hills. Historically, in these parts of the world, land was abundant, but manpower was in short supply. The problem confronting States emerging in the valleys was to have a large enough subject population. Thus wars were not over territory, but about capturing subjects and slaves. The labor-starved States of the plains could not capture the dispersed and mobile populations in the hills for forced labor or military service; nor were tax collectors able to monitor their numbers or their holdings and income. Thus non-transparency in relation to the surveillance systems of the lowland States was the very rationale of the life-styles of the hills and might even explain their ethnic landscapes (Scott 2000: 2).

In this part of the world there was a symbiotic relationship between the non-State spaces in the hills and the State spaces in the lowlands. Thus the categories such as hill tribes and valley peoples are 'leaky vessels'. There were back-and-forth movements between the hills and the plains. Wars produced movements in both directions. While the attractions of commerce and what the lowlanders like to call civilization may have generated movements of hill peoples downwards, it was by no means a one-way flow. Thanks to the extortionist labour demands of the lowland States and, the vulnerability of wet-rice cultivation to crop failures, epidemics and famines, there were also movements to the hills where more subsistence alternatives were available (Scott, 2000: 3-4). This is the material context of the situation described by Miri as one of languages living close to one another and people living in multi-visionary worlds (Miri 2005: 55).

The transformation of non-state spaces and peoples into state-spaces has taken place all through history and in all parts of the world. But that does not make it – or at least all aspects of it – desirable. The transformation of non-state spaces has meant among other things the "massive reduction of vernaculars of all kinds: of vernacular languages, minority peoples, vernacular cultivation techniques, vernacular land tenure systems, vernacular hunting, gathering and forestry techniques, vernacular religion, etc" (Scott 2007). Incidentally, vernacular religion is a much better term to think of the traditional religions of the peoples of the old non-state spaces of Northeast India than the style of thinking that assumes that the faiths of the whole world can be divided into the standardized categories of major world religions such as Hinduism, Islam or Christianity.

Northeast India's enormous linguistic and cultural diversity reflects the resilience of the legacies of historic non-state spaces despite powerful odds. For pre-colonial States in the region such as the valley States of Assam (the Ahom State), Manipur and Tripura, the project of transforming these non-state spaces into state spaces was, to use Scott's phrase, no more than "a mere glint in the eye." But the modern Indian State, both in its colonial and postcolonial incarnations, is able to mobilize the resources necessary to realize such a project. Thus for more than a century, the vast Asian transnational non-state space has been going through what Scott terms the world's last great enclosure movement – "albeit clumsily and with setbacks" (Scott 2007).

Some long-term trends in the agrarian history of South Asia give concrete evidence of this process at work in Northeast India. During the century after 1880, "when statistics appear for the first time", permanent cultivation expanded at extremely high rates in Northeast India, "faster than almost anywhere else in South Asia." Much of this expansion was the result of "people in the agrarian lowlands investing in land at higher altitudes." Indeed "the physical expansion of cultivated farmland remained the major source of additional increments of agricultural production in South Asia until 1960" (Ludden, 2003: 17). The expansion of agriculture has also meant massive immigration into the region from other parts of the subcontinent and consequent increases in the density of population.

This transformation – including the multiple forms of resistance to it and, in postcolonial times, the reformist impulse of a liberal democratic order mediating the process – provides the backdrop to some of Northeast India's conflicts. In the same mix are the proto-national projects that developed around the old valley States – especially Manipur and Assam –, 'entrapped in the linguistic imaginary of the territorial State' (Appadurai 1993: 418). With less and less influence over the drama unfolding in the historic non-state spaces around them, they feel marginalized and besieged in the colonial and subsequently post-colonial, pan-Indian dispensation. The other important historic valley state, Tripura, however, has had a somewhat different postcolonial history.

That colonial Assam was seen as a frontier – an area with vast tracts of 'wastelands' – and that the story of tea in Assam begins with those 'wastelands' being made available to European entrepreneurs, is well known. But tea is only a part of the frontier story. While present-day Assam was the core of this new frontier with its tea plantations, oil wells and coalmines, the rest of Northeast India too had its place in this frontier story. The Inner Line that is still in force in today's Arunachal Pradesh, Nagaland and Mizoram formed the security parameter of the colonial economic frontier. Designed to keep "primitives" bound to their "natural" space in the hills, the Inner Line defined the limits of the "civilizational" space beyond which the colonial State would not provide security of property.

"Development through modernization," is not the same as "development through frontier." There are important differences. "Frontier societies assault and ultimately replace traditional societies" and migration plays a key role in "detaching their populations from the sources of their pre-frontier traditions." On the other hand, non-frontier societies develop through "modernization." Change happens there "in place so that their people have never been detached from their traditional environments; instead they have had to modify their traditions in place" (Elazar 1996: 184).

With the advent of British colonial rule in the 19th century and the "discovery" of tea, Northeast India initially seemed destined for a frontier model of development as a matter of State policy. However, political resistance made this policy frame difficult to justify and "development through modernization" became the default policy model. But the policy shift did not necessarily halt the social and economic forces let loose by the frontier model of development introduced by British colonial rulers. Indian policy-making, whether in the matter of economic development, or peace building strategies, must be sensitive to this conflict-prone context.

Despite the ubiquity of the process of non-state spaces being transformed into state spaces, frontiers are not natural, they are man-made. It is unequal political power – often conquest that turns territories into other people's frontiers. It is not surprising therefore that political resistance in a frontier typically makes an appeal to the principle of self-determination. Yet once an area becomes a frontier, the process is not easily reversed. It may be difficult and, sometimes even undesirable, to reverse some changes in what was once a frontier landscape. For instance, development projects intended to improve conditions may face the constraint of limited labor supply, thus forcing at least a reformist version of the frontier model to be revived.

Policy Challenges of a Post-frontier

This essay is part of a larger work that seeks to identify issues that are specific to Northeast India's post-frontier predicament. Among these challenges are: (a) the legacy of prohibited and unprohibited spaces, (b) the transitional state of property rights, (c) areas of labour shortage, (d) subsidy as a permanent condition of most Northeastern states, (e) mobility-intensive livelihood strategies of settler communities, (f) the transnational dimension of population movement, and (g) an unsustainable two-tiered citizenship regime. Here I will elaborate on just two of these challenges.

a. Accommodating the Livelihood Strategies of 'Char' Settlers

Among places regarded as 'wastelands' by British colonial officials and thus considered suitable for settling new migrants were the *chars* – unstable temporary islands or braid bars – of the Brahmaputra river system. Though some *chars* become permanent, many do not. But since sediments make for very fertile soil, people settle in *chars* despite the hazards of floods, erosion and submergence, temporary as well as permanent.

In pre-colonial times some of the *chars* were used to grow winter crops like mustard and pulses and a variety of paddy called *ahu*. The colonial policy to settle East Bengalis on this frontier was a source of conflict because local cultivators lost their seasonal access to that land. Further, the decision of colonial officials to permanently settle people in the *chars* did not suddenly make them hospitable to round-the-year living.

Yet nearly 2.5 million people – nearly 9.4 percent of Assam's population – now are counted as inhabitants of *chars* and, not surprisingly, 68 per cent of them live below the poverty line (Government of Assam, 2005: 4). A very large part of Assam's Muslim population of East Bengali descent is *char* settlers. Indeed the Assamese term, *Sorua Musalman* (Muslims of the *char* or *sor* in Assamese) is almost synonymous with the term, Muslims of East Bengali descent, as opposed to ethnic Assamese Muslims.

The sedentary bias in development thinking cannot fully grasp the condition of *char* settlers. Often politicians and officials talk about giving *patta* or permanent settlement rights to *char* dwellers. There is talk about cadastral survey and land records as a way of avoiding land disputes. But while it may be possible to do that in some cases, the basic fact is that a flood plain is not meant for permanent settlement.

In wealthier countries, one could have considered the option of gradually weaning people out of some of the most vulnerable and flood-prone *chars* – and having only seasonal cultivation as in pre-colonial times and thus avoiding the annual political theatre of flood control and flood relief.

Mobility is an essential part of the strategies of livelihood for people settled in the *chars*. Lost in the controversy over illegal influx from Bangladesh is this aspect of *char* living. Movement of *char* settlers takes many forms: one or two members of a family, including children, may work in other places; there may be seasonal migration of males; or entire families may move elsewhere. Thus over the years, descendants of those settled in the *chars* of Assam have dispersed to all parts of Northeast India and beyond.

One sees evidence of this dispersal at election times in Assam. Muslims of East Bengali descent go through enormous trouble to vote. Trains to Assam during elections carry large numbers of poor people of 'Bangladeshi' descent – some living in slums in other parts of the country. They travel to Assam to vote in villages – mostly in *char* areas – where they are registered. In Guwahati there is a noticeable shortage of rickshaws and vegetable peddlers on election day, because many people in these occupations leave the city and return to places where they are registered to vote. Voting is clearly more important to this segment of the subcontinent's multitude than to many upper and middle class citizens. This is because their claim to being in the country could rest on something as fragile as a 'voter's slip', given the conflation in public discourse between the dispersal of earlier generations of settlers and the question of illegal immigration.

The Indian discourse on 'Bangladeshis' takes attention away from the question of what attracts outsiders to the once prohibited parts of this post-frontier region, notably places like Arunachal Pradesh, Nagaland and Mizoram. Descendants of *char* settlers have responded to the growth of informal land markets and are getting dispersed all through the region.

b. Still a Frontier?

While the dispersal of the descendants of earlier generations of *char*-settlers is an important dimension of India's 'Bangladeshi' discourse, there is little doubt that significant levels of cross-border migration from eastern Bengal has also continued. The Partition could not suddenly change the logic of a frontier and switch off the flow of people from one of the subcontinent's most densely populated areas, to a relatively sparsely populated region that was once regarded as a frontier open to new settlements, but is now separated by an international border. Indeed from the point of view of Northeast India, the effect of the Partition was mostly to intensify the migration pressure from East Bengal, with Hindu refugees now becoming part of the flow.

It is often difficult to distinguish a Muslim Bangladeshi from a mobile *char*-settler – mostly Muslims of East Bengali descent. At the same time the political consequences of the perception that this migration is unstoppable cannot be exaggerated. In my book *India against Itself*, I had suggested that there is affinity of the situation of Assam with that of Malaysia and Fiji because in all three places large-scale colonial-era immigration had produced a stubborn pattern of conflicts between groups seen as immigrant and those with claims to being indigenous. There are demands on the part of groups claiming to be indigenous for primacy in terms of official cultural symbols, economic opportunities, and even political power in all three places. Cultural policy and immigration policy are especially sensitive issues and they have seriously threatened democratic stability.

Assam's long slide into political instability including the present era of insurgency and counter-insurgency began in 1979 as a social movement protesting immigration. The situation is structurally similar to the political crises in Malaysia and Fiji. But while Malaysia and Fiji managed to develop institutions and practices – albeit fragile ones – that are responsive to indigenous demands, in Assam there has been little acknowledgement that the immigration question requires a robust policy response. The continuation of immigration into Assam in the postcolonial era has made an already precarious demographic and political balance worse. The fact that Malaysia and Fiji are independent sovereign countries with jurisdiction over immigration policy, while Assam is not, has made all the difference in producing these very different outcomes (Baruah 1999, 67-68).

Anindita Dasgupta has pursued the comparison between Assam and Malaysia in greater detail. While Malaysia officially froze immigration and "clamped the lid firmly on the citizenship issue," she writes, thanks to the Partition and the emergence of "a new migrant-exporting state, East Pakistan/Bangladesh," Assam did not. The settlement of refugees in Assam took place despite significant Assamese opposition, and it "re-opened the matter of citizenship time and time again." The absence of an effective immigration policy has produced, in her words, "a sense of a demographic disaster" from the perspective of the indigenous population of Assam (Dasgupta 2005). However, both immigrants and locals in Assam have adapted to the demographic transformation more creatively than is usually recognized.

A passage that often appears in the literature on immigration to Assam is that of C. S. Mullan, a British colonial official responsible for the census report of 1931. He had predicted that, "immigration was likely to alter permanently the whole future of Assam and to destroy more surely than the Burmese invasion of 1820, the whole structure of Assamese culture and civilization" (cited in Sinha, 1998).

In retrospect, Mullan was both right and wrong. The demographic transformation of Assam did indeed take place exactly as Mullan had predicted. But contrary to Mullan's prediction, as Monirul Hussain points out, "the entire East Bengali Muslim peasant community" adopted Axomiya or Assamese as their mother tongue (Hussain 1993: 207). This has produced a cultural politics very different from what Mullan had in mind. Thus the real fears of the ethnic Assamese today, as M.S. Prabhakara argues, are quite different from the "standard" view. It is not so much that they fear that Bengali speakers would eventually outnumber them and that the existence of the Assamese and their culture are in danger. Their real fear is that the new generation of Assamese speakers – mostly Muslims of East Bengali descent – would claim Assamese as their own language "stealing away, as it were, a crucial cultural patrimony which defines the Assamese people" (Prabhakara 1999: 70).

But while Assam may have adapted creatively to its massive demographic transformation, its present political troubles also are, to a significant extent, the result of the seemingly un-resolvable nature of the problem of illegal immigration from Bangladesh. The issue has become further complicated by trends towards Islamicist cultural radicalization in Bangladesh.

But while Indians talk about millions of Bangladeshis living illegally in India, official Bangladesh flatly rejects the notion. There are no mutually agreed upon procedures between India and Bangladesh for identifying – not to speak of deporting – illegal immigrants. Thus when Indian law-enforcement officials deport a Bangladeshi national, they drop the person in the no-man's land between the two countries. A person is literally thrown out of the country and s/he is at the mercy of two armed groups – the Indian Border Security Force (BSF) on one side and the Bangladesh Rifles (BDR) on the other.

This is a rather pathetic performance of sovereign power by a State with big power ambitions. No sovereign country would like to accept a person unilaterally deported by another country. There is little recognition in India that a deportation decision involves two countries and not one. Were official Bangladesh and official India to find a way to talk about cross-border population movement rationally and as equals, at least some aspects of it could be better managed.

A post-frontier policy paradigm would necessarily mean recognizing the transnational dimension of many of Northeast India's challenges including the question of the cross-border movement of people. Turning the region's international borders from spaces of confrontation into spaces of cooperation would facilitate policy-making more generally in areas such as developing water resources and transportation.

The Bangladeshi question, however, is only a part of the larger question of immigration and demographic transformation of the region, and the perception of minoritization by indigenous groups, that animates many conflicts. Last month the Hindi-speaking migrants in the area around Tinsukia in Upper Assam became a focus of attention when the community was targeted for attack by ULFA seeking to open a third front, when faced with the pressures of a counter-insurgency operation.

Tinsukia as a railway junction and urban centre developed in the last century primarily to take out coal, oil, tea and timber to the rest of India. Before its twentieth century transformation, Tinsukia, then called Bengmora was the capital of the independent Muttock (or Motok) kingdom that came under the British colonial rule in 1842, fourteen years after the rest of Assam. Today for all practical purposes Tinsukia is a Hindi-speaking city where the Assamese and other indigenous communities are a minority, while the villages around it are dominated by the Motok-Moran people proud of their history of political resistance. These villages have been a solid source of support for the ULFA. That the hinterland of an urban area marked so clearly in terms of its contemporary political economic niche and a Hindi-speaking cultural profile would be a natural magnet for ULFA is not surprising. There are few other places in Assam where ULFA's thesis that natural resources are being sucked out to the rest of India in a classic colonial relationship seems more plausible.

Towards an Alternative Policy Frame

Siddharth Deb's *The Point of Return* is a poignant novel on the lives of the refugees of the 1947 partition and their descendants in a nameless Northeast Indian hill state. In a region where the idea of ethnic homelands appeals to local political activists, as well as to policymakers looking for ways to put a lid on conflicts, the Partition refugees are seen as interlopers. As a result, the refugees after leaving "their homes forever to try and find themselves within the nation," discover that their journey is not over. "The hills that appeared beyond the horizon were only another mirage, their destination just another place that would reject them." The narrator on a visit to his 'hometown' remembers the 'life time of fear' that the protagonist had felt, and from which the son, the narrator, had run away to escape. A hill-town that had "drummed in the message of death" to the protagonist, he imagines, must have seemed "like a lost spot on the map of the nation, its remote beauty and even more remote violence surfacing in the national newspapers only as little single-column reports of 'disturbances'" (Deb 2004: 292, 295).

Finding ways to compensate the indigenous peoples of Northeast India, symbolically or substantively, for the historic injustice done to them by the colonial imagining of the region as a land (almost) without people, should undoubtedly have been a priority in India's approach to Northeast India's postcolonial future. That did not happen, at least not as an explicit goal of Indian policy. This is undoubtedly a major reason for Northeast India's troubled postcolonial politics.

But at the same time it is in the very nature of what is once a frontier that not all changes in its landscape can be wished away and undone. Thus in Assam we intuitively accept that tea plantation and *char* lands cannot be returned to their original claimants. But ironically, we do not accept that reality when it comes to, say, land occupied by impoverished descendants of tea workers. However, the issue has not been explicitly presented this way to the public, thanks to the mystification by a policy discourse that makes ethnic homelands seem to be the epitome of social justice – a discourse that is in fact completely out of sync with the region's actually existing political economy.

Compensating for historical injuries in a frontier can sometimes take the form only of symbolic justice.

In a post-frontier condition, trying to undo history by enforcing hard boundaries between the indigenous and the outsider – as Indian policy seeks to do in many parts of the Northeast – restricts the capacity to aspire to certain ethnically defined groups and not to others, and risks perpetuating a politics of violent displacement and ethnic cleansing.

The recent reorientation of Indian policy towards Northeast India is mostly a commitment to spend money to bridge what officials see as a developmental gap. It is not a break from the tradition of incremental policy-making by muddling through. It is unlikely to get the region out of its present "low-level equilibrium" of poverty, non-development, civil conflict and lack of faith in political leadership (World Bank 2006: 30). What is needed is a radically new paradigm for Northeast India's future.

When Amitav Ghosh went to the Thai-Burmese border in 1996 after visiting the leader of the Burmese democracy movement Aung San Suu-kyi in Rangoon, he had hoped to find that democracy would have an answer to Burma's unresolved civil war. But by the time he left he was no longer sure (Ghosh 1996: 49). On democracy's ability to resolve civil conflicts, Ghosh would not have found grounds for more certitude and optimism across Burma's border to India.

For while formally democratic through much of its history, the postcolonial Indian State has asserted sovereignty in the Northeast with significant display and use of military power.

Indian policy towards the Northeast is at a crossroads today. The debate on the Armed Forces Special Powers Act underscores a policy impasse. The Reddy Committee, to its credit, recognizes that the law has become "a symbol of oppression, an object of hate and an instrument of discrimination and highhandedness" in the region and it recommends repealing the law. But it also wants the key elements of AFSPA to remain. So it recommends that some of its provisions be incorporated into a pan-Indian counter-terrorism law, in effect proposing a significant reform with one hand and taking it away with the other. The stated goal of this contradictory recommendation, remarkably enough, is to end Northeast India's sense of being discriminated against (Government of India, 2005: 75, 77).

AFSPA is about to enter its sixth decade – it is almost as old as Indian democracy. Arguably, illiberal democracy is the only kind Northeast India has known. Yet if the current debate on AFSPA is any guide, no one expects a sudden outbreak of tranquility. There is no credible roadmap to get Northeast India out of what the World Bank calls its present "low-level equilibrium" (World Bank 2006: 30). Surely, it is time to recognize errors in old habits of thinking, ask some hard questions about how we have come to this point, critically examine prevailing policy frames, and envision a strategic course reversal.

While commenting on the dysfunctional nature of the institutional arrangements governing water resources in Northeast India, the World Bank warns of the dangers of path dependency – of being locked into bad choices even when better alternatives are available. What is needed in order to build a more accountable institutional framework, it says, is "strong political will to counteract the tendency of a society to follow the path it has already taken due to the political or financial costs of changing it" (World Bank, 2006: 14). This applies not only to managing water resource, but to India's entire approach to the Northeast.

While in Burma, Amitav Ghosh had pondered over the inherent arbitrariness of national boundaries in this especially heterogeneous part of the world with many "putative nationalities." He concluded that on balance, Burma's best hope for peace "lie in maintaining intact the larger and the more inclusionary entity that history, albeit absentmindedly, bequeathed to its population almost half a century ago" (Ghosh 1996: 49). The same can be said of Northeast India.

But to be able to break away from the region's troubled past and present – its post-frontier blues – a new policy vision must also be post-national: one that is not entrapped by the national security manager's narrow imaginary of the nation state, where nation building as a metaphor becomes "a handsome neoclassical building in which political prisoners scream in the basement" (P.T. Bauer, cited in McCloskey, 1990).

References

Appadurai, Arjun (1993) "Patriotism and its Futures", *Public Culture*, vol.5, no.3, pp.411-29.

Baruah, Sanjib (1999) *India Against Itself: Assam and the Politics of Nationality*, Oxford University Press, New Delhi.

Dasgupta, Anindita (2005) "Postcolonial Ethnic Management: Assam Through the Prism of Malaysian Experience" (Unpublished paper).

Deb, Siddhartha (2004) *The Point of Return*, HarperCollins (Ecco Paperback edition), New York.

Elazar, Daniel J. (1996) "The Frontier as Chain Reaction" In Yehudah Gradus and Harvey Lithwick, eds., *Frontiers in Regional Development*, Rowman and Littlefield: Lanham, MD, pp. 173-90.

Ghosh, Amitav (1996) "A Reporter at Large: Burma," *The New Yorker*, August 12.

Government of Assam. (2005), Assam Administrative Reforms Commission, *Interim Recommendations*, Part IV.

Government of India (2005), Ministry of Home Affairs, *Report of the Committee to Review the Armed Forces Special Powers Act, 1958*. Available online: http://www.hindu.com/nic/afa/

Hussain, Monirul. (1993) *The Assam Movement: Class, Ideology and Identity*, Manak Publications, Delhi.

Jacobs, Julian, Alan MacFarlane, Sarah Harrison & Anita Herle. (1990) *The Nagas: The Hill People of Northeast India: Society, Culture and the Colonial Encounter*, Thames and Hudson, London.

Ludden, David. (2003) *Where is Assam? Using Geographical History to Locate Current Social Realities* (CENISEAS Papers 1). Guwahati, Assam: Centre for Northeast India, South and Southeast Asia Studies, Omeo Kumar Das Institute of Social Change and Development.

McCloskey, Donald N. (1990) *If You're So Smart: The Narrative of Economic Enterprise*, University of Chicago Press, Chicago.

Miri, Mrinal (2005) "Community, Culture, Nation," *Seminar* (New Delhi) 550, June.

Mohan, Rakesh (2003) "Economic Development of the North East Region" (incomplete)

Prabhakara, M. S. (1999) "Of State and Nationalism", *Frontline* (Chennai) 16 (21) October 22, pp. 68-70.

Scott, James C. (2000) 'Hill and Valley in Southeast Asia. . . or Why the State is the Enemy of the People who Move Around . . . or . . . Why Civilizations Can't Climb Hills' in http://www.artsci.wustl.edu/~symp2000/jscott.PDF (2 November 2002).

Scott, James C. (2007) Chapter 1 of unpublished book manuscript.

Sinha, S.N. (1998) "Report on Illegal Migration into Assam", Report submitted by the Governor of Assam to the President of India, November 8. Online at: http://www.satp.org/satporgtp/countries/india/states/assam/documents/papers/illegal_ migration_in_assam.htm (Accessed 28 March 2006).

Some Reflections". Keynote address delivered by Dr. Rakesh Mohan, Deputy Governor, Reserve Bank of India on the occasion of the 8th anniversary of North East Development Finance Corporation (NEDFi), Guwahati, Assam on September 19.

World Bank (2006) *Natural Resources, Water and the Environment Nexus for Development and Growth in Northeast India*. Strategy Report. (June 28), Washington D.C., World Bank.

2

Democracy and Dialogue: Lessons For and Lessons From India's North-East

B P Misra

Democracy requires that the people give themselves a government of their choice. Cutting across cleavages, a 'we'-feeling therefore becomes a necessary precondition for the democratically constituted modern states. The nation which epitomises this 'we'-consciousness remains no longer a transcendent category but becomes immanent in practice.

But, generally speaking, a modern state is only notionally associational, and as a matter of fact, it remains culture and community specific. In its ideal type, the total banal geographical space of the globe was carved out in patches among a few territorially demarcated nations to form the different political spaces called states that had served primarily the purposes of market sharing for the rising middle classes and the capitalists once upon a time. But in such cases where the modern state was created on the ruins of empires or conquests of the old, multiple cultural groups have been incorporated in a single political space thereby creating the problem of multiculturalism and national integration. Many of these latter groups were also incidentally the less developed countries for whom their developed forerunners provided the role model. Due to this imitative approach, they have often failed to articulate their specific situation in their own light, and be selective in their borrowed wisdom. For them, the political space, the cultural space, and the economic space were no longer coterminous. The incongruities of political space and cultural space pose a challenge for them from within, while the rapidly expanding economic frontier on the heels of global liberalisation affects the stability from without.

The problem is thus in-built for the new states; but interestingly enough it has not spared the old developed ones either during the contemporary period because of different reasons. In the western countries the problem of multiculturalism has made a permanent place for itself in the political discourse because of the pressing compulsions of accommodating suitably the large influx of migrants from the less-developed countries of Asia, Africa, or Latin America.

India's north-east, however, provides a very curious mix of several attributes that defies a strait-jacket fit with any other. The area is economically backward, not developed. A very large number of communities are autochthonous and native to this region, or else the history of their migration is a few centuries old. But their respective status, claims of nativity, and spheres of jurisdiction are increasingly being contested vis-à-vis one another leading to intolerance and strife. At the same time comparatively fresh immigration - both legal and illegal - of the presumed 'others' raises the possibility of marginalisation of the pre-existing people thereby impelling some of the latter to go for organised violence against the late-comers with the avowed object of achieving a fuller but sectional autonomy in disregard of the democratic norms and practices that could be shared by all.

II

What, then, can be the source of unity in a multination state? Classical Marxism and modern Liberalism - both formulated in the tradition of Enlightenment - have been hopeful of rapprochement among all people despite their plurality.

Among the liberal thinkers, Rawls claimed that in a plural society, public agreement on questions of political and social justice supports ties of civic friendship and secures the bond of association. While trying to understand the nature of the European Community, Habermas argued that European unity cannot be based upon the shared traditions, cultures, and languages that characterised the nation states. Instead, European citizenship must be founded on a post-national constitutional patriotism.

But this vision often faces various problems on the ground because the states are not pure associations of Ferdinand Tonnies' binary conceptualisation. Further, even if the state is held to be an association to begin with for the sake of argument, there is a certain rigidity about its existence, unlike that of associations, because of which it tends, once it comes into existence, to legitimise itself with the stable nuances of a community. Every nation struggles to discover its approved anthem, costume, language, religion, heroes, festivals, birds, and even animals in as much as a community may have its own totems and taboos. Taylor has pointed out that even the model experiments in constitutional patriotism, France and the United States, have always fallen back upon some of the trappings of other nation-states like founding myths, national symbols, and ideals of quasi-ethnic membership.[1] It was noted by Navlakha that the inevitable idiom of majority group nationalism in most of the new states of Asia suffers from an inherent contradiction. "While it provides the necessary national identity of the majority community in the international arena, it divides the majority, from other groups within the country..."[2] Kymlycka and several others have pointed out that the fact of two national groups sharing the same principles of justice is not a sufficient reason for them to join (or remain) together, rather than remaining (or splitting into) two separate countries. The case of Norway's seceding from Sweden or the several recent attempts by the francophones in Canada to separate themselves off from the Anglophones, even while sharing the common ideals of liberal democracy, show abundantly the limitations of the liberal hope.[3]

Marx and Engels had said that national differences and antagonisms would gradually vanish 'owing to the development of the bourgeoisie, to freedom of commerce, to the world-market, to uniformity in the mode of production, and in the conditions of life corresponding thereto. The supremacy of the proletariat would cause them to vanish still faster'.[4] Prior to the Russian Revolution (1917), Lenin had echoed the same sentiments as above, and said that the aim of socialism was 'not only to bring the nations closer together but to integrate them'.[5] But, within a few years of the Revolution, Lenin came to realise that national and state distinctions among peoples and countries 'will continue to exist for a very long time to come, even after the dictatorship of the proletariat has been established on a world-wide scale', and any demand for 'the elimination of variety' was nothing short of 'a pipedream'.[6]

After another couple of years, Stalin affirmed that "the period of the victory of socialism in one country does not create the necessary conditions for the amalgamation of nations and national languages, that, on the contrary, this period create favourable conditions for the renaissance and efflorescence of the nations".[7] It may be noticed that Stalin identified the weakness to be 'the victory of socialism in one country', but Lenin was, much earlier, not hopeful of reaching the Marxist millennium 'even after the dictatorship of the proletariat has been established on a world-wide scale'.

In one of his 1925 addresses, Stalin had noticed that the Revolution had awakened to new life 'a number of hitherto unknown or little-known nationalities', by 'stirring up the lower ranks of humanity and pushing them into the political arena'. "Who could have imagined", exclaimed Stalin, "that old, Tsarist Russia consisted of no less than fifty nations and national groups?"[8]. And, then, in September 1989, when the Soviet Russia was heading towards disintegration, Mikhail Gorbachev pronounced, "As a result of historical developments, even if they were contradictory, a single federal socialist state took shape inhabited by more than 100 ethnic groups."[9]

The policy adopted by Soviet Russia towards multiculturalism had, broadly speaking, the following features:

1. A policy of federal consociation was followed in the case of large, geographically well-defined, and comparatively more developed nationalities by granting them statehood within the federation, together with the acceptance of the right of nations to self-determination;

2. Regional, but not national autonomy was awarded to those communities who were not as large or developed as above, but whose aspirations for self-rule could not be ignored due to various reasons particularly because of their regional concentration;

3. Cultural rights were given to those minorities who had a developed culture but were not regionally concentrated

enough to claim a well-defined area for themselves; and, finally,

4. A policy of assimilation was forwarded for 'the belated nations and peoples', 'each possessing a primitive culture, a separate language, but without its own literature', people 'in a state of transition' - to help them all 'cast off the shell of small-nation segregation' as also to facilitate their 'access to the benefits of higher culture'.[10]

The collapse of the Soviet Union in recent years was hastened not so much by its failure to contain the aspirations of its diverse ethnic groups, but because of the ubiquities of its political involvement outside, coupled with the crisis of the command economy within, and the penetration of its boundaries by the modern technology of mass communication favouring the culture of consumerism. It is no small wonder that the Soviet Union could successfully inherit the vast expanses of the Czarist Russia at a time when the right of nations to self-determination was considerably a strategic legitimation after the First World War to help carve out separate states on the ruins of the Austro-Hungarian Empire, the Ottoman Empire, and German expansionism.

But, be whatever it may, at the global level, along with the growth of ethnic, cultural or national identities, there has been a tendency for nations to proliferate. Not to speak of the subjugated colonies asserting independence, even the co-sharers in a common political milieu appear to opt for partition. As a result, the system of organising the world's land and population into sovereign states has grown rapidly during the last one hundred years, expanding from around 50 states in 1900, to 75 on the eve of World War II, to 160 before the disintegration of the Soviet Union, to 192 member states of the United Nations as at present. But, even now, only a small number of these states are sufficiently ethnically homogeneous. According to some estimates, there are over 5000 ethnic minorities in the world constituting a potential seed-bed of adverse political fall-out for the global state system. The much-hyped Globalisation continues its forward march being overshadowed by the prospect of fragmentation, notwithstanding the promises of Liberalism or Marxism.

III

The question therefore arises - what is there about the modern world system that hinders multicultural harmony and promotes ethnic nationalist movements? Let us first try to understand the problem briefly at both the political and economic levels before turning to cultures.

First, the ideology of the global political order embracing such conflicting principles as self-determination and representative democracy on the one hand, and sovereignty and territorial integrity on the other, generates group-consciousness at various levels that are sometimes not in unison. During anti-colonial struggle the nationalists could hold these two positions simultaneously when advocating self-determination in opposition to colonial rule. But, the harmony of interests that combined against imperialism fractures into a cacophony *of* sub-national challenges to state boundaries once independence was attained.

Secondly, the development of underdevelopment of the new states was already a fait accompli during the colonial rule. And, then, after gaining independence, the uneven economic development within a country due to either a deeper penetration of capital or because of late incorporation into the fold of capitalism may create a situation resembling internal colonialism, thereby impelling some of the ethnic groups to mobilise themselves and demand separation.

Lastly, the situation becomes complicated because it is not always practicable to draw and redraw the country boundaries at will. It has to be remembered that despite the realist conception of the world system as being anarchic, redrawing of boundaries cannot be negotiated exclusively between two contesting parties without the tacit consent or even encouragement of some of the more important global players. Considerations of geo-politics and balance of power in a canvas of continuously shifting equilibrium may either help or hinder the growth of few state.[11]

Jackson and Roseberg have coined the concept of the inhibited state in order to explain the maintenance of African boundaries. Their common vulnerability to internal ethnic turmoil restrains them from supporting efforts to change boundaries.[12] Keohane's notion of specific reciprocity in which the behaviour of each state is contingent on that of others supplements the above view.[13] Riggs argues that all the members of the United Nations now belong to a self-preservation club in which the maintenance of existing state boundaries has become a top priority.[14]

But all these should not be taken to imply that the global or the regional hegemons in the marketplace of international competition are always constrained by their mutual inhibition or reciprocity that may be more of a characteristic of the small and the weak in Asia or Africa. The major and regional powers may support dissident ethnic groups in a third country as they themselves compete for economic and geopolitical advantages in the global arena. With the world capitalist system being divided into the core, periphery and the semi-periphery, consolidation of one's own and fragmentation of the others along ethnic lines may be a desirable strategy of the powerful, because these would provide an additional support to the system as a whole to perpetuate itself. On the one hand, the myriad of small states would remain dependent on the goodwill of their overlords; and, on the other, it would be easier to manipulate national inequalities among states rather than living with the uncertain prospects of regional inequalities within states creating a permanent tension for the system as a whole.

The basic structure of the capitalist world economy may be assumed to be organized along an axial division of labour reflected in a core-periphery polarisation, and a political system of theoretically sovereign but practically a few sovereign and many dependent states bound together within an inter-state system. This singular historical system has what Wallerstein calls a geo-culture, meaning that there are norms and values which serve to legitimise the world system as a whole and provide it with the much needed institutional support. What Gramsci had termed as 'the war of position' has been decisively won as at present by the western capitalist civilisation.[15] The Romanticists, and then Vico, or Herder, or even a Hegel had placed an important role upon the 'folk-spirit' or different patterns of social mind or national character of different people. But now the irony is that the easterners, the backward and 'the people without history' have won their political freedom only to be subjugated culturally by the western mind in their fresh wave of global conquest.

Elaborating further upon the idioms of Wallerstein I would place some of the principal geo-cultural values of the age as follows:

(1) People are divided into nations sharing among them a common language, history, territory, and a self-awareness of their distinction from others;

(2) Nations have the right of self-determination;

(3) Self-determination requires statehood;

(4) States are Bonapartist[16] or they represent the 'general will';

(5) All states enjoy sovereign equality in international relations;

(6) All states can be developed to enjoy equal material progress.

The very first proposition is a static view of the world. Its validity lies only in its pragmatic and heuristic level of application. It freezes the multilayered evolutionary history and porosity of cultures for all their future growth and makes boundary maintenance an absorbing obsession for statecraft. But, these myths have stirred the imagination of people everywhere. Consequently, these have the effect of pressing people to find solutions to their problems and look for salvation in their state, their own state. If they get frustrated, they turn against their state, engage in subversion, redefine their own identity, and finally seek to create a separate state for themselves with the help of global or regional hegemons. The people are thus politicised in a very specific direction, a latent function (a la Merton) of which is that the world system together with its attendant geo-culture is spared of any serious challenge. Since the world system generates inequality and the individual states become the shock-absorbers, there will be a systemic propensity for multicultural and uneven states to generate communal fissures leading to political fragmentation.

There are many who believe that globalisation together with multicultural ferments have eroded in recent years much of the authority and centrality of the state. They however fail to notice that the ownership and management of the most important carrier of globalisation, namely the multi-national corporations, are very much concentrated within the orbit of a few developed countries. The proceedings of the United Nations, World Bank, International Monetary Fund or the World Trade Organisation are largely dictated by the sectional interests of the Euro-American states. At the same time while it is true that the existing state framework has become vulnerable to the rising tide of ethnic assertions, it does not necessarily imply that the centrality of nation-state per se in popular imagination is on the wane. On the contrary, communities of people defined along any of the primordial vectors are increasingly on the warpath to carve out a state of their own (rather than attaining any other nebulous objective) because they are in the grip of the geo-cultural myths woven around the centrality of state. The less developed plural societies thus become susceptible to breaking into several states due to the intensity of multicultural misunderstanding. But, I repeat, they break apart politically only to reap sectional advantages but partake conjointly with all others in a shared notion of progress and development.[17]

This dialectic convergence is being further facilitated at present in the following way. The welfare capitalism in the developed west had faced two great problems of cost escalation in production and environmentally negative externalities without any inter-generational concern in their rush for more and more of material progress here and now. On the other hand, against the backdrop of a developmental consensus, the less developed countries want to overcome the adversities of unequal exchange by developing themselves through rapid industrialisation. Under the circumstances, a paradigm shift is taking place in the world capitalist system. A redefinition of core and periphery, and a newer network between them is in order at present. The core countries, through suitable co-option here and there, are aiming to become what Rosecrance had said, 'virtual states'. These virtual states are being designed to become, apart from being industrially and militarily strong, the storehouse of both finance capital and superior knowledge.[18] Meanwhile the tide of liberalisation has broken all resistance to relocation of industries anywhere in the third world to the satisfaction of the latter while serving the purposes of being cost-effective and eco-friendly for the already developed countries. Going beyond what Lenin had said at the beginning of the 20th century, monopoly of capital is being supplemented by monopolisation of higher science and technology. The workshop and the garbage are free for all, but the study and laboratories will tend to become restricted territories - an indication of which is available in the debates over intellectual property rights, weapons of mass destruction, or agreement on trade in services.

Against this background, the tandem operation of globalisation and localisation, called 'glocalisation' by some and 'fragmegration' by James N. Rosenau is no longer a puzzle. Globalisation is flattening the boundaries while localisation is heightening the same. Rosenau said that "there is no inherent contradiction between localising and globalising tendencies.....the more pervasive globalising tendencies become, the less resistant localising reactions will be to further globalisation. In other words, globalisation and localisation will coexist, but the former will set the context for the latter."[19] To me it appears that Rosenau stops a step short of the actual dynamics. Multiculturalism and ethnicity leads to localisation, localisation leads to fragmentation of the less developed thereby peripheralising them and making them dependent upon the prevailing world system to the advantage of the prosperous core countries and, hence, to globalisation at large. The demands of economic forces from without and cultural factors from within bring about the dynamic equilibrium of globalisation, and help reinstate each other. We shall be committing a genetic fallacy in our understanding if we restrict ourselves to the internal genesis and solidarity of any ethnic phenomenon being oblivious of the larger realities that provide additional luster and direction to the same.

IV

There is a certain universalistic appeal of both Liberalism and Marxism. The question therefore arises - whether and to what extent they could be fitted into the particularistic grooves of nationalism. Many scholars who have been nourished under the tradition of John Stuart Mill would uphold the view that the inter-subjective consciousness is circumscribed for political purposes by the limits of nationhood, and as such an expression like 'liberal nationalism' is not an oxymoron.[20] Mill himself had the following to say:

> Free institutions are next to impossible in a country made up of different nationalities. Among a people without fellow-feeling, especially if they read and speak different languages, the united public opinion, necessary to the working of representative government, cannot exist....An altogether different set of leaders have the confidence of one part of the country and of another. The same books, newspapers, pamphlets, speeches, do not reach them....and each fears more injury to itself from the other nationalities than from the common arbiter, the State.[21]

In short, Mill was of the view that there are different determinants of political judgment if there are different nationalities, and 'the grand and only effectual security in the last resort against the despotism of the government' - 'the sympathy of the army with the people' - is also missing. In a multi-national setting a government can long continue to rule in the fashion of foreign conquerors 'by keeping its Hungarian regiments in Italy and its Italian in Hungary'.[22]

Partitioning of nationalities into separate states was therefore the general prescription of Mill. But he was aware that partition might not be possible because of geographical hindrances. If the people are so mixed up as to be incapable of separation, then, Mill said, "there is no course open to them but to make a virtue of necessity, and reconcile themselves to living together under equal rights and laws".[23] Again, partition may not be necessary when one nationality is merged or absorbed in another creating through this admixture a 'united people, like a crossed breed of animals', who 'inherits the special aptitudes and excellences of all its progenitors'.

This merger or absorption (Mill did not use the term assimilation) can be of different types in his opinion. In a situation of two nationalities put together in a common territory, the nationalities may be graded by the abundance of their numbers or by the superiority of their civilisation. Accordingly two different combinations could arise - numerically majority may have an advanced culture (which is the same as saying numerical minority has an inferior culture), or else numerically minority may have an advanced culture (which is the same as saying that the numerical majority has an inferior culture).

According to Mill, the merger of numerical minority possessing inferior culture into the stream of numerical majority with an advanced culture is always good, but not vice versa. Of this latter type 'the absorption of Greece by Macedonia was one of the greatest misfortunes which ever happened to the world', said Mill. Numerical minority having a superior culture should not merge into the numerical majority with inferior culture, but may rule over the latter as subjects, instead of sharing among them the same free institutions as in a democracy. In Mill's judgment, the rule of the Macedonians reinforced by the Greeks over Asia, or the rule of the English over India were thus justified because they offered gains to civilisation.

But where the nationalities are evenly poised in all elements, they might fail to negotiate and compromise, because 'each cultivates with party obstinacy its distinctive peculiarities; obsolete customs, and even declining languages are revived to deepen the separation'. Each feels itself tyrannised by the other, 'and whatever is given to one of the conflicting nationalities is considered to be taken from all the rest'. Such nations, Mill said, should better be 'under a despotic government which is a stranger to all of them' till such time when they are fit for either union, or federation, or partition.[24]

The classical democratic thinker like Mill therefore does not offer any clue as to how democracy could be operationalised in a multicultural milieu. In, any democratic discourse which offers precedence to 'the liberty of the ancients' over 'the liberty of the moderns',[25] that is republicanism over liberalism, the situation could not be otherwise. Republicanism, leaning upon utilitarianism, would tend to become in a plural society cultural majoritarianism, exclusionary, and oppressive using some as means to the happiness of all- making reconciliation of divergent groups on an equal footing almost an impossible task.

We have mentioned in passing of Rawls and Habermas at the introductory stage.[26] It is beyond impossible for me to present their views satisfactorily. But we shall be doing an injustice to ourselves if we fail to remember that Rawls offers a justification of those principles on which a modem society must be constituted if it wants to ensure the fair cooperation of all its citizens. In an 'original position'(1) where everyone is entitled to possess equal system of basic liberties with equal access to public offices (named, the liberty principle), and (2) where social inequalities are acceptable only when they are also to the advantage of the least privileged (named, the difference principle), the basic framework of a constitutional state could be obtained from an 'overlapping consensus', says Rawls, provided the parties are subject to the constraints of a 'veil of ignorance' about their present position and future placement in terms of race, language, religion, class, income level, and such other attributes. If the parties are unaware of which position they would individually occupy in the society that it is their task to order, they would be constrained enough by their self-interest to reflect on what is equally good for all.

Habermas has serious reservation about the modalities offered by

Rawls because, in his opinion, there would be a crisis of legitimation unless the liberty of the moderns is supplemented by the liberty of the ancients. He, therefore, prefers dialogical discourse in the public sphere in place of mono-logical reasoning in private among all the participants, and that too, in the rich luminance of information instead of retreating behind the veil of ignorance. Notwithstanding this familial dispute, Habermas shares with Rawls the liberal project, and says:

> On the one hand, the idea of equal individual liberties for all satisfies the moral standard of egalitarian universalism, which demands equal respect for and consideration of everyone. On the other hand, it meets the ethical standard of individualism, according to which each person must have the right to conduct her life according to her own preferences and convictions. The equality of all citizens is expressed in the generality of laws, while actionable rights, derived in each case from laws, guarantee to every citizen a well-defined latitude in pursuing her own way of life.[27]

But the disembodied self of political liberalism has been contested for valid reasons by many, and some of these critics (including Sandel, Walzer, or Taylor) are therefore inclined to offer communitarianism with group-rights as a supplement to liberalism. Lijphart has also offered a particular variant of Communitarianism which he names as consociational democracy. It is intended to provide a working solution by instituting an elite cartel among the different groups that may survive in the short run basing itself upon pragmatic and opportunistic alliances. But, with the introduction of collective rights, Habermas points out, conflicts may arise: (a) when different identity-groups dispute each other's rights, or rather, privileges; or (b) when one group demands equal treatment with other groups; or (c) when non-members see themselves as disadvantaged in relation to members of privileged groups; or (d) when group leaders violate the individual rights of dissenters within the group in the name of stabilising the collective identity.[28]

But the most disturbing are the foundational norms of democracy. For all people to cooperate on the basis of equal freedom and respect for everyone, the source of universal moral norms, and the particular ethical values of either the egoistic individual or that of the ethno-national group in which the individual is embedded should converge and not run at cross purposes. Both the disembodied self as also the embedded self may refuse to submit to universal moral norm either because of self-interest wrongly understood, or because of the ethical-cultural tenets traditionally handed over to them, in which case the inter-community discourse may remain a non-starter.

I do not know if only a Hobbesian solution is available to such moral dilemma when acting according to self-interest would require transcending self-interest for universal good under threats of survival for each. The geographical determinism, it may be remembered, was the only exceptional situation for Mill when diverse people may be compelled to make a virtue out of necessity and agree to live under equal system of rights and liberties for all.

Or else, the exercise of political power may offer a way out of certain coordination problems called "prisoners' dilemma", as has been pointed out by Tim Heysse. There may be a situation where no cooperation takes place, because every agent fears that others will take advantage of his or her willingness to cooperate. And, in fact, the worst possible scenario emerges when one works for collective interest but the other is guided by self-interest only, either because of lack of confidence or information, or because of a myopic vision of the future. However, if there is a body that has the power to enforce cooperation thereby removing the fear of opportunism, cooperation is a rational choice that will, as a rule, be adopted. The exercise of power achieves a more attractive outcome than that which would have been achieved without the use of power.[29]

V

Before I offer any precise suggestion for its solution, let me be forthright about the multicultural problem confronting India in general and the northeast India in particular. If we make a morphology in the light of all that has been discussed so far about multicultural accommodation it would look as in the accompanying table.

India herself opted for Partition at the dawn of Independence in 1947. But that Partition was ill-conceived and carried out in unseemly haste by the power-hungry politicians. Made wiser by hindsight we may now say that the burden of judgment of the Muslim League claim of Muslims in India being a separate nation having the right of self-determination lay with all Muslims everywhere in India, and therefore, the issue should have been decided first by a referendum among all the Muslims of India. And, then, if Partition were the outcome it should have been followed by a peaceful population transfer. Territory-specific and selective referendum as was forced upon the Sylhet district in Assam served to satisfy the communal among both the Muslims and the Assamese ruling classes.[30]

In *The Assam Tribune,* dated 20th July 1947, less than four weeks before Independence, it was reported that Dr. B.K. Barua, a noted Assamese litterateur and historian, had said, "Culturally, racially, and linguistically, every non-Assamese is a foreigner in Assam. In this connection we must bear in mind that Assam from the very ancient times never formed a part of India."[31]

But the most blatant version of this idea (and one is not sure whether it violated the laws of the land) was pronounced by Akbar Hydari, the then Governor of Assam. Speaking on behalf of the provincial Congress cabinet, when the Assam Assembly met on 5th November 1947 for the first time after Independence, he said:[32]

Monism	Adjusting People to Border	Genocide Ethnic Cleansing Disenfranchisement Voluntary Assimilation Forced Assimilation
	Adjusting People to Border	Partition

Pluralism	Accepting People and Border as they are	Federalism	Territorial and/or subnational
		Communitarianism	Cultural & Minority Rights Regime
		Consociation	Elite Cartel Bicameralism Veto Power
		Liberalism	

The natives of Assam are now masters of their own house. They have a Government which is both responsible and responsive to them. They can take what steps are necessary for the encouragement and propagation of Assamese language and culture and of the languages and customs of the tribal peoples who are their fellow citizens and who also must have a share in the formation of such policies. The Bengalee has no longer the power, even if he had the will, to impose anything on the peoples of these Hills and Valleys which constitute Assam. The basis of such feelings against him as exist is fear - but now there is no cause for fear. I would therefore appeal to you to exert all the influence you possess to give the stranger in our midst a fair deal, provided of course, he in his turn deals loyally with us.

After the Partition had run its course, ethnic cleansing, assimilation and disenfranchisement have been tried over the years for different categories of people to bring about a cultural homogenisation of the political space and also to establish an overall Assamese hegemony into the body politic.[33] We should remember that the present day 'land of seven sisters' (states) in north-east India was virtually contained within only three entities in 1947 - Assam, Manipur, and Tripura - before Assam alone was bifurcated into five different units in different phases.

The Bardoloi Sub-Committee Report on the North-East Frontier (Assam) Tribal and Excluded Areas (1947) which was a part of constitution making process on the eve of independence did not visualize full 'absorption' of the hill areas and hill people, but their 'political and social amalgamation'. It also observed that 'contact with outside influences is necessary though not in a compelling way until there is a change in the way of life brought about by the hill people themselves'. As far as the plains tribals were concerned it was noted that '(they) have gone a long way towards such assimilation'. Creation of autonomous districts in the hill-tribal inhabited areas of Assam, and District Councils as organs of their autonomy was forwarded by the Committee, with the additional observation that 'the population of the plains tribals which is being gradually assimilated to the population of the plains, should for all practical purposes be treated as a minority'.[34]

In the 1950s a strategic assimilation was made of the immigrant Muslims of the Brahmaputra valley and these were incorporated as *Na-asamia* or new Assamese to derive definite numerical edge over others. Then, in the 1960s, it was decided to adopt the Assamese as the only official language throughout the state. The resentment against this decision was voiced by the Bengalis of Assam first, and then it gradually spread among different categories of people including both the hill as also the plains tribals forcing ultimately the official acceptance of Bengali and Bodo languages, but at the same time hastening the dismemberment of Assam.

In the late 1970s the movement against the alleged 'foreigners' — the Bangladeshis — was started demanding their disenfranchisement and, wherever possible, deportation. In 1985 the movement was called off after the Assam agreement was signed accepting the pre-1971 migrants from erstwhile East Pakistan as citizens. But two irritants have remained unresolved: (a) the detection of post-1971 foreigners from Bangladesh, and grant of citizenship identity cards for the rest; and, (b) the non-fulfillment of Clause 6 of the Assam Accord which stipulated that "Constitutional, legislative and administrative safeguards, as may be appropriate, shall be provided to protect, preserve and promote the cultural, social, linguistic identity and heritage of Assamese people". It is possible to construct both a strong as also a weak version of Clause 6, the stronger leading to the persistent and belligerent demands of the ULFA.

I do not find much hope for recovery of the present turmoil for as long as the 'liberty of the ancients' is accorded primacy over the 'liberty' of the moderns'. In a society with communal cleavages if one agent represents many principals having varied interests, the representative government would tend to keep majority satisfied, more so where the first-past-the-post system prevails. The system would under the circumstances sacrifice some at the altar of others, and remain permanently communal by inculcating the spirit of utilitarianism.

The problem becomes more acute when a soft state is instituted in a milieu where allegiance to customary bonds is valued. And, since the bureaucracy is not rule-governed in such a universe, the role of politicians would be reduced to the status of brokers between the government and the people. More than any other form of capital it is the amount of 'social capital' or extent of social network (a la Bourdieu) which would then play the decisive role for anyone's survival and development. Under the circumstances the obsessive insistence upon retaining advantage in terms of numbers or representation is well understood.

Further, there is an ethical tenacity of what could be termed borrowing the Khasi phraseology as the *Ki Khun Nyngkong* principle which accords a greater respect for the earlier settlers in any place. This principle is obeyed in the public transport system where no one forcibly unseats an already seated passenger unless some compelling reasons of morality demands the vacating of seats in favour of the disadvantaged. The Assamese, the tribal people, and even the Bengalees in parts of north-east have every right to be recognized as the *Ki Khun Nyngkong* in their respective places.

But this principle cannot be invoked to look upon the latecomers as, what could be termed borrowing an idiom of Ahom statecraft, the *Thapita-Sanchita* or the protégé of the earlier occupants and hence, not entitled to equal freedom.

Looked at from the larger Indian perspective, there is of course a silver lining in the horizon. Even though the apprehensions have a longer local history let it not be forgotten that the configuration of the present imbroglio appeared on the surface in the 1970s when the Sino-American-Pakistan axis did not look kindly upon India's leaning towards Soviet Russia, and also her role in the liberation of Bangladesh. 'Specific reciprocity' demanded that India be taught a lesson, and therefore, the aggravation of problems and the secessionist demands in the Punjab, Kashmir, and the north-east India served also a wider purpose. But, it seems, after the Cold War had been over, India was lifted as the regional hegemon in the new search for international balance of power. So, right at this moment her political fragmentation is least likely to be engineered by any major world power. The fading away of vacillation and resorting to firmness instead on the part of the Indian state vis-à-vis the north-eastern situation may only underwrite her future consolidation.

But force must in the ultimate analysis be fortified by consensus. India's experiments with federalism consociation may preferably be modulated by progressive extension of cultural secularism and withdrawal by the state from all cultural survival projects so that neither envy nor pride is generated at any level. We must first appreciate that ours is not a complete liberal democracy where all citizens are incorporated universally. Rather we also have a complex structure of group-differentiated rights in the fashion of a consociation incorporation, and since the group-differentiated rights are not territory-neutral all demands for special representation or cultural rights tend to degenerate into territorially based autonomy demands or demands for secession.[35]

The shared political culture and common civic identity may be kept separated from the traditionally given subcultures all of which have equal rights to co-existence within the polity. In other words the state should remain neutral with respect to all pre-political forms of life by, what Habermas says, the decoupling of the majority culture from the political culture with which it was once fused.[36] Cultural matters should better be left at the helms of the civil society to enjoy what might be said negative liberty for all of them. This would definitely deflate the paranoid in searching any essentialist connotation of territorial nomenclature and acting on the same. We may then realise that unless we are overtaken by an anomie we all have a hope for the future only because we can shed off the limitations of a historically given identity.[37] Through an additive and continuous acculturation into a creative blend of severe idioms of life drawn from sources far and near rather than assimilation, all of us can enrich ourselves for ever.

References

1. Will Kymlicka and Norman Wayne, 'Return of the Citizen: A Survey of Recent Work on Citizenship Theory', *Ethics*, 104 (1994)
2. Navlakha, Suren, 'Ethnic Diversities in the New States of Asia: A Model for Analysis', in *Studies in Asian Social Development,* no.1, (ed) Ratna Dutta and P.C.Joshi, (Tata McGraw Hill, Bombay, 1971)
3. When the Roman Empire came into being on the ruins of the petty Greek state as also through expansion, the diverse subject people

lacking any customary bond among them had to be united in their outlook, and their interpretation (The natural laws were supposed to provide the foundation upon which this could be done. Marcus Aurelius Antoninus, the Roman emperor who was born in Rome of a family that was originally Spanish, declared, "My city and country so far as I am Antoninus, is Rome, but so far as I am a man, it is the world". Epictetus, who was a Phrygian slave brought to Rome but rose to be a Stoic philosopher of repute, said that if God and men were akin, there is but one course open to men, to do as Socrates did: never to reply to one, who asks his country, 'I am an Athenian', or' I am a Corinthian', but 'I am a citizen of the universe'. For Cicero, there could not be different laws for Rome or Athens because true law was right reason in agreement with nature, and it was of universal application, unchanging and everlasting. See William Ebenstein, *Great Political Thinkers,* (Holt, Rinehart & Winston, New York, 1965).

Generally speaking there are two types of responses when people of different descriptions come together - Herodian and Zealotlike. The accommodation or the segregation is projected depending upon mostly the exigencies and requirements of a particular situation rather than a reasoned argumentation of the same on a transcendental plane. See B.P.Misra, 'Dynamics of the Construction of Social Identity', *Journal of the Anthropological Survey of India*, 50 (2001).

4. K. Marx & F. Engels, *Manifesto of the Communist Party,* first published in 1848.
5. V.I. Lenin, *Critical Remarks on the National Question,* first published in 1913.
6. V.I. Lenin, *"Left-Wing" Communism – An Infantile Disorder,* first published in 1920.
7. Joseph Stalin, *The National Question and Leninism,* first published in 1929.
8. *Ibid.*
9. CPSU Central Committee, *Plenary Meeting: Documents and Materials,* (Novosti, Moscow, 1989)
10. The policy summed up here was first outlined by Stalin during the prerevolutionary period. It underwent marginal changes and adjustments from time to time while the basics remained the same. See Joseph Stalin, *Marxism and the National Question,* first published 1913. The Soviet experiment was watched and emulated by many

with local modifications. In a new edition (1954) of the *Fundamental Unity of India,* Radha Kumud Mookerji made the following observation:

> No state can ever be a homogeneous social composition made up of only one community. It is bound to be made up of different communities, one of which must necessarily be the majorit.... [The] plan of reconciling the minority to the rule of the majority in a comprehensive political system is now universally applied in all democracies. The best example of this system is the Stalin constitution of the U.S.S.R.

11. In a certain sense all states fit ideally or loosely into the mould of what Morton Fried has named as Secondary States that are not ontogenetic.

12. R.H. Jackson & C.G. Roseberg, 'Why Africa's Weak States Persist: the Empirical and the juridical in Statehood", *World Politics*, 35, (1982).

13. R.O. Keohane, 'Reciprocity in International Relations', *International Organisation,* 40 (1986).

14. Fred W. Riggs, 'Ethnonationalism, Industrialism and the Modem State', *Third World Quarterly,* 15(1994).

15. Machiavelli had pointed out long ago that in the struggle between rulers, 'there are two methods of fighting, the one by law, the other by force'. Specifically, the ruler must imitate both the fox and the lion, 'for the lion cannot protect itself from the traps, and the fox cannot defend himself from wolves'. At the beginning of the twentieth century, Pareto interpreted 'foxes' as the symbol of cunning and manipulation, and 'lions' as the symbol of power and courage. Force and consensus were thus equally necessary for the effective continuance of a political system. And, then, between the two World Wars, Gramsci wrote how in the developed western countries 'the war of manoeuvre' has progressively turned to be 'the war of position'. Hence, the crucial role of ideology and also the means by which consciousness is mediated and protected behind a whole complex of institutions that legitimise bourgeois dominance, rendering its values universal, a task in which the intellectuals – 'the experts in legitimation' - play a crucial role.

16. Possibly the use of the term - Bonapartisan - would be more appropriate to catch all the nuances it seeks to convey.

17. The *Taliban* movement or Islamic fundamentalism in Afghanistan or elsewhere is obviously an exception to this generalization. One cannot however vouchsafe about what would survive as the distinctive characteristic of such upsurge in the long run because many self-proclaimed Islamic states are creatively engaged in reinterpretation of Islamic texts to suit the purpose of modernity. See e.g., A.G. Noorani, *Islam and Jihad,* (Leftworld, New Delhi, 2002); Timur Kuran, *Islam and Mammon: the Economic Predicaments of Islamism.* (Tulika Books, New Delhi, 2006).

18. It should be noticed that there is a gulf of difference between using AK-47 and producing and marketing the same while carrying on research to find still more sophisticated weapons in its place.

19. James N. Rosenau, 'The Complexities and Contradictions of Globalization', *Current History, 96(1997).*

20. See e.g., Sanford Levinson, 'Is Liberal Nationalism an Oxymoron: An Essay for Judith Shklar', *Ethics* 105(1995); Andrew Mason, 'Political Community, Liberal Nationalism, and the Ethics of Assimilation', *Ethics,* 109(1999)

21. John Stuart Mill, *Consideration and Representative Government,* Chapter 16, first published 1861. Mill was however categorical that the distinction between one's own community members and others is 'more worthy of savages than of civilised beings', but he lamented that 'this object, one of the worthiest to which human endeavour can be directed, can never, in the present state of civilisation, be promoted by keeping different nationalities of anything like equivalent strength under the same government'.

22. *Ibid.*

23. *Ibid.*

24. The imperial ethnocentrism and the overbearing enlightenment outlook reflected in these writings may appear repulsive to some of us at this distance; but, in the context of the contemporary conflicts there is something to learn from them. The achievements of India's freedom struggle in 1947, and also her inter-community relations since then may be reexamined in the light of Mill's prognosis which to my knowledge has not been sufficiently highlighted in the historical writings on the subject.

25. See Benjamin Constant, *The Liberty of Ancients Compared with that of Moderns,* 1819, in <http://www.uark.edu/depts/comminfo/

cambridge/ ancients.html>

26. Apart from the basic texts by Rawls or Habermas that may be consulted, there is a rich literature on their writings which are no less useful. I base myself primarily upon their debate in the pages of *The Journal of Philosophy,* March 1995, where the following articles appeared: Jurgen Habermas, 'Reconciliation through the Public Use of Reason - Remarks on John Rawls's Political Liberalism'; and, John Rawls, 'Reply to Habermas'.

27. Jurgen Habermas, 'Equal Treatment of Cultures and the Limits of Postmodern Liberalism', *The Journal of Political Philosophy, 13(2005)*

28. *Ibid.*

29. Tim Heysse, 'Consensus and Power in Deliberative Democracy', *Inquiry,* 49(2006)

30. J.B. Bhattacharjee, 'Sylhet: Myth of a Referendum', *Indo-British Review: A Journal of History,* 17(1989); Bidyut Chakraborty, 'The "Hut" and the "Axe": the 1947 Sylhet Referendum', *Indian Economic and Social History Review,* 39 (2002)

31. Sujit Chaudhuri, 'A God-Sent Opportunity', *Seminar,* February 2002

32. Mahitosh Purkayastha, *The Anatomy of Assam,* (Puthighar, Silchar, 1980), Annexure VI;

    The Assamese-Bengali relations suffered reverses along with the progress of the freedom movement and extension of self-rule. The same was true of Hindu-Muslim relations at all-India level. The presumption of eternal bitterness would therefore be out of place. For an objective assessment of Assamese-Bengali relations during the colonial period, see e.g., Prosenjit Chowdhury, *Socio-Cultural Aspects of Assam in the 19th Century,* (Vikas, New Delhi, 1994).

33. For a detailed analysis of how the class character and the community character of the Indian state conjointly created a problem for peace and security by succumbing to the project of the local chauvinists over a long period of time, see B.P. Misra, 'Security Problems in North-East India, or the Tale of the Bird *Bharunda',* in *Perspectives on India's North-East,* (ed) Sanjukta Bannerji Bhattacharya & Rachana Das, (Bibhasa, Calcutta, 1998)

34. B.L. Hansaria, *Sixth Schedule to the Constitution,* (Universal Law Publishing, Delhi 2005), Appendix 21

35. B.P. Misra, 'Quest for Peace and Development in North-East India', *West Bengal Political Science Review,* 8(2005); see also M.S.Prabhakara, 'In the name of Tribal Identities', *Frontline* 22 (24) 2005, for further elucidation of this problem.

36. Jurgen Habermas, 'Multiculturalism and the Liberal State', *Stanford Law Review,* 47(1995)

37. That there are quests in this direction can be illustrated by referring to what Udayon wrote even though he could not fully transcend the assimilation syndrome. See Udayon Misra, 'Identity Transformation and the Assamese Community: Illusion and Reality', in *Dynamics of Identity and Intergroup Relations in North- East India.* (ed) Kailash S. Aggarwal, (Indian Institute of Advanced Study, Shimla, 1989)

3

The Sino-India Peace Process As I see it

Amalendu Guha

I am elated and grateful to the organizer of this National Seminar and especially to the Director of the Indian Institute of Technology, Guwahati for asking me to deliver a lecture in this national seminar on "Peace in Dialogue: Reflections on North-East India". Hurdles in the way of peace are many with threats both from Internal as well as external forces. Let me talk today on the Himalayan border conflicts and their resolution with particular reference to North-east India.

There was a time when both People's China and free India wanted to be friends–close friends with faith in *Panchashila* (five principles) and the Non-Aligned Movement (NAM), but had a hitch to overcome first–the Tibet question. We wanted to retain our extra-territorial rights in Tibet, a gift from British imperialism, said to be derived from the Simla Convention of 1914. Though its proceedings were initialed by Britain, Tibet and China, the latter refused point blank to ratify it. She was in no mood of having any track with what Britain wanted to thrust on her. Free India promptly recognized liberated People's China, but pressurized her to voluntarily surrender her sovereignty over Tibet and to halt her army's march towards so-called outer Tibet. She refused her army entered Tibet, intervened in the ongoing civil war, dislodged the pro-British party that had seized power in Tibet's local government and put the pro-China party in power in its place. Under the circumstances, India abandoned her former attitude and resolved the Tibet question amicably through a peace process. People's China and Tibet's governments signed on 23rd May 1951 an Agreement on measures for Tibet's peaceful liberation bringing to an end the internal situation of civil war and partition conspiracy. Another important step taken in 1954 was the Sino-Indian Agreement on Trade and Intercourse. Thereby free India was allowed to retain the already established trade agencies of colonial India in Tibet (but without military escorts). Chinese trade agencies in India too began to operate on equal terms. Through peaceful negotiations, free India also agreed to sell to People's China the postal and tele-services she had set up when under the British. But one legacy of imperialism, the border question, was not taken up by default. However a year later in 1955 both accepted the five principles of peaceful co-existence (Pancha Shila) in the Bandung Conference of third world countries. The peace process thus amicably settled the dispute over Tibet's status *vis-à-vis* China and India.[1]

I

The two Asian nations were good friends since then until the end of the 1950s. We maintained peaceful co-existence, without interfering in each other's internal affairs while going ahead for development. However, towards the end of the decade skirmish took place between India's and China's armed border guards along the Himalayan border both in its westernmost and north-eastern sectors. And these ultimately led to a costly a month-long war in 1962. Despite a phase of peace dialogue during 1958-62, because both had adamant positions as regards their mutual overlapping territorial claims. India was not agreeable to put on the agenda the North-East Frontier Agency (present Arunachal) as a disputed area, while China insisted on a political settlement of the border problem as a whole on a *quid-pro-quo* basis.

China was not prepared to admit in advance that the North-East Frontier Agency, or NEFA, which was already in India's de-facto possession, belonged also traditionally to her. She wanted that the disputed Aksai-Chin area, i.e., the western sector of the Himalayan border, which was in her de-facto possession, be also discussed together with NEFA so that a solution could be arrived at for both at the same time and on the basis of the same principles of scientific border-making. India rejected this proposal. She insisted that the undemarcated Himalayan Border's three sectors – western, middle and north-eastern – be each negotiated separately and not together for a package deal.

Both sides having remained adamant, no meaningful negotiations could start at all. However, the aborted dialogue was followed up by the publication of two official documents-one containing the reports of the officials of the two governments on the boundary question and another containing notes, memoranda and letters exchanged between them during 959-63.[2] Meanwhile, the war could not be avoided. After a few minor border clashes on the western and north-eastern sectors, our exasperated Prime Minister Jawaharlal Nehru announced on 12 October 1962 that he had already asked the army to push out the Chinese beyond the eastern frontier, i.e., the 850 mile McMahon Line.[3] About its origins and legal status, I am yet to give the details.

Within days the war was lost and hundreds of our six thousand soldiers on this front were taken prisoners while not a single Chinese soldiers was captured. In hot pursuit of our retreating troops, the Chinese army units marched downhill across the NEFA upto its border with Assam and then halted. It unilaterally declared Cease-Fire on 20 November and went back to their original positions beyond the McMahon Line as drawn on a controversial map by its author.

Understandably, after such a situation, our country's political climate became cloudy and chilly, lacking fresh policy initiatives, but only for a while. With grim determination, our defense system was thoroughly reformed and made strong enough to prevent any such humiliation again. However at long last, realizing the futility of remaining enemies forever, the two Asian nations have now agreed to settle the whole border dispute peacefully through a series of dialogues. After nine sittings, we see a ray of hope in the matter of signing a bilateral border treaty in due course, accommodating both countries' national interests. This could have been achieved long back early in the 1960s, but for a mass frenzy on Indian streets manipulated by irresponsible conservative political forces, thus compelling our government to take unwise bellicose decisions. Let us hope, this time such a mass frenzy will not be allowed to intervene by well-informed and enlightened public opinion.

II

I shall now try to look into the background of the crisis in the Sino-Indian relations we faced during 1958-62. As I have already pointed out, it was an inherited legacy from the colonial times. In pre-colonial times, both India and China believed that the Himalayas belonged to them by tradition from both sides expansionist drives were carried on into the Himalayas, but vast areas still remained unadministrated no-man's land and *terra incognita* even as late as the coming of the British East India Company.

North-east frontier became Britain's concern for the first time only after annexation of Assam to her Indian empire in 1826. The previous Ahom regime, limited to the Assam plains, had developed special relations with some of the neighbour tribes who used to come down and camp in the plains every winter for trade and extortions. To protect the local people from their oppression, the Ahom government paid them *posa*, i.e. an annual payment on condition of their maintaining peace and order while in Ahom territory. For occasional unfriendly acts, their *posa* was withheld, their trade routes blocked and their hill villages beyond the foothills raided and burnt down, until they once more submitted to the Ahom authorities. Beyond the foothills, these tribes were autonomous in their respective habitats and, in many cases, had similar relations with Tibet, as with Assam. After the regime change in 1826, the same old Ahom policy of appeasing these freebooters continued under the British. Payments in kind being gradually replaced by their cash values under fresh treaties.

The Tawang monastery, 17th century the Drepung monastery of Lhasa, and colonies of Tibetan Buddhists were established south of Tibet proper. In a narrow strip of Monpa, a tribal territory bordering Bhutan, Lhasa's loose political control since then gradually expanded further south through this monastery almost touching the Assam plains at Amratol. We have records of their agreements, dated 1844 and 1853 with the British, acknowledging the receipt of *posa* and mentioning the Lhasa government as 'our government'.[4]

The making of the McMahon Line has a history. Without an understanding of how this line was conceived in 1913-14, the significance and complication of the Sino-Indian frontier crisis of today cannot be comprehended. In this lecture, my focus is particularly on the north-eastern sector and its by-now-notorious McMahon Line, a colonial legacy.

From times ancient, India or Bharat was known to be bounded in the north and China bounded in the south by the same Himalayan Range. But the actual delimitation of this boundary, not to speak of its actual demarcation on the ground, came for serious consideration only later. It happened so when the East India Company began to expand its Indian empire in every direction in search of 'ethnographical, political and military frontiers of the East-India continent'.[5] These were fixed by the British through a gradual and prolonged process of colonial warfare. When the British took over medieval Ahom kingdom of Assam in 1826, the latter did not include the uncharted heights of the Himalayas beyond the foothills. The hill tracts, east of Bhutan and north of the Brahmaputra Valley were inhabited by several independent tribes, namely, Tibetanised Monpa, Sherdukpen and Sherchokpa as well as others like Aka, Dafla (Nishi), Miri, Abor (Adi) and Mishmi. They were allowed to come down to the plains for trade and collection of *posa*- a payment made to them as long as they did not oppress Ahom subjects and violate other terms of agreement.

The only case of a demarcated boundary, a short distance from the Deosham River at the westernmost point of the Indo-Bhutanese border to the Rowta River to the east, goes back to 1872-73. It was the boundary between Tawang, a vassal state of Tibet, and Assam laid down on the ground by major J. M. Graham. Boundary pillars were set up roughly eleven miles north of Odalguri (now in Bodoland) to demarcate Tawang and its dependencies from the province of Assam. It was indeed an extension of the Indo-Bhutan international border and though called Inner Line, was also in essence an international border, since Tibet was, both *de-facto* and *de-jure*, a part of China until 1914. This Inner Line extended further to the east running close to the foothills. In British-India's view, this link indicated the limits of regular administration, but did not set limits to extension of loose political control over the tribes, living beyond it.[6]

Hence, there was also a concept of Outer Line, a flexible and movable line, that was gradually pushed northward over the no-man's land in search of a scientific border between the two empires– British and Chinese. Sir Robert Raid, Governor of Assam during the period 1937-41, quotes a note of the chief of the general staff issued about 1911-12, which explains the context of forward policy during the years ahead. It says,

> The direction of the frontier line about Tawang requires careful consideration. The present boundary (demarcated) is south of Tawang, running westwards along the foothills from near Udalguri to the southern Bhutan border, and thus a dangerous wedge of territory is thrust in between the Miri country and Bhutan. A comparatively easy and much used trade route traverses this wedge from north to south by which the Chinese would be able to exert influence or pressure on Bhutan…(the) rectification of the boundary here is therefore imperative, and an ideal line would appear to be one from the knot of mountains near Longitude 93° Latitude 28° 20, in the Bhutan border north of Chona Dzong in a direct east and west line with the northern frontier of Bhutan. There appears to be a convenient watershed for it to follow.[7]

This military vision document inspired Sir Arthur Henry McMahon's forward policy in North-east India.

During the early years of the 20th century the Chinese empire was in turmoil. Taking advantage of China's weakness, the British forced her to yield to their demand for extra-territorial rights in Tibet. Britain did not allow Chinese troops to enter Tibet to repress the pro-Independent secessionists. Tibet became virtually a British protectorate, standing as a buffer state between British India and China, though nominally still a part China[8]. At the same time, the *terra incognita* beyond Assam's northern border (the Inner Line) was explored and surveyed, so that the entire area could soon be brought under loose political control of the British. At this juncture, there was a democratic revolution led by SunYat-Sen (1866-1925) against the Mamchu imperial rule, leading to the emergence of the Chinese Republic. But the republican regime too was not strong enough to confront Tibetan secessionism, instigated and nurtured by British imperialism. Tibet could not be totally severed from China and it was annexed due to Anglo-Russian rivalry in the Asian area for empire building.[9]

1910 onwards, instigated and helped by Britain the Tibetan local government (Kashag) tried to assert its independence as did Outer Mongolia, which was carved out of Chinese Mongolia region and brought under Russian domination. For some four decades since then Tibet remained practically cut off from and virtually independent of mainland China. This was so because her only line of communication with Tibet, being then via India was totally at the mercy of the British imperialists. The British took full advantage of this situation to treat Tibet as a buffer state under their domination, though still a part of China. In 1912 only Outer Mongolia recognized Tibet's independence. This compliment was mutual. No other country till date, not even Britain, India and USA did so. Britian had extra-territorial rights in Tibet by a treaty with China under duress in 1906. Up to the last she nourished Tibet's de-facto independence and in 1943 proposed to the USA that Tibet's right to exchange diplomatic mission with other powers be recognized. But the proposal was rejected. Tibet never had any international identity other than as part of China.[10]

In the early 20th century not only the British imperialists, but also the Chinese were moving forward into the *terra incognita* lying between Tibet and Assam, where tribal peoples carried on their primitive agriculture and animal husbandry. While China cum Tibet was pushing their Outer Lines of political control southward, British India pushed forward her Outer Line northward. Chinese occupation of Rima on 10 May 1910 and appearance of small Chinese armed bands to collect taxes and monastic tithes from Buddhist tribal villagers in abor (Adi) and Mishmi countries created an alarming situation. It warranted an immediate forward policy i.e. advancing loose British administration further northward until the natural strategic frontier was established. Accordingly, during 1911-13, several expeditions with survey parties explored the North-east frontier of India. Thereafter a tripartite conference involving Britain, China and Tibet was planned to be held on the cool heights of Simla.

It was on 17 August 1912 that Sir John Jordan, the British Minister in Beijing declared that his government would withdraw its recognition of the Republic of China if it sent garrisons or administrators to Tibet and that it wanted a special conference being held to discuss the matter, pending which all transit of goods and personnel between Tibet and China proper via India would remain blocked under this threat. Weak China had no other alternative than agreeing to talk.[11]

The Simla Conference was formally opened on 6 October 1913 with Sir Arthur Henry McMahon, Foreign Secretary, Government of India in the chair. The only item of the official agenda was the British proposal to get Tibet divided into two zones, Inner and Outer Tibet (such as had recently been agreed upon between Russia and China in

Mongolia) with China's consent. Under the plan, Outer Tibet was to enjoy full autonomy, free from interference by her suzerain China. Over Inner Tibet, comprising parts of neighboring Chinese provinces inhabited by Tibetans as well as Hans and others, China was to retain administrative rights. The proposed line to divide Tibet was shown in its illustrative map. Additionally and as if casually, the proposed dividing line was extended to indicate also Tibet's boundary with Assam and Burma although this matter was not on the conference agenda. China opposed the idea, but her representative failed to take a strong stand, as desired by Peking, at the conference table. Instead of rejecting the very idea of dividing Tibet, he focused on where the proposed line should run. "This was the issue upon which the conference finally broke down."[12]

China's representative refused to sign the Simla Convention. However, "in April 1914 McMahon successfully persuaded the Chinese representative to at least initial the draft treaty and its illustrative map", of course subject to ratification by his government. The latter rebuked its representative even for initialing the draft and in the first week of July declared both at Simla and London that China rejected the convention and that any separate bilateral Anglo-Tibetan agreement, if any, would be regarded as null and void. Hence, the so-called Simla convention and the McMahon Line (red line in the map) had no legitimacy. In fact there had been such an Anglo-Tibetan (Indo-Tibetan) secret agreement about the Tibet-Assam boundary in February and 24-25 March, 1914 in Delhi behind the back of the Chinese representative. This was in clear violation of both the Anglo-Chinese convention of 1906 and the Anglo-Russian convention of 1907. Therefore Tibet's Kashag accepted the alignment of the McMahan line, but made it conditional to securing the buffer state status, along with the proposed partition. The informal discussions were given final shape in the form of exchange of notes between Tibetan and British representatives. These notes in the original together with a copy of the map were forwarded to the Secretary of State for India by McMahon on 28 March. But these were not published in the 1929 updated edition of the aforementioned Aitchison volume XIV as mentioned by Maxwell. Thereafter, "there are no attempts to make McMahon's map line the effective boundary. The McMahon line was in effect, forgotten".[13]

However, from 1936 onward, the issue was once more revived to push Outer Line everywhere up to the McMahon Line. To facilitate and legitimize the map red line, Britain did not hesitate to take resort even to a diplomatic fraud. It was uncovered by researchers after India's China War. Copies of the original 1929 edition of the relevant Aitchison volume were all withdrawn, destroyed and replaced by newly printed revised ones (volume XIV), bearing the same publication date, 1929; and containing the Simla Convention text inclusive of the secret notes exchanged between Britain and Tibet at Delhi.[14]

The spurious revised edition of the Aitchison volume was not yet published in 1936. Even Governor Reid's book, published in 1942, carried no reference to it. Let me present some extracts from the instructions issued to captain G. S. Lightfoot who led a fact-finding expedition to Tawang (Monyub) as reproduced by Reid.

> In the autumn of 1936 Gould had an interview with the Kashag in Lhasa at which Tawang was discussed. Their attitude was that (1) up to 1914 Tawang had undoubtedly been Tibetan, (2) they regarded the adjustment of the Indo-Tibetan boundary as part and parcel of the general adjustment and determination of boundaries contemplated in the 1914 Convention. If they could, with our help, secure a definite Sino-Tibetan boundary they would of course be glad to observe the Indo-Tibetan border as defined in 1914, (3) they have been encouraged in thinking they His Majesty's Government and the Government of India sympathized with this way of regarding the matter owing to the fact that at no time since the Convention... had the Indian Government taken steps to question Tibetan, or to assert British authority in the Tawang area.... I am to say that your whole handling of this delicate situation must be cautions. It is better to go too slow than too fast.[15]

This aforesaid expedition, with an armed police escort, reached Tawang on 30 April 1938 and stayed there during the summer months. The forward policy of 1910-12 was once more activated in Tawang and its dependencies even as Tibetan officials continued to collect 'taxes' and monastic dues. I have already referred to B. J. Gould's discussions with the Lhasa Government regarding the McMahon Line. Lhasa argued that, if China were able to push its boundary with Tibet so far west as Giamdo (as demanded by China in November 1913 at Simla), the McMahon Line would no more remain a (Outer) Tibetan concern, it would become entirely (Inner) Tibet's and hence China's concern.[16]

III

I have so far presented to you an understanding of China's point of view as regards the problem of delimiting, and then demarcating the Sino-Indian Himalayan frontier in its north-easternmost sector. While doing so on the basis of published sources, I have been heavily indebted to the contributions of Israel Epstein, C.U. Aitchison, H. K. Barpujari, Robert Reid (Governor of Assam), and, above all, to Neville Maxwell.

Now I shall take up the Indo-British colonial point of view. In the latter context, even Karl Marx has already been referred to.

After tracing the origins of the Inner Line since 1872-75 along the border separating Manipur State and Sibsagar District from the Naga Tribal area as well as Tawang and its dependencies from Assam, Barpujari has made two important points. First, it is a fact that plainsmen were prohibited under the Bengal Frontier Regulation of 1873 to enter tribal areas beyond the Inner Line or cross it to obtain jungle products, without special permission of the Assam Government. Yet what is to be noted is that the Inner Line was formally laid down only in 1875 "along the northern frontier of the districts of Darrang and Lakhimpur representing thereby 'the limits of the Deputy Commissioner's ordinary as distinguished from his political jurisdiction". The policy towards the tribes beyond-Aka, Dafla, Miri, Abor and Mishimi etc. beyond the Inner Line, as in the case of Naga Tribal areas, was ordinarily one of non-interference, except in the case of outrages on British subjects, violation of the Inner Line and 'interests' of the people dwelling within British area. "Beyond the Inner Line lay the Outer Line–'external territorial frontier' or limits of the British territory. This was demarcated in 1875 as far as the river Burai (93^{0}29^{0}) and beyond which the boundary followed a readily recognizable line along the foot of the hills as far as Nizamghat (95^{0}40^{0}) to be 'throughout well-recognized by usage'.... Beyond Nizamghat, evidently, there was no Outer Line". By "interests" was meant mainly huge British investments in tea gardens, sawmills and trade in proximity to the inner line.[17]

The other point he emphasizes is that the McMahon line was forgotten and then rediscovered only in 1936 is a half-truth. As far back as in 1928, Captain G.A. Nevill, Political Officer, Balipara Frontier Tract, informed Delhi that if China got hold of Tibet, Tawang country would provide a secret and easy entrance to India. Then in 1934-35, a British explorer and Botanist, who had been arrested in Tibet for unauthorized entry there, observed in course of his published paper that Government of India had for a long time been paying an annual subsidy to the de-facto rulers of Monyul (Tawang) under the impression that they were independent Chiefs. "... most of the subsidy went into the purses of the power at Tsona-Dzong and thence to Lhasa....this established practice dilutes the Indian claim to Monyul..... a deal was effected in 1914; Monyul was to become a part of the Balipara Frontier Tract." He advised effective occupation by 1939 or at the latest 1940. The explorer, F. Kingdom Ward thus roused the Government from slumber. Olaf Canoe, Deputy Secretary, Govt. of India, Foreign and Political Dept., then took up the matter for necessary follow-up action for implementing the McMahon Line as the delimited border.[18]

IV

I shall now briefly survey how British political and administrative control thereafter was established in the north-eastern frontier tract step by step, up to the McMahon Line, completing the process by 1951.

To forestall Chinese penetration into India's unadministered north-east Himalayan frontiers and establish therein 'loose political control'. Several expeditions (the Abor Expedition, the Miri Mission, the Dibong survey and Exploration etc.) were sent in the area during 1910-13. This was to prepare the ground for pushing the Outer Line northward as far as possible towards the Red Line. However as the Simla Convention was not ratified, and hence could not be published, nothing was done towards this goal. The Deputy Commissioners of Darrang and Lakhimpur districts maintained relations with hill tribes living beyond their respective Inner Lines along the foothills.

Separated from the afore-mentioned two regular districts, two North-East frontier sections were formed in 1912-13. These were:

(i) the Western Section dealing with Tibetanised Buddhist Tribes and some non-Budhist tribes as well of Kameng District and (ii) the Central and Eastern Section dealing with Abor (Adi), Miri, Mishmi, Khamti, Singhpo tribes. Their respective headquarters were at Chardwar and Sadiya, each in charge of a Political Officer. These were renamed, respectively as Balipara Frontier Tract and Sadiya Frontier Tract in 1919.[19] These together covered no less than 20,000 square miles of territory (i.e. at least two-thirds of the present Arunachal State) as was later pointed out by our Prime Minister Jawaharlal Nehru to Prime Minister Chou-En-Lai on 26th September 1959.

I have already noted how the forward policy of 1910-13 was once more operationalised in Tawang area even as Tibetan officials continued to collect what they called taxes and British officials called blackmail. The Balipara and Sadiya Frontier Tracts came under the direct administration of the Assam Governor on 1 April 1937. Sent to Tawang (Monyul) in April 1938, Captain G.S. Lightfoot informed all concerned that Tawang was by treaty British-Indian and not Tibetan since 1914. He also told them that the Govt. of India would soon decide what was to be done about Tawang, after his return. Lightfoot on return recommended to his Govt. immediate take-over of Tawang, but his advice was not accepted.[20] Meanwhile even before his return to his headquarters, Lhasa smelt foul and vehemently protested and sent a high official with an escort of troops to continue collecting 'taxes' not only in Tawang, but also as far as Rupa and Shergaon, claiming the population there as Tibetan subjects, however in the face of the Govt. of India's strong protest had to concede that the area south of Tawang was within British Control area. The erring officials received orders to stop collecting taxes from Rupa, Shergaon and Kalaktang, but nothing was said about Tawang proper. Lhasa was firmly told that British jurisdiction would be progressively extended up to the McMahon Line and in no case beyond it, but tax collection by Tibetan officials must stop.[21]

In 1944 an Assam Rifles Outpost was established at Dirangjong. In May 1945 J.P. Mills, renowned anthropologist and Adviser to the Governor, visited the place. In 1946 Balipara Frontier Tract was further split into two Sections: (i) the Subansiri Area and (ii) the Se-La Agency, the latter in charge of the area, south of Tawang proper, including its erstwhile dependencies. A memorandum handed out by Gould on 4

December 1944 to the Tibetan Govt. suggested that the Mcmahon Line might be further revised in due course to run to the south of Tawang if Tibetan officials stopped exercising authority south of Se-La. But their response was cold and negative. In 1947, for example, Tibetan officials issued notices on the people of Kalaktang to pay taxes to their representatives and not to the Govt. of India. Even as late as 16 March 1950, our Lok Sabha was informed in reply to D.K. Barooah that Tibetan 'marauders' were still trying "to collect money in the form to taxes or otherwise from the villages on the Indian side".[2 1a] At long last our Government decided to establish its authority in Tawang right up to the Mcmahon Line. Accordingly Major Khathing, then an Assistant Political Officer, reached Tawang, with an impressive armed police escort on 6 February 1951. Within a week Tawang was Liberated peacefully and brought under Indian administration. In 1953 the headquarters of Se-La Sub-Agency was shifted to Bomdi-La from Charduar. In 1954 its name was changed to that of Kameng Frontier Division.[22]

Even as India was continuing the erstwhile British policy of advancing towards the Red Line, People's China failed to lodge any protest for about a decade. The irony of the situation was that India too failed to protest against China's progressive encroachments in the Aksai Chin area during the same time. After years of slumber, the two Rip Van Winkles confronted each other with grim faces late in 1958. Notes on territorial claims, against each other were exchanged, but with no progress towards a road map for a bilateral negotiated settlement. Why, I have already explained. It is said, Nehru was inclined to favorably consider China's offer of NEFA in possession of India in exchange of Aksai-Chin, in China's possession but had to give in to the frenzied public opinion whipped up to a high pitch of bellicose nationalist emotion. It had by then become clear that China was not vitally interested in seizing NEFA so long as she could remain in Aksai-Chin. If this was so in 1962, it is more so today. Thanks to serious research at home and abroad, Indian public opinion now reflects a better understanding of the complicated border issue and its colonial roots.

"It should never have been allowed to develop into a political crisis, far less a military one," wrote Nirad C. Chaudhuri in February 1963, and he ridiculed the patriotic frenzy of the people as the Hindu traditional jingoism.[23] *The Times of India* suggested editorially on 5th July 1965 that India should "Challenge Peking to come to the negotiation table" and on 8th August 1968 further took note of "wider support in the country for a policy of rapprochment with China". Sarvepally Radhakrishnan, in his Presidential address in his Independence Day broadcast to the nation on 15th August 1966 said China and India would sooner or later, sooner rather than later, learn to live in peace and cooperation. A just settlement of the question dividing us is not impossible."

As early as 1963, K.P.S. Menon of the Indian Foreign Service had observed that the NEFA was "of vital importance to us whereas the Aksai Chin area is of little use, being hardly defensible".[24] If so, if Aksai Chin – " where not a blade of grass grows" (Nehru) – has merely a prestige value for us, it is in India's best interests that we settle the question for ever on a *quid pro quo* basis. Achieving a scientific strategic border, demarcated on the basis of a uniform high ridge-cum watershed principle and applied all along the Himalayan frontier with only minor adjustments here and there should be placed above all other considerations. Our claim need not seek legitimacy from intriguing imperialist land-grabbers like Sir Arthur Henry McMahon.

V

Coming to the close of my lecture let me look into the thorny Tawang question once more. Though Lightfoot had recommended immediate annexation of Tawang and its dependencies and G. Hogg the officiating Governor of Assam supported it, Delhi rejected the suggestion in order to continue good relations with Tibet.

Lightfoot's report had pointed out that Tibetan rulers carried on an oppressive taxation policy and, as a result, local tribesmen were emigrating to Bhutan. Trading in salt and rice was done through Tibetan monopolies. Taxes, on behalf of Tibetan Govt. and Monasteries, were collected in kind only and then transported by forced labour. According to Lightfoot's estimates, there were some 112 villages comprising of 2140 or so houses in Tawang and its dependencies, mostly Buddhist by religion. He argued that the miserable conditions of the dissatisfied tribesmen would justify British annexation and it would be also welcomed by them. On 17th March 1939 H.J. Twynam, Officiating Governor of Assam, wrote to Linlithgo the Viceroy on the same issue.

He argued that Tawang proper, the famous 17th Century monastery inclusive, might be spared from annexation to satisfy the Tibetans by way of modifying the Mcmahon Line. For annexing Tawang, if McMahon's object was to have access to the age-old trade route from Odalguri to Tibet, it could be gained by negotiation by posting a native trade agent at Tawang. To secure a natural watershed frontier also, occupation of Tawang does not help and Mcmahon himself also was aware of this fact. Twynam's recommendation was to extend the Control Area only up to Dirang Dzong and Kalaktang so that the Red Line could include Se-La (altitude 16000 ft.) running a few miles south of Tawang to reach the Bhutan border. Lightfoot justified proposed annexation on humanitarian ground, but Twynam justified his own forward policy more on scientific than on humanitarian ground. Besides, he had also reservation about legal and cartographic validity of the drawing of the Red Line. His proposal too was rejected mainly due to difficult war-time budget constraint. Status quo of Tibetan officials' extortions and monastic oppression thus continued unabated.

From 1943 onwards, we have already noted, India's Tibet policy underwent change. On 23rd October 1943 a post of Adviser to the Governor of Assam for Tibet (affairs) was created. And British anthropologist J.P. Mills of the Indian Civil Service was appointed to this post to expedite the ongoing slow process of extending the Control Area by advancing the Outer Line as far as McMahon Line. This policy change was due to increasing Japanese military threats to Assam. Under his over-all supervision, two Assam Rifles' outposts were established, one at Walong, near Rima and another at Dirangdzong, north of Rupa. The number of such outposts increased to 20 in the northern frontier area of present Himachal by the time the British quit India. During his visits to Siang Valley in 1944 and Se La Sub-Agency in early 1945, he took note of the miserable economic conditions of the local tribesmen, as they were to buy salt at exorbitant prices, and pay heavy taxes-in-kind collected by Tibetan officials. The extent of forced labour and slavery in vogue was also alarming.

Throughout the enlarged Control Area, stern measures were taken against the bandit-like Tibetan tax-collectors in an attempt to firmly establish Biritish colonial authority in the whole area up to the McMahon Line. He did so as a humanitarian having faith in the benevolent role of British imperialism. However, at the same time, like Gould and

Twysnum, he had no doubt that Tawang had always been more oriented to Tibet than to India, ethnically, geographically, politically culturally and in religion.[25]

As a keen observer, Mills discovered a basic cultural difference between Tawang and the rest of NEFA. Though commercially as well as culturally tied to Tibet rather than to India, exporting grain and madder to Tibet and importing salt therefrom, the latter area was inhabited by warring primitive tribesmen in contrast to well-settled 'Civilised' and Tibetanised Tawang. He was impressed by its settled population, Buddhist temples, stone house dwellings, plough cattle and cantilever bridges. Yet he favoured Tawang's merger with post-Independence India. More than half-a-century after his return to Britain, the scenario is thoroughly changed. Everywhere the contrast is narrowed down. As a constituent state of the Union of India yesterday's NEFA is developing and catching up fast with the modern world.[26]

After the 10th sitting of the Sino-Indian Peace Dialogue, the 11th sitting is ahead and we are hopeful a compromise will emerge. In this context, both sides should take lessons from the great epic *Mahabharata.* To avoid an internecine war and peace between the Kouravas and the Pandavas, Krishna led a peace mission to the Court of the former with an appeal to grant just five villages to the latter. Vain as he was, Duryodhana declared that even that much land as a needle point could hold would not be gifted away. The result was total disaster for both the camps. I reiterate my hope that under the present circumstances of international imperialist intrigues and uncertainties India and China will soon secure a mutually agreed boundary. I also hope that they will go ahead for another dialogue for fair distribution of the water of the Brahmaputra basin for multiple purposes by involving also Bangladesh, Nepal and Bhutan in that dialogue.

I conclude my lecture by dedicating it to the memory of Bertrand Russell (1872-1920), who was 20th century world's greatest philosopher, pacifist and a common friend of India and China. In his book *Unarmed Victory* published in 1963, he revealed that he tried to mediate between India and China at their critical hour. His open appeal to world's leading citizens and the press as well as his letters to Nehru and Chou En-Lai were appended to this book. He also sent a statement to the Wales Press being annoyed with the British press which refused to publish his appeal. He stated therein

> ... The Chinese had reached the southern slopes of the mountain and had Assam at their mercy. The difficult fighting in the passed was finished and no powerful military obstacle existed to prevent Chinese occupation of the Indian plains. I can not think of any other instance in which a victorious army had been halted in this way by its own government... (p. 48)

Lord Russell like Lord Krishna tried to mediate but failed to stop a disastrous war.

References

1. Israel Epstein, *Tibet Transformed* (New World Press, Beijing, 1st ed. 1983) pp. 476-80.
2. External Affairs Ministry, Govt. of India, Reports of the Officials of the Government of India and Peoples Republic of China on the Boundary Question (New Delhi, 1961) and Notes, Memoranda and letters between the Governments of India and China (White Paper, New Delhi. 1961-63).
3. *The Statesman* (Calcutta Daily) 13 Octtober 1962.
4. C. U. Aitchison, compiled, *A Collection of Treaties, Engagements and Sunnuds Relating to India and Neighboring Countries* (Calcutta 1876) volume I, pp 156-7, 211-12 and 237-3.
5. Karl Max, "East India Company: history and results" in *New York Daily Tribune,* 11 July 1853.
6. G. N. Rao, *The Indo-Chinese Border: A Re-appraisal* (Bombay 1968), p. 61-68; H. K. Barpujari, *Problem of the Hill Tribes: North East Frontier 1873-1962, Volume III, Inner Line to the McMahon Line* (Guwahati 1981), pp 115-17, Also Amalendu Guha, " *The McMahon Line in Contemporary History*" in M. S. Rajen, ed. *Studies in Politics: National and International* (Indian School of International Studies, New Delhi, 1970), pp 431-32 as well as 431, citing G. N. Rao (pp. 61 and 68).

7. *Ibid.* The quote is from Sir Robert Reid, Governor of Assam 1937-42, *History of the Frontiers Areas Bordering in Assam from 1883-1941,* (Shillong, 1942), pp. 280-81
8. Neville Maxwell, *India's China War* (Jaico Impression, Bombay, 1970), pp. 62-64.
9. *Ibid.,* and Epstein, pp. 476-80, *op cit.*
10. Maxwell, pp. 62-64, *op cit.*
11. Epstein, *op cit,* pp. 462-63
12. Maxwell, *op cit,* pp.46-49
13. *Ibid.*, pp. 46-49 and 50-54
14. *Ibid.,* p. 55
15. Reid, *op cit,* pp. 296-97
16. *Ibid.*
17. Barpujari, pp. 117-18
18. *Ibid.*, pp. 236-239
19. Reid, *op cit*, pp. 242-49, 260, 263-66, 281-90 and 303
20. Reid, *op cit*, 246-50
21. Barpujari, *op cit,* 246-50

21a. Questioned as to whether the present boundary of the Mishmi Hills represented McMahon Line, J. H. F. Williams, the then Political Officers at Sadiya, told the Sub-committee of the Constituent Assembly of India:

"Yes, but in the last few years the Tibetans have made encroachments across the McMahon Line at the top of the Lohit Valley. The position there is not still clear and the area is unvisited and unmapped. It has never been surveyed".

"Then so far as the area is concerned" remarked G. N. Bordoloi, Assam Chief Minister and Chairman of the Sub-Committee "the McMahon Line exists only in theory". This was on 26 May 1950. See Constituent Assembly of India, *North East Frontier (Assam) Tribal and Excluded Areas Sub-Committee* (Delhi), vol. 2 part 2, p.27.

22. L. N. Chakrabarty, *Glimpses of the Early History of Arunachal.* (Research Department, Arunachal Pradesh Administration, Shillong, 1973), p. 119.

23. Nirod C. Choudhari, *The Continent of Circe* (Bombay, 1965), p. 119.
24. K. P. Menon, *The Flying Troika* (London, 1963), p. 320.
25. Maxwell, *op cit*, pp. 58-62 and Barpujari, *op cit,* pp. 58-61and Barpuajri, pp. 257 and 262-63.
26. Maxwell, pp. 58-62 and Barpujari, p. 265.

Section II

Redefining Peace: Issues in Governance

4

Dialogues for Peace or Dialogues for Justice?

ULFA and the (Im)Possibilities of Peace Dialogue in Assam

Samir Kumar Das

Much of what goes on in the name of peace dialogues in the Northeast focuses more on peace per se than on its *quality* – widely considered as one of the preconditions of its durability and resolution. While the quality of peace is a function of rights, democracy and justice (Das 2005: 11-14), peace viewed in the negative sense as merely an absence of war is fragile, keeps war in abeyance and yet is constantly haunted by it. Peace in the second instance is an outcome of the balance of power reached at any given point of time between the two or more parties engaged in war. Such Peace obviously marks a continuation of war through dialogues and is therefore entered or broken as part of a strategic move to eventually checkmate the enemy in what looks like a prolonged war of attrition. While individual leaders have been seen to be involved in dialogues with various agencies of the State, right from the days of the first army operation (codenamed 'Operation Bajrang' in late 1990), the United Liberation Front of Asom (heretofore ULFA) as an organization has consistently kept itself as an organization outside all these dialogues. Yet, there have at least been two occasions (in 1991-2 and 2006-7) when ULFA came close to holding dialogues with the State. These are instances of *almost* dialogues, which had never taken place. The possibilities were created, but never actualized.

This paper probes into these aborted and unactualized possibilities and argues in favour of taking a more cautious view about war and peace commonly seen as binaries. For, many an impossibility is built into these apparently created possibilities of peace dialogues and the aborted and unactualized possibilities should be seen more as part of the same continuing war between the two parties. The possibilities and impossibilities do not form a set of unsurpassable opposites, but are integral to the same war game that otherwise sets forth the terms of the relationships between two mutually hostile parties. Thus at one level, peace for the State means that the insurgents need to be sufficiently weakened by the ongoing security operations and *consequently* brought to the negotiating table so that some 'solution' can be forced on them. At another, insurgents view it as a temporary breather that gives them opportunities for regrouping and rearming themselves particularly at a time when continuous security operations push them into the defensive and thereafter striking a blow to the State with full might at an opportune moment. For both of these parties, peace dialogues are only the tools and instruments of the larger strategic maneuver in the otherwise grand game of war. We assume that it is by way of bringing the larger perspective of rights, democracy and justice to bear on our understanding of peace dialogues that we gain insights into the possible roadmap to durable and sustainable peace and the resolution of the outstanding problems that divide the warring parties.

The paper also seeks to drive home the argument that the terms of present-day peace dialogues are caught in the midst of an apparently irresolvable dichotomy between nation and rights and is therefore unable to overcome the democratic deficit produced by it. While the State always insists that all the markers and symbols of the State (the Constitution, for example) and the (Indian) nation it represents are adhered to and respected while reaching any solution, the insurgents including the ULFA want to keep *all* possibilities open and refuse to commit themselves to any solution that unduly forecloses the other non-national alternatives even before the dialogues are initiated.[2] What we call 'democratic deficit' is accumulated precisely because of the inability of the world's actually existing democratic states to transcend (but not necessarily negate) the order of nations and resolve the dichotomy between nation and rights. Dialogues that are conducted without violating the sanctity of the given Indian nation in any way are called *policy* dialogues, while those that are free, unencumbered and open-ended are regarded as *rights* dialogues. The first part of our paper reflects on the complexities of this dichotomy with special reference to the series of 'almost dialogues' between ULFA and the Indian State. The second part argues that one way to come out of the impasse is to reorient the peace dialogues and predicate them on the principles of justice. Justice is the site where the hiatus between the claims of the nation and the particular rights claims of such insurgent organizations as ULFA are likely to be reconciled and bridged over. Justice dialogues constitute the site where the dichotomy between policy and right, between the nation and the insurgents, between the whole and the indissoluble parts can be sublimated and resolved. The paper makes a plea for framing the terms of peace dialogue within the principles of justice.

Democracy and Its Modes of Dialoguing

It was Alexis De Tocqueville who made a categorical distinction between democracy and justice and warned us against the otherwise commonplace tendency of confusing one with the other. While democracies of modern times have for all practical purposes become representative and are ruled by the majorities, majority rule according to him is no guarantee for justice. As he observes:

> A general law exists that has been made or at least adopted not only by the majority of this or that people, but by the majority of all men. This law is justice ... (W)hen I refuse to obey an unjust law, I do not deny to the majority the right to command; I only appeal from the sovereignty of the people to the sovereignty of the human race. (Tocqueville 2000: 240)

In pursuance of this distinction, it is also argued that democracy defined as procedure does not necessarily have any impact on the substance of justice and vice versa, implying thereby that justice is conceivable in undemocratic or even antidemocratic political systems as much as democratic political systems do not necessarily promote justice. The distributive performances of such 'non-democratic' states as the former Soviet Union and Saddam Hussein's Iraq are said to be better than many of the democratic states. There is thus no necessary and invariable correlation between (representative) democracy and justice. But how are we to ascertain justice? While for Tocqueville, understanding 'the law of the human race' does not pose any problems for they are too self-evident, historically however human race has more often than not suffered from people who seem to have 'known' the law of the human race and accordingly throttled the voice of the majority. Former Soviet Union or Saddam's Iraq are a standing testimony to this. Democratic procedures are designed to facilitate a dialogue between the rulers and the ruled. Dialogue per se may have its importance in a democracy. The communication between them may have its intrinsic worth in a democracy. But, more than providing and facilitating communication between the rulers and the ruled, we have to keep in mind that the way we conduct our dialogue with the rulers has its implications for the substance or content of justice. How we talk also has its implications for what we (can) talk and what we probably do (can) not. The procedures set forth the terms and range of what our talks are. There is no one way of conducting dialogues even in a democracy. The emphasis on democratic form does not make our contention formalistic. We may have to redesign our democratic dialogues in keeping with the imperatives of justice. Democratic dialogue is not necessarily a justice dialogue. Majority rule may not be apt for the purpose.

We have to understand that there is no one single way of conducting dialogues. I propose to take the cue from Ronald Dworkin who in his *Taking Rights Seriously* (1977) makes a distinction between 'policies' and 'rights'. Rights, as he argues, tend to disarticulate the collective (the nation, for example) that policies seek to organize, sustain and stabilize. Rights therefore are to be regarded as particularistic or at times exclusive claims against the collective. It seems that our dialoguing with the State can accordingly be conducted in either of the two languages: the language of the collective or that of rights. These two languages are distinct in many ways. The language of rights does not have any obligation of remaining bound by the imperatives of keeping the collective body of nation intact. Policies and rights in this view are clearly dichotomous. We define the existing peace dialogues as the ones that seek to subordinate the rights claims to the imperative of allowing the already existing collective to thrive and continue. The insistence by the insurgents on holding an open-ended plebiscite in what they consider as their homeland thus clashes against the State's acceptance of the nation it represents and its territorial integrity as given and unalterable. Secondly, they also argue that these parts were incorporated into the national body without giving them any freedom of choice whatsoever. Their incorporation has been a fait accompli and therefore cannot be reversed. The State, for example, always emphasizes that the dialogues should be held within the basic framework of the Indian Constitution. This insistence actually rules out many alternatives of possible solution. One of the State's worries has been to determine the representativeness of the insurgent organizations they are called upon to dialogue with. The State, for example, shot down a couple of years back the All-Party Hurriyat Conference's (APHC) institution of an Election Commission outside the purview of the Indian State to conduct free and fair elections in the Indian State of Jammu and Kashmir. Many of the insurgent organizations on the other hand argue that since their incorporation into the Indian Union was done without offering them any freedom of choice and right to contract in this respect, the process itself should not be taken as fait accompli and would have to be revisited. Besides ULFA, the United National Liberation Front of Manipur (UNLF) makes a critique of Manipur's forcible incorporation into the Indian Union. The 'Merger Agreement' that was signed between Maharaja Bodhachandra Singh and the representative of the Government of India in 1949 was signed, as UNLF maintains, when the King was 'under duress' and taken outside his kingdom. It may be recalled that the Agreement was signed in Shillong.

We know that the putatively democratic states have not been able to come completely, if at all, to terms with the language of rights. We are now living in an age of policies rather than rights. As the inside of the State has become exposed to influences coming from across the borders, thanks to the forces and processes of globalization and the State's growing inability to exercise ideological hegemony over its people, Indian State too has been facing the problem of reconstituting 'the inside' by way of initiating a package of policies that basically aim at holding the inside together and keeping it from falling apart. Globalization has shifted the terms of discourse from rights to policies as much as it has turned the spotlight from the outside to the inside. We are passing through a phase of policy explosion particularly since the 1990s. National Agricultural Policy, National Employment Guarantee Act, The Policy of Resettlement and Rehabilitation of Project-affected Families etc., provide only some examples of this larger policy explosion in India. A change in Government's policy is discernible particularly since the mid-1980s in its insistence on holding dialogues with various independentist and armed groups of the region. This seems to be based on the new realization that the imperative of peace, quietly and often unrecognizably, expands the realm of what the State is willing to negotiate and concede and thereby stabilizing the national body. Thus dialogues – unlike the previous ones, are mostly held outside India in such places as Chiang Mai, Bangkok, Amsterdam, Geneva or Copenhagen and more often than not without any preconditions. In some cases like the Naga one, the State did not raise any objection to the third part involvement of foreign NGOs in the peace process.

These policies are primarily meant for rebuilding the collective now facing the threat of being disarticulated and fractured by a plethora of forces commonly associated with globalization. The threats that the nation-State faces today emerge both from within and from without the nation. At one level, there is what is euphemistically called, the global civil society. The Unrepresented Nations and Peoples' Organization (UNPO) is a classic example. The National Socialist Council of Nagalim (IM) became a member to this organization notwithstanding the Indian State's strong objections to it. ULFA's soliciting for membership however was not granted. At another level, the indigenous rights discourse is increasingly gaining momentum. (Barbora, 2005) The discourse is based on the principled dichotomy between the 'indigenous peoples' of the region and the 'settler' Indian State. The State, whether colonial or postcolonial, is held as alien, external and 'colonial' to the region. It is also referred to as 'occupier' State by several insurgent organizations including ULFA. The relationship between the State and the indigenous peoples of the region has not been contractually negotiated unlike in other cases. The discourse also envisages the reemergence of the cultural continuities historically evolved across the sub-Himalayan region throughout the ages but snapped only recently with the formation of nation-states and reorganization of administrative and international borders in its wake. As security operations turned the heat on the insurgents and as the cadres are on the run, they seek shelter in the neighbouring countries like China, Bhutan and Bangladesh, interestingly on the ground that they have been one till the subcontinent was partitioned and international borders were reorganized.

Peace with ULFA?

Although ULFA was born on 7 April 1979, it was not until 1983 that ULFA surfaced in the public arena and people could become aware of its political presence in Assam. ULFA first came to the limelight when it joined hands with the All-Assam Students' Union and All-Assam Gana Sangram Parishad in enforcing the boycott of polls in 1983 till the names of the illegally settled 'foreigners' were struck off from the electoral rolls. The first four years may therefore be regarded as the period of silent consolidation. But, as ULFA shot into prominence whether by way of organizing exceptionally daring bank dacoities or by initiating rural development works particularly in areas where State presence was cosmetic or even by conducting retributive killings and meting out summary justice in those areas or any of their combination, there is reason to believe that the State for whatever reasons did not come down heavily on the insurgents. As one ULFA leader subsequently acknowledged that they had no idea that this could be such a cakewalk for them: they asked for little but the impact was enormous. (in Roy 1991: 98). For one, ULFA was declared illegal only as late as on 27 November 1990. For another, the ruling Asom Gana Parishad (AGP) regime that came to power in 1985 was reportedly 'hand in glove' with them. (Hazarika 1994: 175) In many cases, its penetration into the State police was almost complete so much so that it was admitted by a police officer, then serving in Assam, that 'ULFA cadres are un-uniformed policemen and the policemen are the uniformed ULFA cadres'.

One wonders how such a State-insurgent nexus could operate in Assam almost uninterruptedly during the first ten years of ULFA's existence. Part of the nexus may be explained with reference to the fact that both AGP, including its earlier incarnation, All-Assam Gana Sangram Parishad (AAGSP) and ULFA, owe their common origin to the Assam movement that rocked Assam between 1979 and 1985. Although their organizations were ideologically distinct, many of the ULFA cadres were personally close to a section of ministers and leaders sometimes across party lines and were indirectly instrumental in bringing them to power both in 1985 and also in 1996. (Das in Phukon & Adil-ul-Yasin 1998:1-18) Although ULFA has consciously stayed away from all the polls, it carefully created, almost in each of them, the conditions that helped in launching a particular party into power and edging past its adversaries. Obviously, they harboured a sense of gratitude towards them, as they would come to power and form the Government with their tacit support. It was too much to expect that they would do anything to alienate their former comrades in arms. Partly the immense popularity that ULFA enjoyed in the 1980s especially by providing instant justice to the offenders and criminals and initiating rural development works was a factor that none of the established political parties had had the courage to overlook or even firmly deal with. ULFA served as the para-State in the remoter areas, where the presence of the Indian State was cosmetic, if not non-existent. Most of the political parties were keen on deriving maximum political mileage from out of their presence without ever trying to crack down on them. The nexus proved to be beneficial for both the parties and continued unabated till the first army operation against them began in Assam in 1990.

The year 1990 marks the watershed as the army moved in and the first ever army operation was launched in Assam with the objective of 'liquidating' ULFA. But, it came as a surprise both to the army as well as to the insurgents. ULFA by its own admission was least prepared for 'taking on the army'. As Siddhartha Phukan, the then publicity secretary pointed out, even as late as in the middle of 1990, that is to say, a few months before 'Operation Bajrang':

> In fact the members of our organization are not yet prepared for taking on the army, we want the direct fight with the State machinery sometimes later. Over and above, common people have not yet been ready for this type of military conflict. If we start military operation with the armed forces dispatched by Delhi, frightening (State) repression will be unleashed in the places of operation, like in Manipur and Mizoram. Since our common people are not yet mentally habituated with the armed struggle, and if State repression is unleashed at this time against them, the people will blame us; we will not allow that. And for this reason we are trying to avoid the patrol by the security forces. In order to get hold of ULFA (cadres), they will repress the common people so that they start getting disenchanted with the ULFA... we will have to prepare the people very slowly. The people will have to resist in a united manner against the aggression and repression of State machinery. And that process has taken off on its own now. (quoted in *Budhbar*, 6 June 1990).

In simple terms, ULFA evidently was preparing for a prolonged engagement. On the other hand, Lt. Col. K. S. Brar – the GOC-in-C, Eastern Command, pointed out that the secret documents seized from ULFA hideouts by the army suggested that warnings were given to them from the central headquarters to shut off their military training camps on 19 December 1990. It only shows that ULFA leadership was aware of the impending army operations and reveals the depth of ULFA penetration into the State and its decision-making machinery. It is interesting to ponder what led the Government to strike against ULFA. The murder of Surrendra Paul, a planter and an eminent industrialist, radically changed the scenario and inaugurated in the words of *India Today*, a 'new era of capitulation' of the Government to the tea industry. (Gupta & Sengupta, 1990: 23) This is revealed in the Government's decision to act simultaneously on two fronts: First it decided to rehabilitate the top management cadre of tea industries, facing threats for ransoms from ULFA, to safe havens. On 8 November 1990, in the early hours, Indian army and air force were involved in airlifting top executives of Brooke Bond, Lipton and Doom Dooma tea companies from the airstrip controlled by the Aviation Research Centre working under the Research and Analysis Wing (RAW) in Tinsukia. Secondly, the Government also decided to call the army on 29 November 1990. Thus began direct and armed confrontation between the State and ULFA. And as the operation began, the ULFA too realized the importance of military preparations. Sunil Nath alias Siddhartha Phukan for example points out: "... the events of Lakhipathar and Charaipung (where the ULFA camps were busted by the army and mass graves were discovered, SKD) have proven that it is a primary condition for any revolutionary organization to put emphasis on military discipline and ultramodern weapons." (quoted in *Budhbar*, 16 June 1990) While 'Operation Bajrang' turned out to be a damp squib insofar as all the camps had been vacated before army troops marched in, another military operation codenamed 'Operation Rhino' began in September 1991 with the objective of flushing out the 'terrorists' and isolating them from the people of Assam. Unlike 'Operation Bajrang', the objective of the second operation was quite different. It seems that the State too realized that complete 'liquidation' of ULFA might not be possible in the short run.

Peace dialogues to begin need first of all a breach in the State-insurgent nexus and the commencement of armed hostilities. For, as long as the nexus is put in place, and continues to be mutually beneficial, neither the State nor the insurgents is in any pressing need to negotiate with the other. It is only with the commencement of hostilities that they feel the necessity of initiating dialogues and stand the chance of facing reverses. Nexus is mutually beneficial while hostility may not necessarily be so. Hostility or war is a precondition of dialogues. Initiating peace talks with ULFA proves to be quite a long haul and seems to be moving through a roller coaster. The reference to talks has been made intermittently right after the first-ever army operation against the outfit. It was in the middle of 1990, the Government of India extended its first peace offer to ULFA and expressed its willingness to hold talks 'at any State, anywhere'. Dinesh Goswami, one of the cabinet ministers hailing from Assam, even went a step further and remarked that he had 'full respect' for the 'sincerity' of ULFA members. Back in early 1990, however, ULFA looked upon any offer of negotiations as 'a clever means employed by the capitalist groups and the State of disarming ULFA' and of creating 'rift within its ranks'. ULFA's general antipathy towards dialogues is much too well known to be recounted here. Again in 1991 when the second military operation was in full swing, the Government and ULFA were reportedly engaged in dialogues with the help of mediators consisting mainly of the locals from the central services and the journalists. There were also reports of ULFA leaders secretly meeting the chief minister of Assam and working out the terms of future dialogues between them. These back channel negotiations are common in such cases but usually take time to bear fruit. It seems that by the middle of 1991, ULFA was clearly divided on the question of whether to enter into dialogues with the Indian State or not. According to *Budhbar*, it was possible to identify the 'moderates' and 'extremists' on this crucial question. (*Budhbar*, 30 October 1991) In an interview with *Budhbar*, Raju Baruah, then chief of ULFA's Nalbari unit, observed: "There has been no change in our position on freedom (*swadhinata*). The struggle will continue. The question of compromise with the treacherous State or its representatives is absurd." (*Budhbar* 8 January 1992) On the other hand, there were reports that five ULFA leaders under the leadership of Arabinda Rajkhowa acquiesced to the Constitution and signed what Parag Kumar Das termed, 'a treaty of compromise' with the Government of India. (*Budhbar* 22 January 1992).

Way back in 1992 immediately after 'Operation Bajrang', a section of ULFA leadership was involved in peace talks, which however broke off when one of its delegations led by Arabinda Rajkhowa decided to withdraw due to 'the pressure from his uncompromising "commander-in-chief" Paresh Barua. (Misra 2000:139) Baruah is said to have expressed his 'dissatisfaction' with the 'unconditional surrender of arms' and 'one-sided acquiescence to the Constitution of India'. Rajkhowa subsequently walked away from the talks describing his compromise-seeking colleagues as 'Government revolutionaries'. Finally on 22 July 1992, a full-house General Body meeting of ULFA was held at an undisclosed place in Bhutan. The meeting was attended by Arabinda Rajkhowa, Paresh Baruah and Anup Chetiya etc. All the 18 District units including that of Karimganj took part in it. The meeting arrived at a 'unanimous decision' that the question of 'falling into the trap laid by the Indian State through deceit and treachery in the name of discussions does not arise.' (*Budhbar* 29 April 1992) The meeting also decided to prepare a list of compromise-seeking leaders, described them as 'counter-revolutionaries' but did not assign to itself the responsibility of punishing them. It resolved that the people would 'judge and punish' them.

There is reason to believe that a serious ideological churning within ULFA on the question of entering into peace dialogues with the Government of India did exist. In January 1992, Sunil Nath – ULFA's the then Publicity Secretary -- with a few other leaders, came out openly against the organization and said that instead of "Swadhinata" (Independence) they wanted "Swadhikar" (Right to self-determination) of the Assamese people. The change in semantics was associated with at least two major strategic changes in ULFA's political practice that helped in creating conditions for peace dialogues with the Government of India. One, it was clarified by the concerned circles that the assertion of the right to self-determination ought not to be confused with a demand for secession. Drupad Bargaohian – himself an ULFA member, who wanted the organization to be part of the forthcoming peace process, even implied that the right to self-determination could actually be enjoyed within a 'Federation'. Besides both Kamal Bora and Siddhartha Phukan, 'lieutenant' and 'second lieutenant' of ULFA respectively, argued for instance that talks were a means of transforming ULFA into a 'mass organization' and would help them in organizing 'a movement within the so-called Indian democracy.' (*Budhbar* 1 April 1992) Two, it seems that a section of ULFA members too realized that a movement that remained confined to a small region could not finally achieve its objectives unless it could widen itself and was organized on an all-India basis. (*Budhabar* 29 January 1992) Arabinda Rajkhowa, ULFA's Chairman, along with five of his colleagues, was believed to have writnen a letter on 12 January 1992 to Rajiv Gandhi, the then Prime Minister of Assam, in which he expressed his willingness to enter into some form of negotiations with the Government of India and agreed to (a) accept the Constitution of India for the resolution of the Assam problem, (b) abandon the path of violence, and finally, (c) surrender their arms at an appropriate time. In return, the same 'compromise group' requested the Government to (a) withdraw military operations, (b) stop indiscriminate arresting of ULFA members, (c) withdraw the ban imposed on ULFA and the Armed Forces (Special Powers) Act clamped on parts of Assam, (d) transfer all ULFA members arrested by the police to jail custody, (e) extend general amnesty to all the supporters and sympathizers held in prisons. (*Budhbar* 22 January 1992).

But as army operations went on, in January 1991, Siddhartha Phukan publicly expressed ULFA's willingness to enter into negotiations with the Government. The outfit declared unilateral ceasefire from 28 February 1991. The Government however did not take any step in this direction and ULFA's call for peace went unheeded. After a long ceasefire, the organization resurfaced again on 1 July with the kidnapping of an industrialist in upper Assam. The Government sources read ULFA's reported insistence on holding talks in a 'third country' under the UN supervision and exclusively on the issue of 'sovereignty' of Assam as a ploy to avoid talks and take a breather while preparing for further escalation of violence in future. Government on its part clearly looked upon the peace process as a means of making ULFA surrender and compromise. The Government reportedly imposed many a condition on the compromise-seeking leadership and April 1, 1992 was given as the deadline of surrender. Surrender was held as a precondition for the initiation of talks. The Government sources also made it clear that no talks were possible unless Paresh Baruah was personally present. Given his unbending attitude towards peace dialogues, the condition put the compromise group into clear disadvantage. The other condition was that surrender of arms had to be completed before peace dialogues could begin. (*Budhbar*, 18 March 1992) It is only obvious that the Government viewed the almost peace process only as an extension of its war game, while the compromise group involved itself in serious ideological rethinking and hard strategic reviews.

In a signed statement issued by Mithinga Daimary, its publicity secretary in July 1996, the ULFA extended an offer of peace to the Government and set immediate stoppage of 'the forceful Indianisation of the people of Assam' as one of the preconditions. However, the statement stuck to its formulation of 'Sovereignty and Independence of Assam' as the only issue of discussion. Even as late as in September 1998, ULFA did not seem to be reconciled to the idea of holding peace talks with the Government of India in a way that might lead 'national liberation struggle astray'. The organization reiterated that the talks would centre on the issue of 'Assam's sovereignty' and be held in 'a third country' under the UN supervision.[7] As Swadhinata Phukon, one of the members of ULFA's Central Publicity Cell, pointed out, there was "no alternative to a prolonged mass armed struggle to end killings and atrocities by the Indian State". Again in 1999, S(urrendered) ULFA reportedly sent 'feelers' to the Government circles expressing its willingness to enter into some form of peace negotiations with the central Government. Immediately after the operations in Bhutan that led to the busting of its headquarters and killing of a number of its top-ranking cadres (December 2003), an offer of peace was made by the organization although the same issues of 'sovereignty of Assam' and 'venue of third country' were set as preconditions by Paresh Baruah – its "Commander-in-Chief". ULFA cadres, who escaped the operation and fled away, made a 'dramatic appeal' to the Chairman of the People's Republic of China: "At this moment, they (the cadre) have no option but to enter the territory of the People's Republic of China extra-legally to save their lives, negotiating subzero temperature and starvation... We would like to request you and your people to permit them safe passage to your territory and temporary shelter necessary for their survival". The Government of India's response has been very cautious in the sense that it accused ULFA of initiating peace talks with a view to regroup itself usually after any army operation. Indira Goswami, one of the highly respected Asomiya litterateurs, in her letter to the Prime Minister written in November

2004 urged the New Delhi Government on taking steps for holding talks with the insurgents. Arabinda Rajkhowa, the outfit's Chairman, also expressed his willingness to begin dialogues, provided it receives a formal invitation on "the Government of India's letterhead with a signature and office seal". In an email message to the media, Rajkhowa made a case for plebiscite on the contentious issue of 'sovereignty' of Assam as 'sovereignty' according to ULFA, rests with the people of Assam. The ULFA-Centre peace process was highlighted at a recent Jatiya Mahasabha (national conclave) held in Guwahati. Organized under the aegis of the People's Committee for Peace Initiatives (PCPI), the two-day conclave urged the Centre to start talks with ULFA on sovereignty or hold a plebiscite. The meeting adopted several resolutions highlighting various burning issues of the region, including groups to facilitate direct talks with the ULFA and various other militant groups. The Assam Government has however rejected the demand for plebiscite. Chief Minister Tarun Gogoi rubbished it as "a futile exercise" since the Centre would never concede to the demand. He also argued that the question of a plebiscite did not arise since elections were held democratically and the people had been exercising their franchise despite calls for boycott of elections by various outfits, including the ULFA.

The ULFA however seems to have moved a step ahead by dropping the first two conditions and Paresh Baruah has reportedly agreed to come over to New Delhi or Dispur to attend such talks. As he pointed out in a statement issued in August 2004: "Sovereignty is the core issue for us and we are willing to sit for dialogue anywhere if this is discussed."

Mamoni Raisom Goswami's memoir entitled *Dastabejar Natun Prishtha* (the new pages of document) is expected to be published shortly. Publication of her memoir is also expected to throw light on her role as a facilitator of the recently initiated dialogue. On November 16, 2004 Goswami met Prime Minister Manmohan Singh and handed over a memorandum drafted in consultation with the academics from Delhi University including Manoranjan Mohanty. On November 18, Arabinda Rajkhowa – the chairman, confirmed that ULFA would enter into a dialogue if the organization were invited on the Government of India's letterhead with a signature and office seal, and with 'sovereignty' on the agenda. Both Goswami and the Government of India have been consulting legal experts for an interpretation of 'sovereignty' and its place in the Indian Constitution. She has also consulted Soli Sorabjee – the then Solicitor General of India. As *The Telegraph* reported it: "Legal opinion seems to be that there could be various kinds of sovereignty, some of which are not against the Constitution. Economic sovereignty is a possibility, for instance."

On 19 November 2004, in one of her meetings with the Prime Minister, she was successful in attracting the attention of the Government to the serious problem of insurgency in Assam. She appealed to the Prime Minister to initiate a process of dialogue on the outfit's demand for "sovereignty" for Assam, but the Prime Minister put to rest any such speculation and said in Guwahati on 22 November 2004 that "if they shun violence, then I will invite them for talks but violence and talks cannot go on simultaneously." Responding to Singh's categorical rejection of ULFA's 'sovereignty' demand on 22 November, the ULFA commander-in-chief Paresh Baruah said, "The commitment made by the PM was not unexpected and not different from that made by his predecessors. It is evident that the Centre's colonial policy will continue." Both Paresh Baruah and Mamoni Goswami maintain that the latter is talking with the PM in her own capacity and initiative but Baruah lauds her effort in bringing the issue of 'sovereignty' into the agenda. Goswami has reportedly been briefed not to make any press statement in this respect.

Goswami's move was preceded by similar moves by different organizations in the State. In September 2004, the Assam Jatiyatabadi Yuba Chhatra Parishad (AJYCP) for instance, initiated a Jatiya Mahasabha (People's Council) on the dialogue process. The Mahasabha called for a unilateral ceasefire by the Government, and asked the ULFA to give up violence. None of these demands was fulfilled. The AJYCP initiative was followed by several meetings organized by the intelligentsia, and research organizations in Guwahati, which reiterated the demand for continuing negotiations. Notably, the All Assam Students' Union (AASU) called for a 100 hour unilateral ceasefire by the Government. While the Government was in no mood to concede to these demands, ULFA was critical of such multiple forums and in a media statement in the last week of October 2004, Paresh Baruah asked these organizations to desist from such efforts.

Sometime in early 2005, Indira Goswami met Prime Minister Dr. Manmohan Singh (who happens to be one of her ex-colleagues from Delhi University), requesting the start of a dialogue between ULFA leaders and the Government. In December 2004, ULFA leaders rejected the first peace offer made by the Prime Minister's office; but Goswami has not given up hope. Despite a series of blasts in Assam apparently triggered off by the ULFA, Goswami has again written to the Prime Minister to issue a fresh call to the ULFA for talks. During her visit to Guwahati jail (January 1, 2005), she met three prominent ULFA leaders– Pardip Gogoi (vice-chairman), Bhimkanta Buragohain (political adviser) and Mithinga Daimari (publicity secretary). She requested them to talk with the Government with an open mind. In the past the Government of India invited ULFA for talks, but most of the requests were turned down by the latter. After telephonic conversations with some top ULFA leaders, she is believed to have submitted a draft to the Prime Minister's office justifying the need to discuss the issue of 'sovereignty'. The draft does not include two of the earlier demands: peace talks should be held in another country and under UN supervision. Goswami seems to have managed to convince ULFA to confine their talks to the issue of sovereignty. She maintained that "sovereignty" of Assam was an issue, which had to be discussed, even though it should not be seen as a 'precondition'. On a number of occasions, she said that there was no harm in talking about 'sovereignty' of Assam. In an interview to Nava Thakuria, she observed: "The issue of sovereignty per se should not be seen as a precondition ... I understand that he (Prime Minister) will have to find out some middle path and some solution after consulting all parties and experts. However, without the sovereignty issue, the ULFA leaders are unlikely to come." In fact, Arabinda Rajkhowa reportedly requested her to continue her efforts despite the early setback in December 2004.

It is interesting to see why she takes an abiding interest in the initiative? It largely springs from the deeply rooted personal commitment of a highly respected litterateur of Assam. Goswami's non-political past and her extraordinarily deep belief in the innate goodness of human beings, whether in Government or in ULFA ranks or outside, literally catapulted her overnight into the rough and tumble of politics. She too realized that it was too much for her to handle – although she was very clear from the outset that her intervention is restricted to the task of bringing both parties to the negotiating table and it is for them to find out a solution for themselves. She blamed both the Government and the ULFA for the carnage against 'the Hindi-speaking Indians' – a euphemism for the Biharis perpetrated by the insurgents. "There was lack of transparency on both sides," as she claimed. The carnage took a toll of over 70 persons and a string of bomb blasts all over Assam. Goswami says that she met ULFA leaders 'by accident'. She had gone to a remote village in Assam to attend a public meeting. Here, she came to know that many of the organizers of the meeting were either directly involved with the ULFA or sympathetic to the cause. The writer decided to interact with the 'boys': "The Government should listen to the boys. Why have they taken to the path of violence? They are our boys, with guns in their hands. We have maintained the armed struggle for the last quarter of a century. So we cannot simply ignore them."

It is in such a context that an 11-member People's Consultative Group (PCG) consisting mainly of well-known civil society activists was set up by the ULFA to conduct negotiations with the Government. This is the first time that ULFA inducts the civil society persons into the peace process. It too seems to realize the necessity of involving the larger civil society in the peace process so that the issue gets widely discussed and as part of the process, a collective self can eventually come into being from an otherwise badly battered society. The Prime Minister met them in late November 2005 and the members of PCG expressed satisfaction over their first meeting with the Prime Minister. The personal appearance of the Prime Minister without sending an emissary at the very first meeting is unusual. First of all, it speaks of his personal interest in resolving the problem especially when he is a member of parliament from the State. Secondly, it also shows that much groundwork might have already been done before the first meeting took place and both parties refused to let their discussions get embroiled in procedural niceties.

Yet there are many hiccups in the way. First, it seems that the signals are conflicting and the Government too is fragmented and is not one in accord. The military operations against ULFA in the Dibru-Saikhowa forests of upper Assam are enough to jeopardize the peace process. Peace talks with PCG continued without any ceasefire declared by either side. There was letup in the military operations while talks with PCG were carried out. While according to one estimate at least 13 rounds of talks were held between the Government of India and PCG, no less than 36 ULFA cadres were killed by bullets of the security forces. Moreover, the talks with PCG could not dispel the mutual hatred and suspicion between the two adversaries and clear the decks for reaching any negotiated settlement with ULFA. While ULFA stuck to its demand for release of five of its top leaders who were arrested in course of the Bhutan operations in 2003 on the ground that they might take part in the peace dialogues, Tarun Gogoi– Assam's Chief Minister wanted a written response from the organization assuring the Government of its commitment to talks. Given ULFA's earlier record of breaking off talks even after the release of their arrested leaders, the Government probably considered it to be too risky to act on the basis of its merely verbal commitments. The Centre therefore insists on an official letter from ULFA for 'direct talks'. Gogoi went a step further and conceded that talks could be held on 'any matter' including that of 'Assam's sovereignty'. But no Government on earth, he pointed out, could make the offer in black and white because of its own inherent compulsions. It may not be irrelevant to note in this connection that ULFA too insisted on written assurance from the Government on the question. The formalistic stand on both parts caught both the parties in a stalemate. ULFA went on a rampage and claimed responsibility to the carnage that killed over 70 'Hindi speakers' – mostly Bihari brick kiln workers whose families, as subsequent findings indicated, had migrated to and settled in Assam more than 100 years ago. ULFA'a attacks were meant mainly for acquiring a certain visibility that it had reportedly lost as a result of the stalemate and avenge the alleged death of five ULFA cadres in Kakopathar in early January by the Bihar Regiment deployed there.

Secondly, it is also reported that there is strong pressure from Inter-Services Intelligence (ISI), the Pakistani espionage agency, that compels ULFA to stay away from any peace talks. Indeed, Mamoni Goswami expressed her surprise when she had come to know that ULFA was very close to the Pakistani agency and its moves were masterminded by it. "I would have given up, if only I was told", she exclaimed. Goswami however conceded that she did not get a specific denial when she broached the subject with ULFA Chief, Paresh Baruah: "He said that they (ULFA cadres) were independent and can have ties with anybody." (quoted in Mohan 2007: 7)

Although 'deadlocked' from September 2006 with the resumption of army operations on 24 September 2006 and PCG backing out from talks, the Government has never ruled out the possibility of holding peace dialogues even at the height of army operations. The history of such almost talks with ULFA is as old as the history of war with them. Indeed, as we argued, peace is viewed by both the warring parties as only a part of the game of war. Even after the recent army operations began, V. K. Duggal, the then Home Secretary to the Government of India, for example observed: "Let them (ULFA) come for talks". He also dismissed a question whether there was lack of will on the part of the Centre to open talks with ULFA. The war game is clear from the army brief, the objective of which this time is to exert pressure on the insurgent outfit to give up violence and come to the table. J.J. Singh, the Army Chief for example pointed out: "The Army has been given as assignment to perform. If we can compel them to come to the negotiating table and abjure violence, the peace and prosperity will come back to Assam." (quoted in Pandit 2007: 7) But then, making them come back and join the peace dialogues is not going to be peaceful. It is going to be a messy affair involving the prolongation of the same war. War and peace in this great game of chess are inextricably tied together.

Dialoguing for Justice

The struggles for particularistic rights including that of self-determination are attended to by the policies. This has substantially enriched our policy fund. Rights are showing signs of being appropriated by the language of policies. Locating rights at the level of policies implies governmentalization of justice – a process whereby the rough and particularistic edges of rights are blunted and their claimants are made an integral part of the collective body – the object of the State's government. If the State's intent is to governmentalize the rights, the ULFA has consistently stood back and refused to convert the almost talks into talks.

That does not mean that I am making a plea for locating justice at the level of rights. Since rights – as Dworkin points out, are claims against the collective, a society dialoguing in the language of rights is a potentially unstable society. The language of justice is not particularistic and cannot be expressed through particularistic let alone exclusivist claims against the collective. This is required to be universal. It implies a redefinition of the rules and principles and as a corollary to it, the re-imagining and reconstruction of the collective. Justice is not what you consider as just for you; it should also be just for all others in the world. The ethnic or nationalistic vision will have to transcend itself into a universal vision. While the nation will have to find a place for the particularistic rights of the ethnics and nation/alities, the latter will have to come to terms with the nation. Only justice as a discourse has the potential of reconciling policies with rights and vice versa. A justice discourse can come about only by appreciating the other in a just social and political order. The partition of social bodies does not beget a justice discourse. Recognition of division within the social body – not its partition is the key to justice. Hence, justice is predicated on the principle of responsibility towards others and its scope cuts across narrow and particularistic identities. Kant's plea for autonomy of the self is incomplete without the corresponding obligation towards others in compliance with the imperatives of moral universalism. (Kant 1966: 118-211)

It is only when the State recognizes the insurgents as the insiders to the body politic and a just political order that a dialogue for justice can begin in right earnest. Recognition is the first step to justice. The double nature of recognition should not escape our notice. Recognition requires that those who seek justice are considered as part of the body politic. Neither the slaves amongst the ancient Greeks nor the Blacks amongst the White Americans were recognized as autonomous justice-seeking agents by the respective states till they were registered as parts of the body politic. Justice presupposes first of all the recognition that the society we live in is a divided one. A homogeneous society is one that does not include them and therefore does not recognize them as a problem. Divisions can only be mapped within the same social body. Divisions between various social bodies do not make justice a public issue. It is interesting to see how the colonial policy of keeping the 'primitive' and 'savage' tribals at bay by way of drawing lines and organizing punitive raids in order to save the subjects 'who have submitted to our authority' (Allen 2002: 16) changed into the postcolonial policy of treating them as parts of India. 'Terrorism', as I argued, becomes a problem only when there is the underlying expectation of the State that the so-called terrorists are potential insiders to the nation. (Das 2006 mimeo) While the State's recognition cannot stop at the point of mere incorporation, justice has to do with the terms of such inclusion. Similarly, insurgents cannot remain oblivious to and must recognize the rights claims of others. It is in that context that larger civil and political (and not merely military and strategic) unity is necessary for questions of justice to be raised and discussed.

The language of justice will have to be salvaged from those of the nation and rights. Of course the distinction between rights and justice is too thin to be always noticed in our lived experiences. Justice dialogue makes its beginning through the rights dialogue and if the latter were to succeed, it must gradually be transformed into a justice dialogue. The transformation is crucial. I argue that justice demands a language of its own – autonomous from those of policies and rights. Democratic theory has hitherto focused more on rights than on justice. A vision of justice helps in de-ethnicizing the agenda of rights. Rights are not bound to be inclusive of justice and at times they may sound contradictory. But it is important to note that they can be *made* inclusive. Justice is essentially dialogical and cannot but be so.

References

[I thank Walter Fernandes and Sanjib Baruah for their comments on an earlier draft of this paper. Lapses – if any, are however mine. All translations from original non-English sources are mine. The author]

Allen, B. C. (2002) *Gazetteer of Naga Hills and Manipur*, Mittal, New Delhi. First Published 1905.

Barbora, Sanjay (2005) "Quiet History, Unquiet Peoples: The 'Tribal' Question in Assam" (mimeo).

Budhbar (Assamese weekly) [various issues mentioned in the text]

Das, Samir Kumar (1998) "Community Goes to Polls: An Interpretation of the Assam Elections of 1996", In Girin Phukon & Adil-ul-Yasin, eds., *Working of Parliamentary Democracy and Electoral Politics in Northeast India*, South Asian, New Delhi.

Das, Samir Kumar (2002) "Peace and the Limits of Democracy: Some

Reflections on the Naga Peace Process", In C. J. Thomas & Gurudas Das (eds.), *Dimensions of Development in Nagaland*, Regency, New Delhi.

Das, Samir Kumar (2005) *South Asian Peace Studies: Vol. II: Peace Accords and Peace Processes*, Sage, New Delhi.

Das, Samir Kumar (2006) "Terrorists in India's Northeast and Dialogues with Them? The Improbables in the Hypotheses", mimeo. Paris: College Internationale de Philosophie.

Das, Samir Kumar, *ULFA: A Political Analysis*, Ajanta, New Delhi.

Dworkin, Ronald (1977) *Taking Rights Seriously*, Harvard University Press, Cambridge.

Gupta, Shekhar & Uttam Sengupta (1990) "A Violent Mess", In *India Today*, 15 September.

Hazarika, Sanjoy (1994) *Strangers in the Mist: Tales of War and Peace from India's Northeast*, Viking, New Delhi.

Kant, Immanuel (1966) *Critique of Practical Reason and Other Writings in Moral Philosophy*, trans. & ed. Lewis White Beck, University of Chicago Press, Chicago.

Kumar, Madhuresh (2005) *Globalization, State Policies and Sustainability of Rights*, Policies and Practices 6, Calcutta Research Group, Calcutta.

Misra, Udayon (2000) *The Periphery Strikes Back: Challenges to the Nation-State in Assam and Nagaland*, IIAS, Shimla.

Mohan, Vishwa (2007) "PM to visit Assam next week" in *Times of India* (Kolkata), 13 January.

Pandit, Rajat (2007) "Army Brief: Bring 'em to the table'", In *Times of India* (Kolkata), 13 January.

Roy, Amit, ed. (1991) *Communist Chintay Bharate Jati Prasna* (*in Bengali*) Radical Impression, Calcutta.

Tocqueville, Alexis de (2000) *Democracy in America*, University of Chicago Press, Chicago.

5

Identity and Underdevelopment: On Conflict and Peace in Assam

Gurudas Das

Identity and underdevelopment are the two basic issues that have kept Assam on the boil for long. The problem with identity arose due to the incongruity between the aspirations of the ethnic Assamese to make Assam a "nation province" of the Assamese and the historically developed multi-ethnic social base of territorial Assam of today. The relentless strides made towards homogenization and realization of the goal of making Assam a nation-province of the ethnic Assamese during the 1950s and 1960s not only aggravated the ethnic cleavage developed during the colonial period but also developed new cleavages along the ethnic faultlines leading to the reorganization of Assam in 1972. Although the diversity of ethnic cleavages has reduced in post-reorganized Assam due to the reduction of demographic heterogeneity and has made the ethnic Assamese the single largest community, their aspirations to make Assam a nation-province have remained unfulfilled.

In fact the idea of a nation-province for the ethnic Assamese is basically an unrealizable goal within the present political boundary of Assam primarily because of the fact that these two boundaries, viz., ethnic and political, do not coincide. The political boundary of Assam not only includes the ethnic Assamese but also the Dimasas of N C Hills, Karbis of Karbi Anglong, Bodos, Koches, Miris, Chutias, Kacharis, Deoris, Rabhas, Lalungs, Morans, and other indigenous populations, and Muslims, Hindu Bengalis and tea tribes in Brahmaputra Valley. Thus, historically evolved geographic and demographic structures in Assam are not in conformity with the claim of making

Assam a nation province for the ethnic Assamese. While members of a multi-ethnic society like Assam have multiple identities, i.e., one can simultaneously be a Bodo, an Assamese and a Christian, adoption of singular identity and trying to magnify it only leads to inter-group conflicts and identity disintegration. Identity politics in Assam has many facets rooted in remote as well as recent social history of Assam.

With the adoption of the three language formula for the state of Assam, i.e., Assamese as official language for the Brahmaputra Valley, Bengali for Barak Valley and English for N C Hills and Karbi Anglong, and later on Bodo for the Bodoland area, the ethnic Assamese nationality seems to have realized the futility of their aspiration of making Assam a nation-province for themselves. As the politics of identity, instead of paying any dividends, has reduced the territorial boundary of Assam further, the implications of the presence of a large migrant Muslim population in the Brahmaputra Valley itself, which the ethnic Assamese consider to be their homeland, has become obvious. Having overcrowded Bangladesh across the border, the perceived threat of being overrun by the Bangladeshi migrants looms large in the psyche of the ethnic Assamese.

This paper argues that the root cause of inter-ethnic conflicts and assertion of identities by various ethnic and tribal groups lies in the solitary approach towards identity adopted by the ethnic Assamese in Assam. Efforts to make Assam a nation province for the ethnic Assamese have ignited the identity conflicts, which, in turn, have accelerated the transformation from multiculturalism to plural monoculturalism. The paper seeks to explain the triadic linkages among identity, insurgency and economic underdevelopment based on Assam experience. It also seeks to suggest options available for the resolution of identity conflicts in Assam.

Evolution of Multi-Ethnic Social Base in Assam: The Age of the Ahoms

The process of fusion that has worked in making the modern Assamese identity for about 750 years since the days of Sukapha (1228), the first Ahom king, till independence (1947) is well documented in the annals of history. The rise of Ahoms in the Brahmaputra valley at the cost of the Bodos, Chutiyas, Cacharis, Morans, Moamarias and Koches had set in the process of inclusion of the latter identities into the former either through conquest or through cross cultural social bonding like marriage. As the territorial boundary of the Ahom kingdom expanded overtime, the degree of assimilation of the defeated social groups mentioned above into the Ahom identity started weakening with the distance from the seat of power. The identities of the invaded groups did not vanquish altogether; rather they remained dormant often as a sub-category of the broader Ahom identity. While this process of fusion was under operation, shifting of 'Ahom identity' towards 'Assamese identity' was also taking place particularly under the influence of the Brahmins, who had been brought into the kingdom by the rulers of Assam, particularly from Navadweep, the cultural citadel of the then Bengal. Brahmanical rituals gradually got prominence even in the courts of the Ahom kings and the tribal belief system was increasingly on the wane.

Sankardev's Bhakti Movement has created the 'cultural life world' of the Assamese identity. While the Ahom kings created the political boundary, which varied with the stature of the king – the more powerful the king the wider the size of the kingdom – it was the rise of Sankardev's neo-Vaishnavite movement during the 16th century, which began to melt the different social formations into a singular Assamese identity. It may be noted that the neo-Vaishnavite movement had grown in spite of the initial opposition by the Ahom kings and had finally dragged the royal authority to identify themselves with it. The movement had gained so much popularity that some of the Ahom kings later used the Vaishnavite institutions as cultural ambassadors of the royal court for inculcating loyalty among the people of the newly acquired territory *a la* Christianity by the western powers and Islam by the Muslim rulers. Thus the Brahmanical variety of Hinduism and neo-Vaishnavism together, both based in Aryan religious scriptures like the *Bhagavad Gita, Ramayana, Mahabharata, Upanishads* and *Puranas,* constituted the 'belief system' of the Assamese identity, which is primarily rooted in Hindu heritage. The influence of the 'cultural life world', created by the neo-Vaishnavite movement, was so strong that the Ahom nobility had embraced it in order to legitimize their rule. In course of time, "Tai", the royal language, was replaced by "Assamese", tribal religious practices and rituals were replaced by Hindu/neo-Vaishnavite practices, the identity of the "Ahom" became a part of the broader "Assamese" identity.

Although the neo-Vaishnavite movement had a great potential to mobilize people across caste and creed to form an Assamese national identity, its assimilative capacity narrowed down in the post-Sankardev phase as Brahmanical caste-based social philosophy crept into the *satriya* institutions as well as segmentation of the movement into different denominations. As a result, the boundary of the Assamese identity based on religious and cultural markers, which are largely the offshoots of the neo-Vaishnavite movement, including the Assamese language, was stiffened making way for Christianity to have sway in the hills during the colonial period.

When the Ahoms invaded the territory of the Morans, Bodos and Chutiyas during the 13th century and consolidated their rule in the eastern part of the Brahmaputra Valley centering around the present Sibsagar district, Sen dynasty had been overrun by the Turk Sultanate (1203) and Muslim power continued to grow in Bengal. Even before the Koch kingdom, comprising of Western part of the Brahmaputra Valley and Northern part of Bengal, which, for a considerable time acted as the buffer between the Sultanate of Bengal and the Ahom kingdom, came into being, Muslim invaders from Bengal under the leadership of Ikhtiar Uddin Mahammad Bakhtiar Khilji (1205-06), Giasuddin Bakhtiar (around 1226), and Ikhtiar Uddin Malik Ujbeg Tugrilkha (1254-55) tried in vain to invade Kamatapur (Choudhury : 1982). However, at last, Hussain Shah defeated the last Kamata king Nilambar in 1498 A D and occupied Kamatapur. Shah's son ruled the country for quite sometime centering on Hajo before being vanquished by war with the Ahom kings (Gait: 1981). The void created out of the defeat of the Muslim ruler had later been filled by the rise of the Koch kingdom (1515) on the edifice of erstwhile Kamatapur. There had been several encounters between the Ahoms and the Koch kings as well as between Muslim invading forces from Bengal and the Koch kings of western Assam during the 16th century. Again, for a considerable period, western Assam was under the occupation of the Muslims. This 'eastern thrust' of the Muslim invading forces gained considerable strength during the 17th century with the consolidation of the Mughal power in Delhi. Mughals replaced the Sultanate in Bengal and ruled it through the governor. Althrough the 17th century, Mughal governors of Bengal sent, one after another, expeditions to invade Assam. During the second half of the 17th century, Mughal forces under Mir Jumlah even succeeded to capture Garhgaon, the capital of the Ahoms. By the end of the century, with the capture of Gauhati by the Ahom king Gadadhar Singh in 1682, the Mughal interest in the western Assam had been completely wiped out. Aurangzeb's preoccupation with south India and the weakening of Mughal Empire following his demise in 1707 had caused the 'eastern thrust' to wither away.

The purpose of browsing through the history of the Muslim invasions into Assam is to drive the point home that the two century long interactions (1498-1682) between the Muslims and the different powers in western Assam in particular and the Ahoms in general, has, no doubt, left some legacies in terms of accommodating some Muslim population as war captives in the valley, who later engaged in trade and commerce and settled down there.

During his Kamatapur campaign, Hussain Shah encouraged many Muslim warriors to settle down at Hajo and he built, perhaps, the first Masjid at Rangamati. (Choudhuri: 1982). The Muslim population which settled in the Brahmaputra valley either by compulsion or by choice was gradually mingled with the multi-ethnic social fabric of the then Assam. Muslim settlers were engaged by the Ahom kings as security guards, workers in kings' fire arms manufacturing as well as minting workshops (Choudhuri: 1982). Muslims were good at making copper utensils and this industry was monopolized by them in medieval Assam. They were also employed to carry out finer artistic works in temples. Tailoring was another profession in which Muslims were good at. Their Bengal connections helped them to carry out trade and commerce across Assam and Bengal. In fact, prior to the arrival of Marwari traders during the colonial period, Muslim traders used to play a significant role in this sector. Some of the early Muslim settlers also worked as musicians and singers, shoe makers and *japi* manufacturers (Barua:1989).

Besides the Sultanate and Mughal invading forces, preachers of Islam in general and Sufism in particular had also visited the Brahmaputra valley during the medieval period. The activities of different *Pirs* and fakirs like Jamaluddin Tabriji during the 13th century, Giasuddin Aulia during the 14th century and Azan Fakir during the 17th century had led to the internalization of Islam as one of the components of local medieval culture. It may not be out of place to mention here that Ahom king Surampha (1641-1644), also known as Bhaga Raja, had even conferred land grants to Azan Fakir. Although the Ahom kings vigorously fought against the Muslim invasion all through their reign till the end of the 17th century, there is no single instance of their war against Islam. In fact, Sufism and Sankardev's neo-Vaishnavite movement progressed hand in hand in medieval Assam. Many Muslims became the disciples of Sankardev and some of them like Chand Khan, Joyhari, Haridas and Dheli Darji are well known for their contribution to the growth of neo-Vaishnavite movement in pre-colonial Assam (Barua:1989). Even Sankardev himself referred to the existence of the 'Turuk' (meaning the Muslims) population in Assam during his time (Neog:1985). When the Muhammedan chronicler Shihabuddin visited Assam with the Mughal invading army led by Mir Jumla during 1662-63, he noted that the Muslims settled here had assimilated themselves to such an extent that except the name nothing was left of Islam in them (Gait: 1981, Neog:1985).

Thus, it is needless to mention that the society in feudal Assam was not a monolithic one. Centering around the political power of the Ahom kings and Sankardev's neo-Vaishnavite movement, people of other faiths and origins adjusted themselves in the medieval social order of Assam. Although the political power was in the hands of the Ahoms who called themselves Tais, but whom the indigenous people called Asam (unequalled) (Gait: 1981, Kakati: 1995) and later this exoethnonym was ascribed to the territory under their rule, which subsequently expanded to include the whole of the Brahmaputra valley, the social space was studded by numerous indigenous groups of people as well as early Muslim settlers. Political loyalty to the Ahom kings, gradual adoption of symbols of Asamiya culture including language and neo-Vaishnavite religion of Sankardev had gradually drawn these groups nearer to Asamiya identity. The modern names like Assam and Assamese are the anglicized names of Asam and Asamiya (Kakati: 1995) which Britishers used for the kingdom of the Ahom kings and the people therein respectively following the annexation of the Brahmaputra valley in 1826.

Evolution of Multi-Ethnic Social Base in Assam: The Colonial Era

Before the natural process of ethnic fusion taking place during the feudal era (1228-1826) could galvanize into the emergence of a singular

Assamese identity, annexation of, and subsequent administrative experimentation with, Assam (1826-1947) by the colonial rulers had added an altogether different dimension having far reaching consequences for the Assamese nationality formation and inter-ethnic relations in both colonial and post-colonial Assam. The boundary of the multi-ethnic social base was further widened with the incorporation of new territories within the political boundary of Assam as well as induction of different groups of people from various parts of British India.

Following the victory in the first Anglo-Burmese war in 1826, although western Assam was immediately annexed to the British India, eastern Assam was brought only under direct colonial rule in 1839. Since then for about 35 years Assam remained under the umbrella of the Bengal Presidency till the administrative reorganization of 1874. During this early phase of colonial rule, the British introduced Bengali as the court language of Assam at the cost of the linguistic identity of the Assamese in 1837, which sowed the seeds of Assamese-Bengali inter-ethnic conflict till the restoration of Assamese in 1874. Although the Assamese language was restored to its rightful place in 1874, the inter-ethnic hostility continued all through the colonial period and even spilled over to the post-colonial era. In Assamese history writing, this fact was interpreted as the machinations of the Bengalis in general and Bengali bureaucrats in particular (Neog: 1962, Sarma:1965; Sarma:1972; Weiner:1978). However, the gains from the restoration of Assamese as the official language was more than nullified by the addition of three Bengali dominated areas of Goalpara, Sylhet and Cachar (while North Cachar was transferred to Assam in 1854, the remaining part of the Cachar plains which was a part of Dacca Division was transferred to Assam in 1874) to the reconstituted Assam in 1874, which was taken out of the administrative umbrella of Bengal Presidency and elevated to a Chief Commissionership. In this reconstituted Assam, Assamese became the minority with 38.30 per cent (1871 Census) of the total provincial population (Kar: 2005). As the districts of Sylhet, Cachar and Goalpara had a large population of Muslim Bengali settlers, their attachment led to the sudden rise of Muslim population in colonial Assam. In fact while the Muslims constituted only about 6 per cent of the total population of the five districts of the Brahamaputra valley (Darrang, Kamrup, Lakhimpur, Nowgong and Sibsagar), following the attachment of Sylhet, Cachar and Goalpara, their number had increased fivefold to constitute about 30 per cent of the total provincial population (1871 Census) (Kar: 2005).

The Assamese identity was further threatened with the constitution of the province of Eastern Bengal and Assam in 1905 following the partition of Bengal as part of the colonial strategy to crush the growth of nationalism in Bengal. As Eastern Bengal was dominated by the Muslim Bengalis, Assamese people became a miniscule minority in this newly formed province. However, this arrangement was short lived and Assam got back its pre-1905 status with the annulment of partition of Bengal in 1912. Although Assam was made a governor's province in 1921 and continued to remain so till 1947, no new territories were added to it any longer. Following the Sylhet referendum in 1946, Assam got rid of the Bengali dominated Sylhet which largely paved way for the claim to make Assam a nation province of the Assamese (now being the single largest community). However, both Goalpara and Cachar remained parts of Assam thereby making both the Hindu and Muslim Bengalis constituents of the polity of Assam. Thus territorial reorganization had simultaneously expanded the political boundary as well as multi-ethnic social base of colonial Assam.

Besides British political interest in territorial reorganization, colonial administrative and economic interests brought the Bengalis, both Hindu and Muslims, Marwaris, tribal people from central Provinces to Assam. Hindu Bengalis were brought to run the British administration as well as to provide professional services. Muslim Bengali peasants were settled particularly in western rural Assam as peasants. Marwaris came as comprador to British capital and made a deep penetration in state's trade and commerce. Tribals from Cental Provinces particularly from Chotanagpur region were brought to work in the tea gardens in eastern Assam. Besides these groups, Nepalese came as soldiers of the colonial army and Biharis as manual labour-force to work in construction activities. The story of migration of different ethnic groups in colonial Assam is well documented (Hussain: 1993; Barua: 1999; Kar: 1990; Weiner:1978; Nag:1990, Das :1996; Das: 2002) and we do not intend to repeat the same. However, it is important to note that of all these groups, large immigration of the Muslim peasants into the wastelands of western Assam and the tribals into the tea gardens of eastern Assam had radically changed the demographic composition of colonial Assam. While the Muslim population in Assam was a little more than 2 lakhs in 1881 (Nag: 1990), following the addition of Sylhet, Cachar and Goalpara as well as settlement of Muslim peasants in the wastelands, this number had gone up to 35 lakhs (Kar: 1990) on the eve of independence. Thus, just before the Sylhet referendum, Muslims constituted 34 per cent of the provincial population while the Hindus were 39 per cent (Kar: 1990). From 1902-03 to 1937-38, a total of about 17 lakhs of tea labourers were brought in Assam (Guha: 1977).

Thus, colonial Assam no longer remained the homeland of the Assamese. Although tea labourers (popularly known as Adivasis or tea tribes) remained isolated and did not transform themselves into a political community, Muslim Bengalis under the banner of Muslim League contested for political power against the Assamese Hindus organized under the banner of Indian National Congress in colonial Assam. Assamese nationalism, articulated by the ethnic Hindu Assamese middle class, thus, had to have a three-pronged struggle viz. struggle against British colonialism, struggle against Muslim political and territorial interests and struggle against Hindu Bengali domination in cultural and professional spheres, in colonial Assam. These struggles had created, on the one hand, some sort of centripetal forces which helped the indigenous communities like the Bodos, Chutiyas, Cacharis, Morans, Muttaks and Deuris to increasingly gravitate towards Assamese nationalism and simultaneously, on the other hand, centrifugal forces which intensified Hindu-Muslim conflict particularly during the first half of the twentieth century. All other ethnic equations were overshadowed by the Hindu-Muslim conflict in colonial Assam. In fact, it was the Assamese political leadership who, by opposing to group Assam with Bengal, as proposed in the Cabinet Mission Plan and supported by the Muslim League, had in a way ultimately saved Assam as well as the North Eastern States for India. Thus, besides being anti-colonial, strong anti-Muslim as well as anti-Bengali currents were embedded in the ideology of Assamese nationalism.

Evolution of Multi-Ethnic Social Base in Assam: The Post-Colonial Era

The inter-ethnic relations based on religion and language and the cleavage structures developed during the colonial era took a new turn following partition and independence. Muslims in Assam in general and Brahmaputra valley in particular had to compromise with their fate and provincial Muslim league was dissolved and the followers joined en masse in the congress (Kar: 1990). Following the transfer of Sylhet to East Pakistan, Muslim population in Assam had reduced to 25 per cent (Kar: 1990) which further declined to about 22 per cent immediately after the 1950 communal riot. Henceforth, Muslim politics in Assam was rechristened as minority politics shedding away the pro-Pakistan position and seeking integration with the host society.

Multi-ethnic social base of Assam was further widened with the inclusion of 'excluded" and "partially excluded" hilly areas inhabited by the tribals. The Naga hills, Lushai/Mizo hills, Khasi hills, Garo hills, Jaintia hills and Mikir hills—all were added to Assam as it was viewed as the "last outpost of Indian civilization in the east" by the mainland political leaders. Thus, post-colonial Assam expanded both in terms of territory and population making its name a misnomer where ethnic Assamese became merely one of the numerous ethnic groups having no clear majority in the provincial population.

Assamese National Aspiration and the Politics of Identity

Although the multi-ethnic social base that has historically evolved in Assam stood on the way of making Assam a nation-province for the Assamese, following the rules of the game of carving out provinces in independent India based on ethno-linguistic identity, ethnic Assamese elites vigorously strived for it. The expediencies of electoral politics as well as the aspiration for making Assam a nation province for the Assamese led to the widening of Assamese linguistic identity in order to accommodate the Muslims of Brahmaputra valley as well as the tea tribes within the fold of Assamese nationalism. Muslims of Assam were rechristened as *Na Asamiya* (New Assamese) and encouraged to barter their identity for security by way of reporting Assamese as their mother tongue in census returns in order to strengthen the claim to make Assam the nation province for the Assamese. It may be pointed out that, at this stage, the Congress-led ruling elites in Assam tacitly encouraged the immigration of Muslim Bengalis from East Pakistan. As the immigrant Muslim Bengalis readily shifted their ethnic identity in favour of the Assamese, they became useful not only as a 'safe vote bank' but also to realize the majority claim of the Assamese (Das: 2001a).

It may also be noted that this game plan of the ethnic Assamese elites also suited the needs of the immigrant Bengali Muslims. They came to Assam in search of a *lebensraum*. Faced with strong push factors at home arising out of a 'failed state syndrome' in East Pakistan, economic security for them was much more important than their cultural symbols. In fact, their decision to barter their cultural identity against economic security was also essentially political. While indicating this, it is not intended to deny the fact that this has also created a space, albeit a limited one, for naturalized assimilation of the new generations of immigrant Muslims. But primarily, the relationship between the two communities may, at best, be described as a marriage of convenience. The immigrants needed a living space and the ethnic Assamese elites needed their political support to stake a majority claim in multi-ethnic Assam (Das: 2001a).

But this strategy of assimilation that had been attempted through the practice of majoritarian politics did not work. The segmented social space in post colonial Assam, instead, presented an altogether different political reality. Majoritarian politics practised in a multi-ethnic society led to unequal development of various socio-economic formations, particularly of the minorities and peripheral groups (Das:2001a).

It may not be out of context to note that, while the process of unequal development within a homogeneous society leads to class-cleavages, the same process, within a multi-ethnic society, leads to ethnic cleavages. While class cleavages do not pose any territorial threat in terms of separation or secession, the ethnic cleavages do pose a threat, particularly when different ethnic groups are territorially concentrated. And the geo-political location of a territory, undoubtedly, plays a crucial role in setting the political goal of a deprived segment. While the separatist goals are feasible, irrespective of territorial location, secessionist goals are more feasible for the communities living along international borders (Das:2001a).

Be that as it may, the relentless efforts made towards homogenization and realization of the goal of making Assam a nation-province during the 1950s and 1960s had resulted in unmanageable discontent among various groups, which ultimately led to the reorganization of Assam in 1972 along ethnic lines. It has already been discussed elsewhere (Das: 2001b) that both external security threats to India's north east arising out of the consequences of cold war rivalry and internal insecurity arising out of imposition of the linguistic identity of the ethnic Assamese in post-colonial multi-ethnic Assam had intensified the inter-ethnic rivalries to such an extent that reorganization of the province had been considered to be the best option by the Indian state. Naga Hills were taken out much earlier in 1963 to form the province of Nagaland and under the 1972 reorganization plan, Garo, Khasi and Jaintia hills were taken out to form Meghalaya and Lushai hills were made the province of Mizoram. Thus the post colonial territorial gain was lost in post-reorganized Assam.

Although the diversity of ethnic cleavages has reduced in post-reorganized Assam, the faultlines continue to persist. Though the 1972 reorganization has reduced the demographic heterogeneity and rendered the ethnic Assamese as the single largest community in Assam, their aspirations to make Assam a nation-province has remained unfulfilled. Instead, a new dimension came into sharp focus in post-reorganized Assam, i.e. the steady ingress of the Muslims into the political power structures. It is, indeed, an irony of the politics of ethnicity in Assam that the immigrant Muslims, who had been instrumental in making Assamese the single largest community at one point of time and helped them to advance the claim of making Assam a nation-province, are now viewed as the principal threat to the political security of the ethnic Assamese in the State. In approximately 23 electoral constituencies out of a total of 120 Legislative Assembly segments, Muslims are now believed to enjoy majority support. In another seven constituencies, they are the deciding factor (Das: 2001a).

In order to counter the growing electoral strength of the Muslims whose strategic support is no longer important in post-reorganized Assam, the ethnic Assamese elites wanted to get rid of them and, thus, demanded their deportation by setting 1951 as the cut-off year. The anti-foreigner agitation or the Assam Movement (1979-85) has, thus, lent support to our hypothesis that Assam's policy of assimilation of the immigrant Muslims had been a tactical move intended to gain mileage over other ethnic groups in multi-ethnic Assam during the 1950s and 1960s. They were used as pawns in the number game to realize the aspirations of the ethnic Assamese. And with the failure of the strategy of assimilation in realizing the goal of making Assam a nation-province, the attitude of ethnic Assamese towards immigrant Muslims changed. From a constituent of the Assamese linguistic community, they were suddenly branded as foreigners in Assam (Das: 2001a). Besides language, religious and racial attributes were emphasized to define the identity of the Assamese in social and political discourse of the Asamiya ethnic civil society movements and organizations obviously to bracket the Muslims in Brahmaputra valley.

In spite of sensitizing some of the security concerns arising out of fresh illegal immigration of Bengali Muslims from Bangladesh, the Assam Movement has failed in realizing its goal as far as the deportation of immigrant Muslims is concerned. Like the agenda of making Assam a nation-province, the 'deportation-goal' was also unattainable, given the constitutional and legal framework of the country. On the contrary, the ethnic ideology of the movement has made it amply clear that the inclusion of a group within the 'Assamese ethnic boundary', or for that matter its exclusion (from it), is defined exclusively by the interest of the 'ethnic Assamese'. Linguistic symbols alone are not sufficient to claim Assamese identity. Rather, non-existence of an 'other' cultural/ sub-cultural base has become the prime criterion. The Movement, thus, in a way, drew an implicit boundary in a hitherto open-ended process of Assamese nationality formation. The exclusionist ethnic ideology of the Movement alarmed ethnic minorities and encouraged them in a compelling way to construct their identities in rigid terms in order to claim politico-territorial autonomy in their respective traditional homelands. Besides, the Bengalis of Barak valley, who have all along opposed the Assamese idea of making Assam a nation-province, the Bodos, Karbis and Dimasas have also started pressing hard for complete autonomy. The Tiwas, Deuris, Lalungs and Koch Rajbanshis have also made conscious efforts to dissociate themselves from the Assamese identity. Thus, instead of mellowing down in post-reorganized Assam, the residual faultlines have widened further (Das: 2001a). The "singular identity" approach, as Sen (2006) has described it, adopted by the ethnic Assamese has led to the narrowing down of their ethnic boundary which, in turn, has created multiple identity boxes paving the way for the emergence of "plural monoculturalism" in place of "multiculturalism" in post-colonial Assam.

Who is an Assamese in Assam?

Although, as it has already been discussed, the social space of Assam is multi-ethnic in nature, there is hardly any term available to capture the concept of "people of Assam" or "citizen of Assam". The etymology of the term Assamese may be traced to Ahom>Asam>Asamiya>Assamese. The term "Assamese" has been and is being used at least in four senses: (i) to mean the residents of Assam, (ii) to mean the Asamiya linguistic group, (iii) to mean the ethnic Assamese, and (iv) indigenous Assamese, the *Bhumiputras* (sons of the soil).

The term "Assamese" is often implicitly used to refer to the residents of Assam in political and social discourses in post-colonial pre-reorganized Assam (1947-1972). It may be noted that this has been the time while ethnic Assamese elites were facing the challenges of integration of the ethnically most heterogeneous groups of people placed under the political and administrative leadership of Assam. The political leadership of the Indian state sought integration of the hills of north east and people therein through Assam and not through the Assamese linguistic community. Nehru's idea of integrating the hills through Assam while reading along with his approach towards tribal development in the region makes the issue amply clear (Elwin: 1958). If the term "Assamese" is taken as a territorial identity, then it becomes a generic name for the multitude of identities including the ethnic Assamese, Hindu and Muslim Bengalis, Bodos, Dimasas, Karbis, Koch Rajbongshis, Cacharis and others. However, the term "Assamese" is more popularly used to refer to the linguistic identity of the Asamiyas rather than to the territorial identity of the people of Assam.

In the second sense, "Assamese" refers to the group of people who speak in Asamiya language. In fact the Assamese is the anglicized name of Asamiya. Speakers of Assamese language may broadly be divided into two groups—(i) people whose mother tongue is Assamese, and (ii) people whose mother tongue is different but have acquired Assamese language either formally or informally. Many people belonging to the second category use their mother tongue for private communication but use Assamese for communication in public. Most of the tribal groups, Hindu and Muslim Bengalis of Brahmaputra valley, Bodos, Karbis, Dimasas, Koch Rajbongshis, Adivashi groups in upper

Assam and smaller speech groups from other parts of the country belong to this second category. "Assamese", while taken as a linguistic identity, thus, includes both categories of speakers. In fact, linguistic Assamese nationalism, being open ended, has played a significant role in incorporating people from other cultures and providing them the much needed umbilical cord to be a part of the Assamese society. It is the common Assamese language that acted as the bridge between early and late migrants and galvanized them to form a single speech group.

The word "Assamese", in the third sense, refers to the ethnic Assamese. Besides a shared language, the idea of ethnic Assamese involves some elements of descent and shared culture between the members of the group as well as with their ancestors. Thus, while the civic Assamese nationalism based on territorial identity is inclusive in nature, ethnic Assamese nationalism is exclusive as it can exclude groups of people not conforming to the cultural norms of the Asamiyas including the language, religion and shared history. As the Muslim and Hindu Bengalis, Marwaris and other minority migrant groups, tribals and Adivasis have their separate history, language, religion and culture, they will not be considered as members of ethnic Assamese community in the strict sense of the term.

In the fourth sense, the word Assamese is used to mean the *bhumiputras* (sons of the soil) of Assam. It is only recently, particularly after the Assam Accord (1985) that attempts are being made increasingly to define the term "Assamese" in this sense. The English equivalent of the Assamese word "*bhumiputras*" may be taken as 'indigenous people'. The term "indigenous people" lacks precision. Its meaning differs from context to context. The term is often used as synonymous with the aborigines, natives or the autochthons. From the anthropological point of view, "indigenous people" are those who rely upon subsistence-based production and live in non-urbanized society. United Nations and International Labour Organization use the term to mean "any ethnic group who inhabit the geographic region with which they have the earliest historical connection" (www.wikipedia.org). Thus the principle of first occupation is often used to claim the status of indigenous people. In some cases, the term is also used to mean categories of people who "by a variety of historical and environmental circumstances have been placed outside of the dominant state system and whose traditional practices and land claims often come into conflict with the objectives and policies promulgated by governments, companies and surrounding dominant societies" (www.wikipedia.org). As such, as per the nuances in which the term "indigenous people" is generally used, tribal communities in India largely fit into this category irrespective of the fact whether they have been recognized as scheduled tribe or not by the Indian constitutional-legal framework. If one goes by the strict sense of the term which involves the principle of first occupation, then the Bodos, Cacharis, Chutias, Dimasas, Karbis, Deuris and Koch Rajbongshis better fit for the term than the ethnic Assamese including even the Ahoms. Of course, if the term is interpreted *a la* America, where it refers to those groups and their descendents who inhabited the region before the arrival of European colonizers and settlers, then ethnic Assamese including the Ahoms as well as the Goria Muslims also fit into the category as far as the Brahmaputra valley is concerned. Although both Muslim and Hindu Bengalis, the Adivasis and other speech groups who have migrated into the Brahmaputra valley during the colonial period would not fit into the category of indigenous people, however, people of both Goalpara and Barak valley (undivided Cachar district) can not be left out.

Identity Politics and Identity Retrogression

Having discussed the four different conceptual categories in which the word Assamese has been and is being used, it is important to delineate the role of identity politics in creating the identity dilemma in post-colonial Assam. The metamorphosis of the Assamese identity from territorial to *bhumiputra*, in order of sequence as has already been cited, may be analyzed in terms of two propositions. First, there may be four different parallel schools of thought among the Assamese, viz., liberal, moderate, conservative and extremist who, explicitly or implicitly, define the Assamese identity boundary by way of territorial, linguistic, ethnic and indigenous terms respectively. Second, there may be shifting of position over time by the same stock of people in a retrogressive direction from territorial to indigenous. These two propositions may be interlinked in more than one way. The first might result from the second. The political expediency of making Assam a nation-province for the ethnic Assamese warranted this shift over time, as has already been discussed, which, in turn, might have left the legacies of the past practice of identity politics. The second might result from the first either through the transfer of power from the protagonists of one school to another, assuming that all the four schools exist parallelly, or through mobilization of masses by the competing non-state agencies, like civil society organizations, conforming to one or the other of these four constructs of Assamese identity. The sequence of shifting of the Assamese ethnic boundary, while reading along with political development in post colonial Assam centering around the aspiration of making Assam a nation province for the ethnic Assamese, lends support to the second proposition. The distinction between these two propositions gets blurred in case of the above four-fold ideological categories as they are merely positional rather than real. A political position may sound liberal while in power (as supra-ethnic image helps to govern multi-ethnic polity) and conservative while out of power (for mobilizing the single largest community for electoral gain). In such a case, both the first and second propositions work in an interactive mode to regress the identity boundary. Thus the boundary of the ethnic Assamese identity is being retrograded over time, setting a clear trend towards adjusting the territorial boundary to conform to social identity, albeit unintended, instead of enlarging the social identity to fit with the territorial boundary, albeit intended, of post colonial Assam.

As the ethnic Assamese nationalism defines nationality by *jus sanguinis* (i.e., descent from a person of that nationality) the claim to make Assam a nation province for the Assamese nationality is neither just nor desirable due to the non-coincidence of the political boundary of Assam to that of ethnic boundary of the Assamese. As the population of Assam belongs to different nationalities where no single group has the absolute majority, nationalism in Assam needs to be defined not by *jus sanguinis* but by *jus soli* (i.e. birth within Assam) *a la* Indian citizenship. We need a separate term to capture the idea of "people of Assam", say *Asamian*, like Indian, to make a distinction between the people of Assam and ethnic Assamse people. As the term "*Asamian*" will refer to the permanent residents/ citizens of Assam it will include the members of all the ethnic groups including the ethnic Assamese. If the state vows to protect the interest, and promote the welfare, of the "*Asamian*", not only of the ethnic Assamese, then it will have wider legitimacy across the social groups. It will largely eliminate the crisis of legitimacy that governance in Assam is facing currently as the non-ethnic Assamese social groups view the state symbolizing only the interest of ethnic Assamese in Assam. If the identity problem is to resolve without compromising on the present political and territorial boundary of Assam, multiculturalism has to be inculcated instead of a singular identity. The word "*Asamian*" captures this multicultural basis of the regional identity of the people of Assam in more unambiguous terms than the word "Assamese", which is primarily used to mean the ethnic Assamese group. The shift from singular identity to multiculturalism calls for looking beyond the Assam Accord (Datta:1990).

Looking Beyond Assam Movement and the Assam Accord

Assam movement has been the result of the perceived threat to the identity of the ethnic Assamese arising out of the growing political power of the Muslims in post-reorganized Assam. The strategy of accommodation of the Muslims under the linguistic Assamese nationalism has lost its relevance in post-reorganized Assam. With the reorganization of the political boundary along ethnic lines in 1972, the ethnic Assamese community suddenly found themselves in a precarious position, sharing the Brahamuptra valley with a large Muslim population. For them, the valley became too small to accommodate the Muslims. Dissents against the policy of the ethnic Assamese power elites to bank on the Ali-Cooli (Muslims and the Adivasis) constituency to sail through the electoral politics have been institutionalized through ethnic Assamese civil society organizations like All Assam Students Union (AASU), Assam Sahitya Sabha (ASS) and Assam Gana Sangram Parishad (AGSP). Ethnic Assamese civil society realized that the use of the Muslims as vote banks by the power elites tacitly encourages the illegal immigration of Muslims across the border. The Muslim conspiracy of making Assam a part of Pakistan on the eve of the partition was revoked and the theory of Islamization of Assam was brought into the sharp focus to build a mighty anti-foreigner (anti-Muslim) movement which in due course transformed itself into anti-non-Assamese agitation. Events and dimensions of the movement have already been studied (Hussain: 1993, Gohain: 1980, Guha: 1980, Gupta: 1983, Murty: 1983), we only intend to dwell on the two important lessons having significant bearing for the post-Assam Accord politics of Assam.

First, in spite of the popular support that has caused a regime change in favour of the movement why did it fail its mission in terms of detection and deportation of foreign nationals from Assam? The answer to this question lies, perhaps, in the diametrically opposite compulsions of the politics of ethnicity and parliamentary politics. While the movement has mobilized the masses based on ethnic Assamese identity against illegal Bangladeshi immigrants (read Muslims) without drawing any distinction between the Muslims who are as old in Assam as the ethnic Assamese are and the infiltrators on the one hand, the expediency of parliamentary politics on the other has called for protecting the Muslim interest as without their support it would be difficult for any political party to stake the majority claim in the state legislative assembly. Thus the dilemma faced by the ethnic Assamese political elites is that while, on the one hand, they intend to keep the Muslims out of their ethnic boundary and, if possible, deport them lock stock and barrel to ensure their political and cultural security, on the other hand, they need the support of the Muslim legislators to continue to remain in power as the ethnic Assamese community is divided into several political constituencies. This dilemma largely explains as to why the political elites, parties, and even civil society movements only exhibit positional opposition to infiltration. While in power they go soft, while in opposition they cry hard.

The Muslim factor, indeed, has long been rhetoric in Assam politics. What is to note is that there has not been any appreciable change in this position even after the movement and Assam Accord. Even if the Assam Accord is implemented in letter and spirit in terms of identification and deportation of foreign nationals, it will have little impact on the present electoral strength of the Muslims in Assam. As the peak period of immigration of the Muslim peasants from Mymensingh and other parts of Bengal into Assam had been the first decade of the 20th century, who by 1947 had acquired domiciled status in the independent India and constitutional-legal framework has already recognized them as Indian citizens, there hardly exists any legal covenant to deny them their rightful place as Indian citizen. Similarly, the Hindu Bengalis, who entered into India including Assam prior to or after the partition have also been provided with automatic citizenship due to the 'national commitments'. Moreover, as per the Assam Accord, the anti-foreigner movement has also settled for March 25,

1971 as the cut off date for the identification of illegal foreigners. Only those who had entered Assam illegally on or after this date will be labeled as "illegal foreigners". While nobody knows how many illegal foreigners (read Muslims) are there in Assam, based on fictitious rhetorical figures, the movement branded the whole Muslim and Hindu Bengali groups in Brahmaputra valley as foreigners, but by agreeing to March 25, 1971, as cut off date, ultimately only legitimized all illegal immigrants entering Assam prior to that date. According to one estimate, total number of illegal foreign migrants during 1951-1991 was about 13 lakhs (Saikia, *et al:* 2003) of which about 7 lakhs entered Assam during 1951-1971 and another 6 lakhs entered during 1971-1991. Even if we go by these figures, Assam Accord has legitimized more than half of the illegal foreign immigrants, majority of whom are expected to be Muslims as during 1951-71 ethnic Assamese power elites had tacitly encouraged them for the sake of electoral gains as well as for proving linguistic Assamese majority in order to make Assam a nation province for the Assamese. As far as the Bangladeshi immigration into Assam during 1971-1991 is concerned, majority of them are expected to be Hindus who migrated following the Bangladesh war of liberation and subsequent official declaration of making Bangladesh an Islamic state. Political developments in Bangladesh and Assam during the post-1971 period do not lend any strong support for large scale immigration of Bangladeshi Muslims into Assam particularly in view of reorganization of Assam (1972) that has eroded the *raison d'etre* of political support for cross border Bangladeshi Muslim immigration into Assam as well as Assam movement (1979-85) that has made Assam a hostile region for the Muslim immigrants. Given India's "national commitments", it is not a politically feasible proposition to identify and deport the Hindu Bangladeshi immigrants entering Assam during 1971-91. Thus the anti-foreigner Assam movement has rather legitimized the illegal foreigners instead of ousting them from Assam. As soon as the movement assumed the political power by giving birth to a powerful regional ideology rooted in the identity crisis of the ethnic Assamese and institutionalized in Assam Gana Parishad (AGP), it had to confront with the dilemma of wining the support of the Muslim legislators for ensuring the stability of the government and immediately accommodated the Muslim interest.

An anatomy of the ethnic composition of the present Legislative Assembly of Assam (formed in 2006) reveals that out of 126 MLAs, 25 are Muslims, 24 are tribals, and another 22 are non-ethnic Assamese Hindus belonging to groups such as Hindu Bengalis, Biharis, Adivasis, Nepalis and others (The Assam Gazette: 2006). Together non-ethnic Assamese representatives constitute about 56 per cent of the total Assam Assembly strength. These figures evidently demonstrate the strategic importance of the Muslims in Assam's parliamentary political matrix particularly in view of the fact that while the Muslims of Brahmaputra valley are ready to shift their ethnic affiliation in favour of the linguistic Assamese identity, the tribal groups are increasingly distancing themselves from the ethnic as well as linguistic Assamese identities by reconstructing and asserting their own identities. Thus, while the electoral politics of Assam makes the Muslims a natural ally of the ethnic Assamese, the identity politics makes them their adversary. Resolution of this dilemma lies at the root of building peace in Assam.

Second, the singular identity approach of the ethnic Assamese has not only helped the Muslims of Assam to organize as a political community but also generated "demonstration effects" for other ethnic groups including the tribals to transform themselves as ethno-political groups, many of whom hitherto considered themselves as part of the larger Assamese society, on the one hand, and strengthened the nascent identity movements on the other. The retrogression of Assamese identity from *Asamian* to linguistic Assamese identity and then to ethnic Assamese and finally to *Bhumiputras* has rung the identity alarm bell for others. Following the ethnic Assamese model of identity movement, other indigenous groups like the Bodos, Karbis, Dimasas, Koch Rajbangsis, Morans, Muttocks, Deuris and even the Adivasis are also organizing themselves either to establish or to protect their own respective identities. Besides this, orthodox ethnic fundamentalists of other non-Assamese populations of Assam like the Muslims, Hindu Bengalis and other speech groups have been provided with increased pace to play with the feeling of insecurity that has been magnified manifold due to the assertion of ethnic Assamese identity. All these have resulted into the creation of numerous "identity boxes" increasingly posing greater challenge towards social stability and polity management in post-Accord Assam. As the constituency of the political parties cut across the ethnic boundaries, it is difficult for them to take up the cause of a particular ethnic group for redress particularly when the demands of the groups are conflicting in nature. As a result, intense feeling of deprivation looms large within the group and it is left to itself to protect the interest of the members of the group. Moreover, in a multi-ethnic setting the smaller groups could hardly influence the political decision making through democratic conflict resolution mechanism as their respective political representation in the legislature is too meager vis-à-vis others (Das:2005). This results in the adoption of violence as a strategy to reach out to the authorities that matter. A uniform structure of the organization of the ethnic movements has been observed which includes an ethnic civil society forum led by the students and youths of the community acting as the democratic façade and an ethnic insurgent army ruling the roost from behind. The formation of ethnic insurgent army often gets support from the members of the community due to the failure of the state to provide security to them. This, not only, erodes the legitimacy of the state but transforms the movement into a war between the state and the community. Post-Accord Assam is trapped into such an inter-ethnic stratagem where the values of multiculturalism are fast giving way to singular ethnocentrism. Thus mending the identity barriers to transform the social processes from plural monoculturaliism to multiculturalism is another key for the restoration of peace in Assam.

Identity and Underdevelopment

There are two way linkages between identity and development. Identity conflicts in multi-ethnic Assam have led to political instability, which in turn adversely affected economic development. Conversely, lack of economic development has led to the creation of limited economic opportunities, which in turn has sharpened inter-ethnic competition for access to resources and avenues for livelihood. Economic development in multi-ethnic Assam appears to have been largely biased in favour of the dominant group, i.e., ethnic Assamese. As all major public sector investment decisions are political in nature, the group wielding greater political power is only expected to be the largest beneficiary. Most of the public projects relating to health, education, and infrastructure are located in regions inhabited by the dominant group. The members of the dominant group have grabbed the most of the government jobs. Most of the public welfare schemes are serviced in areas populated by the dominant group. Minority ethnic groups have little say over public decision-making. This ethnocentric view towards development has made the state incapable in playing the buffer role where the market forces have failed to usher development and as a result has created inequality across social as well as territorial spaces. This inequality, in turn, has given birth to ethnic assertion by the peripheral groups suffering from intense feeling of relative deprivation, real or perceived (Das: 1997). Once the ethnic movements have adopted the violent tactics to redress their grievances, this has vitiated the whole business environment where risk premium of investment in general and private investment in particular appeared to have become higher than the expected rate of return. As a result not only businesses investments have shied away from the conflict zones, flight of business capital to other profitable regions has also become prominent following the persistence of the identity conflict. Ethnocentric *developmentality*, an attitude towards development which favours the members of a particular ethnic group and excludes others, coupled with ethnic militancy have created multiple layers of loops which have kept the economy of the state at a low level equilibrium trap.

Unlike market governed development, ethnocentric development leads to inefficiency. While ethnic criterion is used as a choice variable in hiring a person or in allotting a contract, efficiency is sacrificed on the altar of ethnicity. This breeds inefficiency and leads to poor decision-making particularly in public service providing sectors where selection process is largely subject to ethnocentric bias. Inefficient public servants, in turn, contribute to the overall underdevelopment of the economy and society.

The most harmful effect of the ethnocentric *developmentality* is the destruction of social capital. It has vitiated the inter-ethnic relations to a large extent. Trust, bonding and networking across the communities have largely disappeared with the formation of identity boxes. This has not only adversely affected the growth of multiculturalism by reducing the cultural capital, but also stood on the way of building shared opportunities for material wellbeing of the members cutting across communitarian barriers. The banishment of cultural interdependence has led to some sort of economic isolation as well. This has added further impetus to the demands for positive discrimination. The movements by Koch Rajbongshis, Muttoks, Morans, Chutiyas, Ahoms and Adivasis for scheduled tribe status while seen from this perspective make this point self-evident. As the Muslims in Assam, majority of whom are peasants, are subject to distrust and suspicion, capital formation in agriculture is certain to suffer. The feeling of insecurity about their *locas standi* as a bonafide citizen of Assam appears to have crippled their economic motivation. Had this air of suspicion been removed and necessary support services ensured by the state, the Muslim peasants would have made a significant contribution towards the growth of the agricultural sector in Assam. Similar is the case of the Adivasis who have created wealth in the tea gardens of Assam for centuries. Had the well being of the Advasis were taken care of, the tea industry in Assam would have done much better than what it is today.

The phenomenon of insurgency in Assam may be viewed, to a large extent, as the by-product of identity movements. Following the adoption of strategy of violence by the identity movements their adverse impact on the economy have increased manifold. Rent seeking behaviour of these movements not only has jeopardized the prospect of private investment; they also helped in breeding as well as justifying corruption in the society. Extortionist demands from the insurgent groups have encouraged and legitimized corruption in public domain. The wrong doers are in turn protected by the gunrunners. Businesses buy peace by coughing up a part of their profit which is again compensated by raising the prices of goods and services ultimately leading to the decline in consumer welfare. Insurgent-politician-contractor-supplier-nexus siphons the bulk share of development funds leading to the poor quality of development projects, which in turn drastically reduces the rate of return from them. Kidnapping for ransom has made it difficult to get expertise personnel for project implementation. Failures of the state to provide effective and adequate security for the development project agencies have resulted in extraordinary delay and hence escalation of project costs often making many a project economically and/or operatively unviable. As the profitable enterprises are being targeted for extortion, insurgency, thus, has created disincentives for motivation and accumulation. This has caused migration of even local talents and entrepreneurs. All these have made the enterprises non-competitive vis-à-vis their counterparts from other regions by way of higher production and delivery costs leading to the perpetuation of underdevelopment in Assam.

The proliferations of identity movements and, their offshoots, insurgency have made conflict management as the prime focus of polity management pushing the development agenda to the back seat. Popular mandates are sought based on the performance of the political managers on conflict management rather than their ability to deliver goods which are valued for material well being of the people. As a result, the agenda of governance has been misplaced in the state of Assam. Often insurgency and identity conflicts are made scapegoats for the non-performance of the political elites in development front. Identity movements, thus, not only retard economic development, they also provide legitimacy for the perpetuation of underdevelopment in Assam.

Concluding Remarks

If Assam is to maintain its territorial boundary, it is important for the state to work for the welfare of the "Asamian", a term used here to mean residents of Assam, instead of only for the Assamese, the single largest of the numerous linguistic groups in Assam. The areas of commonality cutting across the ethnic boundaries need to be strengthened instead of focusing on the singularity of communal identity. Instead of harping on the "Assam Accord" type solution of the vexed problem of infiltration, all the members of the Muslim community particularly in Brahmaputra valley may be accepted as the bonafide citizen of Assam based on the day of issuance of identity papers in order to prevent future flow of illegal immigration. This option is far better in view of political acceptability, migration history, social ethics and above all legal complicacies than the Assam Accord option. It will be easier to identify future illegal immigrants once identity for the existing stock of people is issued rather than finding the illegal immigrants of the past. Thus accepting the present as the cut off to prevent the future infiltration is, no doubt, the most viable option rather than digging the past and keeping the future open for illegal immigration. Moreover to dig the past the whole Muslim population of the present has to be bracketed as the suspect. It will not be acceptable to those Muslims who have arrived in Assam even before the ethnic Assamese and who have already been naturalized as Indian citizens by virtue of being British citizens in colonial Assam. While the Muslims of these categories could not be denied the citizenship by bracketing them as suspect, Assam Accord type solution would only make them hostile to the political goals of the ethnic Assamese. Instead, since the issue of infiltration is a common concern, it can only be addressed by taking all the ethnic groups into confidence particularly those who reside along the Indo-Bangladesh border. As the Muslims inhabit the Assam-Bangladesh border areas, it is unlikely that any anti-infiltration measure would meet with success without taking them into confidence (Das: 2006). Thus, a fair deal to the existing Muslim population can only prevent the unfair immigration, which the ethnic Assamese views as the threat to their identity.

Besides resolving the Muslim question, polity management in Assam has to be inclusive so that minority tribal and non-Assamese ethnic groups can play some role in decision-making. Practice of consociational democracy (Lijphart: 1989) instead of electoral democracy based on majoritarian principle may be an option to accommodate the interests of the smaller identities in a multi-ethnic society like Assam. Given the existing political process, although it does not appear to be feasible, creation of the Upper House of the state legislature based on consociational principle may bring some respite. This will help in restoring the legitimacy to the governance, which has reduced to a large extent as the tribals and non-Assamese minority ethnic groups view the governance as an instrument of imposition of the will of the dominant ethnic group. Thus, secularizing the political space by way of accommodating the diverse interests of the different groups is the key for the restoration of socio-political stability and economic development of Assam.

References

Barua, Rafiul Hussain, (1989), *Islamiya Oitiya Aru Asam*, Vol 1, Luchi Publication, Jorhat (In Assamese).

Baruah, Sanjib, (1999), *India Against Itself: Assam and the Politics of Nationality*, Oxford University Press, New Delhi.

Choudhury, Medini, (1982), *Luit Barak Aru Islam,* Nandan Prakashan, Guwahati.

Das, Gurudas, (1996), "Migration, Ethnicity and Competition for State

Resources : Cause of Social Tension in the North East", in Mehtabuddin Ahmed and Prosenjit Chowdhury, (eds), *The Turbulent North*, Akshar Publications, New Delhi.

Das, Gurudas, (1997), "Understanding the Insurgency Phenomenon in India's North-East : An Analytical Framework", in B. Pakem, (ed), *Insurgency in North - East India,* 1997, Omsons Publications, New Delhi.

Das, Gurudas, (2001a), "Probable Options : Cementing the Faultlines in Assam*", Faultlines*, 2002, Vol 11.

Das, Gurudas, (2001b), "Understanding India's North East: Security, Integration and Development", Omeo Kumar Das Institute of Social Change and Development, Guwahati, (mimeo).

Das, Gurudas, (2002), "Immigration into North-East India : The Security Dimension", in C. Joshua Thomas, (ed), 2002, *Dimensions of Displaced People in North-East India*, Regency Publications, New Delhi

Das, Gurudas, (2005), "Small Societies in Large Democracy: Problems of Conflict Resolution in India's North East", in Monirul Hussain, (ed), *Coming Out of Violence: Essays on Ethnicity, Conflict Resolution and Peace Process in North East India,* Regency Publications, New Delhi.

Das, Gurudas, (2006), "War and Peace in India's North East: Issues, Complexities and Options-A Plea for Strengthening the Civil Society", in Biswas, Prasenjit and C J Thomas, (eds), *Peace in India's North East: Meaning, Metaphor and Method*, Regency Publications, New Delhi.

Datta, P S, (ed), (1990), *Ethnic Movements in Poly-Cultural Assam*, Har-Anand Publications, New Delhi.

Elwin, Verrier, (1958), *A Philosophy for NEFA*, Adviser to the Governor of Assam, Shillong.

Gait, Edward, (1981), (Second Edition reprint), *A History of Assam,* LBS Publications, Gauhati.

Gohain, Hiren, (1980), *On the Present Movement in Assam*, Shree Bhumi Publishers, Calcutta.

Guha, Amalendu, (1977), *Planter Raj to Swaraj: Freedom Struggle and Electoral Politics in Assam 1826-1947*, Indian Council of Historical Research, New Delhi.

Guha, Amalendu, (1980), "Little Nationalism Turned Chauvinist: Assam's Anti-Foreigners Upsurge", in *EPW,* Special Number, Vol XV, Nos. 41,42,44.

Gupta, Shekhar, (1983), *Assam: The Valley Divided*, Vikas, New Delhi.

Hussain, Monirul, (1993), *The Assam Movement: Class, Ideology and Identity,* Manak Publications, Delhi.

Kakati, Banikanta, (1995), *Assamese: It's Formation and Development*, (Fifth Edition) ,LBS Publication, Gauhati.

Kar, M, (1990), *Muslims in Assam Politics,* Omsons Publications, Delhi.

Kar, Makhanlal, (2005), *Evolution of Constitutional Government and Assam Legislatures*, Akansha Publishing House, New Delhi.

Lijphart, Arend, (1989), *Democracy in Plural Societies: A Comparative Exploration,* Popular Prakashan, Bombay.

Murty, T S, (1983), *Assam: The Difficult Years–A Study of Political Development in 1979-83*, Himalayan Books, New Delhi.

Nag, Sajal, (1990), *Roots of Ethnic Conflict:Nationality Question in North East India*, Manohar, New Delhi.

Neog, Maheshwar, (1985), (Second Edition, reprint*), Early History of the Vaisnava Faith and Movement in Assam: Sankaradev and his Times*, Motilal Banarsidass, Delhi.

Neog, Dimbeswar, (1962), *New Lights on the History of Asamiya Literature,* Suwani Prakash, Guwahati.

Saikia, Anil, Homeswar Goswami and Atul Goswami, (2003), *Population Growth in Assam 1951-1991: With Focus on Migration*, Akansha Publishing House, New Delhi.

Sarma, Hemanta Kumar, (1972), *Asamiya Sahitat Dristipat* (in Assamese), New Book Stall, Guwahati.

Sarma, Satyandranath, (1965), *Asamiya Sahityar Itibrita* (in Assamese), Bani Prakash, Pathsala.

Sen, Amartya, (2006), *Identity and Violence: The Illusion of Destiny*, Allen Lane, London.

The Assam Gazette, Registered No 768/97, Notification No 101, May 13, 2006, Election Department, Government of Assam.

Wiener, Myron, (1978), *Sons of the Soil: Migration and Ethnic Conflict in India,* Oxford University Press, Delhi.

6

Women in Peace: But Are They in Dialogue? A Case Study of Manipur

N. Vijaylakshmi Brara

Introduction

Let me start by giving you a very interesting factual history which is meant for kids. It is in a website called "pitara.com". In its section on super moms, written by Chitra Padmanabhan, she has delineated the following facts.

Japan – Mothers for Peace: Did you know that mothers in Japan were among the first to protest against nuclear weapons? This happened 45 years ago, in 1955. America's nuclear test of 1954, in Marshall Islands, had a radiation effect on Japanese fishermen who were near that area. That made the people of Japan very angry. In 1955, women got together for a Mother's Congress and protested against nuclear weapons. A big peace movement started in Japan after that.

El Salvador – Mothers against Guns: Did you know that more than 15 years ago, mothers in the Latin American country of El Salvador had a big hand in stopping violence and killings in their country? El Salvador was ruled by a military dictator at that time. The people were not free to live as they pleased. Those who protested were taken away by the government's secret service. Many Salvadorans started fighting the government. Some formed guerrilla groups. There was nothing but violence everywhere. Ordinary people were hit hard from all sides. It was then that thousands of women got into action – non violent action. They held peace marches, protests and strikes. They carried posters of their sons who had disappeared. The government accused them of being traitors but they did not care.

Finally, the government and the guerrilla groups reached a settlement. The mothers won.

Sri Lanka – Mothers of Missing Children: While the Sri Lankan army and the Liberation Tigers of Tamil Eelam (LTTE) are fighting a bitter war, women from both sides have formed a Mother's Front. They have protested against the disappearance of their sons in the violence that has been going on for the last seventeen years. Thousands of people have either been killed or disappeared. They have held rallies and they have also asked the government to take action.

A fourth case story given in the same website is of our concern here.

India – Grandmothers against Drugs: A group of old women in India's Northeastern state of Manipur have come together to guard their villages at night. They are trying to see that their children do not end up taking drugs. They have been doing this for almost ten years now. Armed with torches and iron gongs, the elderly women sit at the village entrance under a tin shed. If they sense any trouble, they ring the gongs and warn the villagers. Most of these women are old. Some of them are as old as 80 years, and they have helped save many young lives.

The History of Manipur

The Pre-British Period

We have had a history and therefore a *tradition of women-headed households*. Manipur has been a constant war zone. It has been at war with the Burmese, the Chinese, the Ahoms and also the British. As a result the reign of socio-economic as well as the domestic order has been in the hands of women. Therefore, it is not by choice that women have come to the forefront in the society. They have been bearing the brunt of war and conflict for a very long time. The role of maintaining domestic order has extended to maintenance of social order. This constant turmoil has been not without the benefits, because necessitated by the exigencies, women came to possess individual skills in economic activities, knowledge in marketing and also disaster management to maintain a semblance of the social order and give a coherent life to their progenies.

Before the British landed on this soil, women had a role in the affairs of governance, in economy and in the civil society. The king's rule was marked by an exclusive court for women called the *pacha* court. Here the queen conducted the trials. While in the king's court where the king was the ultimate authority, even his order of death penalty, could be converted to life sentence only by a woman. This woman used to be the wife of the chief of the place called *Sugnu*, where the offender was sent to be executed. If this wife of the *Sugnulakpa* (the Chief of Sugnu) covered the condemned with her *phanek (*women's lower garment), the condemned person was considered to have been given a fresh lease of life. He/she was symbolically considered to be born again and therefore, his/her death sentence was converted to life sentence.

History speaks, that this society has been marked by a series of invasions and conquests by outside forces, more particularly the Burmese as mentioned above. Therefore, the male members of the society were always out for war, from which there was also no certainty of their return. In such a scenario, the women took upon themselves the tasks of bringing up their children, taking care of their economy and, at the same time, ensuring that the social order is maintained. This role was amply demonstrated particularly when the Burmese invaded and occupied Manipur. That period of occupation and havoc wrought by them is called *Chahi Taret Khutakpa* (the seven years devastation) from 1819 to 1826. These seven years were marked by huge demographic shift. The population of able-bodied men was markedly low. Most of them were either killed or captured and taken away to Burma. History therefore compelled the women folk to bear the responsibility to produce as well as nurture the future generation. It was mainly at this time that *Motherhood* of Manipuri women became their social/ collective responsibility.

Many people believe that the system of polygamy, which was earlier only restricted to the kings, spread and got sanctity amongst the masses in this period, because the ratio of men vis-à-vis women decreased substantially as a result of *aggression among men*. Polygamy, which was the result of aggression for the cause of the nation and the issues of nationality, made women suffer the worst humiliation. They were told to tolerate and share their male partners with other women since they had no other choice. In other words, polygamy got sanctity within the realm of love for one's "Motherland" – patriotism.

The British Period

The assertive motherhood of the Manipuri women got manifested in the form of the two *nupilans* (women's fight) against the British. In 1903, the people revolting against the British rule and burnt down the house of the Assistant Superintendent. In 1904, Lt. Col. Maxwell, the political agent at that time, ordered the people of Imphal to supply teak-wood from the Kabaw valley (now in Myanmar) and reconstruct the house. Women did not take it calmly, as in that order they read the re-introduction of forced labour, which their king had earlier abolished. They entered the residency and could not be controlled even by the military. The British were compelled to withdraw their order. This *Nupilan* (an exclusive women's movement) marked the first organized people's protest against the British.

The women rose again in 1939 against the decision to export rice by the British in connivance with the local traders. This led to the acute shortage of foodgrain. Women, who were already playing a significant role in the sphere of domestic trade and commerce, felt the gravity of the situation and once again *gheraoed* the British Residency. A contingent of Assam Rifles had to be called in to rescue the British administrators. This was the second *Nupilan*.

Incidentally, these two agitations transgressed communal boundaries. We have *nupilan* veterans among the Naga women, Kuki women and also Muslim women, besides the Meitei women. But, ultimately when the British left, and when the question of merger of Manipur with India came, none of the state representatives of both the sides or the people asked these women their opinion. It is not that other men were also asked, but women had shown that they were capable of compelling the British to withdraw stringent inhuman laws, couldn't they perhaps change the equation of merger with Indian Union? Today, after 60 years of India's independence every year on 15 October, when we mourn the merger of Manipur with India, no body still asks the women as to what they feel? Even though they are brought on the podium, we know that they are speaking just what they are expected to speak. Our women are powerful only because of their sheer might but we have never thought of empowering them. In fact, increasingly, either consciously or unconsciously there is a trend towards marginalizing them. Do these powerful women's bodies have access to power – political, economic and domestic?

The Present Period

Manipur has for a very long time been witness to the violent conflict between the state and the underground forces. Like any other war situation women have been bearing the major brunt of the conflict. There have been high indices of displacement and mortality among women as well as men. This situation aggravates in the rural areas where mortality means loss of productive labour force and displacement means loss of land and therefore, loss of bread.

People have been too engrossed with the atrocities committed by both state and the non-state actors. Women in trying to save their children's and their menfolk's lives have not yet been able to focus their attention to the crude as well as the subtle violence meted out to them, even though they are the worst victims in such a situation. They are sexually targeted both by state and the underground outfits. They have been victim of mental, physical and sexual violence. It has been estimated that three to four out of ten rape cases go unreported. An incident where the woman was raped by a security personnel right in front of her eight years old handicapped son is still fresh in our minds. The infamous Oinam (name of a Poumei village) incident, where a pregnant woman was compelled to deliver in the open fields has become part of our nightmare. The latest "Monorama incident" of alleged rape and custodial death of a young girl, which has sparked a statewide protest and created a sensation all over the country, is another grim reminder of the continuing fear of the Mothers in zealously safeguarding the modesty and honor of their children. Imagine the extent of mental torture these women undergo when their children are simply picked up and disappear.

The issues relating to rape, molestation and other forms of sexual abuse against women are not seen as gender violence per se, but get subsumed as violation of human rights and assault on the society as a whole. Violence of such kind is not 'genderized' in Manipur. Even in the present protest arising from the death of Manorma, the agitation had revolved around the greater issue of demand for removal of the Armed Forces Special Powers Act from the State of Manipur. While the demand for removal of this Act also needs to be looked into urgently, the issue relating to the dignity of a woman has to be continued to be highlighted, lest it gets subsumed in the so called bigger issue of Nation-state.

According to Rashmi Goswami (*Reinforcing Subordination: An Analysis of women in Armed Conflict Situation*), while all sections of civilian population are affected by situations of armed conflict, "women and girls are particularly affected because of their status in society and their sex.". Women experience greater violations being caught between different violators. On the one hand, the state targets women and uses violence against them as a means of suppression; and on the other, the community is apathetic to the special problems faced by women. Often also, in such situations of ongoing conflict as the one prevailing in large parts of Northeast India, gross violations of civil and political rights prevail because of the political situation. This situation is often used as justification to disregard the violations of women's rights that are either consequence of discrimination against women sanctioned by the community, or of inaction by the state. But as signatories to the Women's Convention, the state is obligated to address discrimination at all levels.

Our women have, not yet got time to concentrate on their own plight. They have only parenthetically looked at themselves and their inside worlds.

Our informal pressure groups, the *meira-paibis*, the Kuki mothers, The Tangkhul *Shanaolong* have been in the forefront in all kinds of injustices. But pessimism is the dominant thought if one sees the future role of our *Meira Paibis*, the reasons being firstly, no new faces are joining the organisation. Secondly, their main role is that of watchdogs, i.e., to protect their men. Both underground and other patriarchal groups in Manipur use them. Thirdly, *Meira Paibi*'s do not seem to have any proactive agenda. *Today we can also say that they are primarily agitationists? They have today become our front covers.* Urvashi Butalia, in one of her article says that

> When women protest the use of their bodies as commodities the world knows what they are talking about, though many do not sympathize with what they have to say. But when women themselves turn their bodies into commodities, people don't know how to react... But the question that keeps bothering me is: what is it that drives women to take this absolutely desperate step? How humiliated, how violated, how angry must a woman feel to think that this is the only way she can make people listen? And

> what must those women feel when they see their protest being trivialized, their bodies further violated?" (*from New Internationalist website*)

They were trivialized no doubt. When the serious 'talk' started taking place in Delhi, where their body was of no more use, they were not even given a chair. That is the reason why instead of demanding exemplary punishment to the perpetrators of such a heinous crime against Manorma Devi, the issue has been degenderized and subsumed under the demand to remove AFSPA. (I don't mean to say that the issue of AFSPA is less serious, but only if it could be dealt with separately).

I think the reason why our women get marginalized at the stage of decision-making is because they are not supposed to enter the formal sphere. On the question as to why women are always pushed out in formal negotiations for peace, Ritu Menon has a response. She says that both war and peace is a contract between men, they decide the terms and also when it is to be waged. They also decide when peace is to be waged and how truce should come about. Both war and peace are discourses of power. When we talk of peace it is a question of sharing of power and women are marginalized. The area of action for our women is presumed to be the informal arena. They can protest, scream, shout but they cannot decide. There is an invisible boundary. This is the reason that in spite of having such formidable women's pressure groups, we do not have any woman leader in the state Legislative Assembly, except the one who has also been given a less serious ministry. Today all the four zilla-parishad presidents are women but they have not been able to cut much ice. In the formal work force sphere, the lower rung jobs are filled with women but one can count them on fingers in the higher levels of bureaucracy. We even do not find any woman leader among the 'formal' revolutionary groups. But, again they do have impressive numbers in their cadres.

How to Break the Impasse

We the women have to shift the dominant paradigm of our region, the existing paradigm being 'identity, territory and sovereignty'. We have to bring the issues to the forefront, which we think are affecting our lives. The issues, which have been our major concerns for such a long time, the issues of livelihood and the paradigm of governance, specially the local governance.

I am associated with a project called NERCORMP/IFAD in Shillong. We have been working on livelihood issues and sustainable development in the villages of six districts in Assam, Manipur and Meghalaya. In these villages our constant attempt has not been to challenge the traditional authorities in spite of they being completely gender blind but instead to create natural resource management groups with a fifty-fifty gender balance, besides the Self Help Groups (SHGs) which gear towards income generation of its members. These NaRM-Gs, as we call them, are the village development councils, which discuss and implement programmes for the development of the village. These NaRM-Gs have an upper level called the Associations. There are three points of dynamism, which I have noticed, due to the change in the dominant paradigm.

1. The fact that the dominant paradigm could be shifted from identity to livelihood issues is itself an important shift.

2. Since we have gender equity, we are actually getting a feedback, of course, from men that it is so refreshing for them to know women's views in the decisions involving the village. In West Khasi hills, the all male traditional authority, the *Dorbars*, are getting a conceptual expansion, whereby they are using the same term for their village development councils, where women are an integral part.

3. Thirdly, I would like to give an example of North Cachar Hills district of Assam. This area has witnessed the bloodiest tribal conflicts. But our project has achieved a breakthrough whereby transcending the tribal differences a combination of Hmar, Kuki, Naga and Meitei office bearers could be appointed for the Associations of the NaRM-Groups. When they come for their meetings, the improvement in their livelihood becomes their prime agenda. They have been able to shed the tribal boundaries and talk on common socio-economic issues.

It is a long struggle, and a long way to go, but in these villages at least the path has been defined and defined not by their leaders but by themselves.

Conclusion

Issues of independence and national liberation have altered women's political consciousness. The imperatives of Sovereignty and freedom commit them to national struggles. They are in the forefront in mounting the barricades beside their countrymen in the wars against "Imperialism"/ "Colonialism". These women subsume their priorities as women in the wider political conflict. I wonder, whether they ever think as to what place they will occupy after the struggle is over, in the process of "National reconstruction"? We therefore need to move from *feminization of poverty to feminization of development*. Today, we need to conduct a very simple study. We need to go to our women and ask them as to what they want and what their priority is. That will give a truly women's perspective to war and peace, and development.

References

Anirban, Bhaumik (2004) "Peace Message from a Land of Myriad Conflicts", *Deccan Herald*.html.

Banerjee, Paula (2002) "Second Civil Dialogue on Peace", A Report, Kolkata.

Bimola, Ksh Devi (2001) "Manipuri Women in the Beginning of the 21st Century", *Manipur Online.*

Brara, N.Vijaylakshmi (1998) *Politics, Society and Cosmology in India's North East*, OUP, Delhi.

Butalia, Urvashi (2001) 'The Body as Weapon', *New Internationalist.*

Butalia, Urvashi (2002) *Speaking Peace: Women's Voices from Kashmir*, Kali for Women, Delhi.

Fernandes, Walter *et al.* (2002) *Changing Women's Status in India: Focus on the Northeast*, Northeast Social Research Centre, Guwahati.

Hodson, T.C. (1989) *The Meitheis*, Low Price Publications, Delhi.

Kikon, Dolly (Unpublished paper) "Political Mobilization of Women in Nagaland: A Sociological Background".

Leslie, Julia I. (1989) *The Perfect Wife*, OUP, London.

Parret, Saroj Nalini (1980) *The Religion of Manipur*, Firma KLM Private Limited, Calcutta.

Raisunriang, (1998) Fourth Edition, Naga Women's Union, Imphal, Manipur.

Sircar, Manjusri Chaki (1984) *Feminism in a Traditional Society*, Shakti Books, Gaziabad.

Women in Action (1999) Reinforcing Subordination – Roshmi Goswami. Isis Manila html, Pitara.com.

Women's Peace maker's Programme, International Fellowship of reconciliation, Pitara.com.

7

Untapped Women's Agency in Conflict Resolution and Peace Process

Deepthi Shanker

Introduction

Peace building is an activity which is important for conflict prevention during pre-conflict period. It is also a process actively engaged during the conflict and post-conflict period. Peace builders are constantly engaged in the peace building and conflict resolution activity in different capacities. But women as peace builders, despite their substantial contribution, often remain unnoticed. Women and men have different access to resources, power and decision-making before, during and after conflicts. Similarly, the experiences of women and men in situations of war and post-conflict reconstruction are significantly different. Feminist discourses have time and again established that war and peace are gendered activities with the needs and responses of women being different. It is argued that while women actively are engaged in local, regional, and community level peace building mechanisms, they are completely excluded from the formal level of peace negotiations, whether it is at the national or international levels. If they are active in the peace movement at the grassroots levels, then their absence at the peace negotiating table needs to be questioned. Unheard women's voices, which is essential for peace process and conflict resolution, need to be explored, examined and critiqued.

Studies highlighting women's agency in peace building are largely ignored by the dominant discourses of peace, conflict and security. As Manchanda (2005) claims, popular discourses on peace, conflict and security, besides configuring women as victims, normally end up devaluing the multiple roles women play during the conflict. Managing community during the conflict, peace building and survival strategies, often silently takes place due to the empowering roles of women during the conflict or post conflict phases. It is important that these new roles, which normally go unnoticed, need to be socially recognized as they have implications for the society. Neglected gender issues during conflict and post-conflict situation, can be recognized more effectively if more attention is paid towards reworking more equitable gender relations during the conflict itself.

Women as Victims of War and Violence

The aftermath of war has serious economic consequence to women as there is a drastic and sudden change in the material and demographic status of women. There is increase in the female-headed households, widows, polygamous marriages, etc., all of which is underreported. Besides, causalities of war and violence, which earlier included just the fathers, brothers, husbands and sons, now largely include women and children. But it has significantly remained unnoticed and neglected. Women and children are now actually been used as deliberate soft targets. On one hand they are the main civilian victims of conflict, while on the other hand they are often powerless to prevent them as they are excluded from the negotiations during resolution. Their role is limited to a marginal role in the post conflict efforts of reconstruction and reconciliation. Thus their general exclusion from the decision making positions prior to, during and after the conflicts only end up reinforcing them as victims. (Assembly debate, 2004). Some of the facts to be noted are:

1. Women constitute 51 per cent of the world's population, i.e., half of the world's resources, but yet they are excluded from effective participation in conflict resolution and peace processes. But why?

2. Even at times, when they are involved in the negotiation process, it is believed that their voices and actions are rather too passive and are actually ignored.

3. The consequences of armed conflict are suffered by the entire community. But women and girls are particularly affected because of their gendered status in the society.

4. Rapes have been a common phenomenon in conflict situations. Other forms of violence affecting women in such situations include murder, sexual slavery, forced pregnancy and forced sterilization.

Women and children constitute about 80 per cent of the 23 million refugees and of the 26 million internally displaced persons in the world. Major threat to women refugees is the deprivation of property, goods and services, besides all sorts of violence and insecurity. They are also deprived of their basic right to return to their homes of origin. Sometimes they might be forced to flee due to sexual violence and other gender-based discrimination and persecution. Consequences of armed conflict are likely to have more lasting impact on women because of their vulnerability. The impact of violence against women and other such experiences is never seriously dealt with. Women in such situations are likely to suffer displacement, loss of home and property, loss or disappearance of close relatives, poverty, family separation and disintegration, besides being the victims of torture, violence and sexual abuse. Several new forms of violence against women is surfacing as a result of the policies of ethnic cleansing, which is never reported and goes unnoticed. It eventually gets compounded into a life long social, economic and psychological trauma for women, which leaves a permanent impact on them even after the armed conflict or the foreign occupation cease to exist in that area. (Linkages, 1995).

Understanding Women's Agency in Conflict Situations

Understanding women's agency in conflict and post conflict situations involves complex paradoxical issues. The dominant image of women as losers and as victims leads to awareness of the differential impact conflict can have on men and women's lives. It also highlights the creative strategies women engage for the survival of their families and communities. It involves the hardships and the compulsions that would have pushed the women into decision-making roles or forced them to enter into negotiations with conflict-perpetrators in public spheres. In order to strengthen women as agents of social transformation and not just to reduce them to victims of conflict situations, it is important that the 'gains' shaped and produced by the experiences of women in conflict situations is focused upon. However, the 'gains' from conflict discourse is indeed a problematic one as it is rooted in loss, pain and hardship. It is quite paradoxical to note that war and conflict situations offer women opportunities to transform their lives in terms of social relationships and also self image. (Manchanda, 2005) On the other hand Rehn and Sirleaf (2002) are skeptical of the sustainability of the impact of conflict upon women. Although women may acquire more mobility, resources and opportunities for leadership, their empowerment is ambiguous. Hence the momentary space in which women take on non-traditional roles may not sustain gender equality in the larger sense.

However, scholars have argued that there is a need to have more nuanced assessment of the implications of women's multiple roles in conflict situation. Feminist discourses attempt to locate agency even in the ordinary activities of women during war time. The language of their resistance decides their survival strategies and the political action which arises from their everyday reality. Forms of agency ranges from the concern women have for the safety of the family to the various struggles they are involved in to sustain the community. There are instances when women have stepped out of the cultural framework of the family and domesticity in order to negotiate with the institutional power structures of the enemy, army, administration and the courts. Women should not just be seen as victims of conflict situations and as sufferers, but we need to go beyond it and understand their roles as peace advocates, negotiators and political leaders. Women's peace activism tends to get obscured by the fact that women's language of support and resistance flows from their cultural experience of being disempowered as the protest strategies they use are symbols of motherhood, mourning or ritual cursing. (Manchanda, 2005)

Women have been in the forefront of politics either to prevent the outbreak of violence or to mitigate it in different forms across the world. It could be nationalistic identity conflicts in Northeast India or Sri Lankas's ethnic conflict. Women's agency is visible in their interventions to protect their families, in the campaigns for justice and in their reconciliation and peace building activities. Examples of women who have stepped in to the public space during the times of extreme violence and terror are many, most of which go unreported. For example, Naga mothers of Nagaland had stepped forward to campaign for 'Stop All Bloodshed'. Similarly, the mothers and grandmothers of Nepal's Dailekh district had protested against Maoist policy of forcible recruitment of one child per family. The powerful agency of mothers is being witnessed even in Kashmir and Sri Lanka in their determination to fight against injustice. The most shocking, strategic and dramatic protest of women against militarism was witnessed in July 2004 in Manipur. Women of the Metei ethnic community organized themselves and protested naked against Assam rifles and paramilitary forces, condemning the rape and custodial death of Manorma Devi. The campaign against the Armed Forces Special Power Act was intense as women went naked before the army with a banner quoting 'Indian Army Rape Us'. Sri Lanka also witnessed Tamil women protesting against violence and deaths outside LTTE camp in 1986 and challenged them. They were armed with chilly powder and kitchen knives. There were instances of mothers fasting unto death in order to pressurize the Indian Peace Keeping Force (IPKF) and the LTTE to declare a ceasefire. The Association of War Affected Women (AWAW), which has originated more recently and which is built on motherhood politics, focuses on the welfare needs of young widows of soldiers missing and dead in Srilanka. (Manchanda, 2005)

The case of Northern Ireland is another classic example. In July 2005, the Irish Republican Army (IRA), which was in violent struggle against the British government over the question of liberation of Northern Ireland, announced an end to its armed campaign and decided to pursue its goal through peaceful political means. What actually compelled and led the IRA to disarm itself and end violence in favour of political negotiations is the sustained campaign waged by six Irish women. The case unveils the strength of gendered resources in peace processes and conflict resolution. The saga of the six Irish women and their negotiations with the IRA furnishes hopes on the mobilization

---

* The evenings of Belfast in Northern Ireland two years ago was known for assaults, murders etc. But the death of Robert McCartney changed the scene completely. Following his murder, his five sisters Paula, Catherine, Gemma, Claire, Dorina McCartney and his fiancé Bridgeen Hagan, started a campaign for justice and demanded that the IRA hand over the guilty to the police so that prosecution could begin. They tried to raise funds so that a civil case could be registered against the IRA men who were responsible for the death. However, they soon realized that the fight with IRA in its home is not simple as it had strong political patronage. So they approached

of untapped women's agency and resources for conflict management.* (Nag, 2006) Thus, there is an underlying pattern in the protests of women, which speaks volumes on the agency women possess to tackle conflict situations and work towards peace building.

Mainstreaming Gender in Conflict and Post-Conflict Situations

Women are compelled to assume new and independent roles and demonstrate capacities for decision making during conflict and post conflict conditions. It could be for community management, peace

---

the European Parliament and addressed their problems where they were welcomed and were assured full support. Being alienated from the European community, the IRA which had initially denied that their men were responsible for murder later offered to capture and execute them to meet the demand for justice. But the six women denied the offer as they did not believe in the laws and decided to approach the US which had been the traditional sympathizer of the IRA cause. They realized that the US support formed the lifeline of the IRA. The ladies did not step back even when the IRA threatened them with dire consequences. The women propagated that the IRA was no more a revolutionary organization but had degenerated into a criminal gang. They told the journalists the facts and the way IRA was using its romantic revolutionary image to murder people on the street and for other criminal activities. Following it, there was a series of formal meetings of these ladies with the officials who showed interest in their demands. The media supported their plea too and it was clearly demonstrated that the women were able to mould the public opinion of the US and as a result the campaign had severe political implications. The US, although a traditional supporter of the IRA, was not ready to ally with it anymore as it was associated with criminal activities. IRA's future was in question and had to face the demands of the public in a more dignified way. Soon it declared that it had decided to give up arms and adopt a dialogic method and ballot box to settle the embarrassing situation. It declared that it would achieve its aims by purely political means and activity. Thus by July 2005 it was unbelievable that the IRA eventually surrendered its arms and by September 2005, the disarmament of the IRA was almost complete. It finally brought to an end the 30 year old violent campaign against British rule for reunification of Northern Ireland. The case sets an international example as it demonstrates the significant metamorphosis of the world's most powerful insurgent organization (Nag, 2006). What actually makes it interesting is the possibility of insurgency being replaced by genuine and mature politics with the initiative and involvement of six women. It signifies and showcases the untapped powerful gender resources which can be mobilized for conflict resolution and peace building activities.

process and reconstruction activities. Women's agency cannot be tapped and due attention to the needs of women cannot be given without mainstreaming gender at every stage of the peace process and reconstruction. The most visible social impact of conflict is the increasing number of woman headed households, widow and half widows who are abruptly thrust into a position of caretaker and breadwinner of the entire family. The welfare of the family is totally and suddenly a woman's responsibility and especially in the situations of instability during conflict or post conflict stages. For instance, the Taliban's official will which excludes women from working outside the home has forced widows to begging or in to prostitution for the survival of the family. Three decades of civil war in Afghanistan has only reinforced culturally sanctioned notions of restrictions and exclusion as women become the site for contesting ideologies of tradition and modernity. It is estimated that there are about 50,000 widows in Kabul alone and approximately about two million in the entire Afghanistan. (Azarbaijan-Moghaddam, 2002). Jaffna in Sri Lanka alone has 19,000 registered widows who are living in the government welfare centers. Similar is the situation of the wives of the disabled soldiers who are forced to take up the responsibility of the family and are vulnerable to exploitation, as they are entitled to claim compensations. As Azarbaijan-Moghaddam (2002) argues, widows and female headed households should not be looked as vulnerable groups as they are largely portrayed. Rather, one has to appreciate the way they have coped and addressed several issues in a better way in the society, which always disempowers them. Projects dealing with the widows should not just end up addressing their welfare, but also focus upon the strategic gender needs. Agency that resides unrecognized among these women should be tapped properly.

Political economy of violence against women in the post conflict situations needs to be examined. Primarily women's socially subordinate position puts them at the larger risk of gender-based violence. Violence women suffer during conflict situations is somehow directly connected to the physical, structural and cultural violence that already exists in normal situations of everyday life. Feminist analysis of the political economy of rape relates violence against women with sexual control and resource allocation, which is an aspect of political and economic violence. (Meintjes *et al.* 2001). Not surprisingly, women are regarded as property by the patriarchal societies and hence value is attached to the productive and reproductive labour of women. Hence abduction and rape become strategies for stripping women of their personal possessions and political assets. Many a time, it is not just the honour of the women which is at stake, but that of the entire community. Manchanda's work maps the complex picture of civilian and militarized women's agency in moments of violent social transformation and particularities of their languages of resistance and empowerment. She argues that Patriarchal biases in the process of state consolidation during post conflict situations manifest themselves through state sponsored projects like compulsory mass abortions, adoptions of the babies of the rape survivors etc. Women's claims as equal citizens are violated in the post conflict situations and thus in ethno nationalist discourses, the productive and reproductive assets of women are appropriated and ideologies of 'purity' provide social sanction for 'honour' killings. (Manchanda, 2005)

Do women withdraw during post conflict situations or are they forced to maintain low profile images? Meaning, those women who were visible during the conflict at the community level, working and striving for peace building and reconciliation, are marginalized when the actual peace table is set and talks are in process. Possibly, the patriarchal dominance and control over women surfaces during these stages and they are left without being consulted. Manchanda (2005) argues that men reassert control through political violence by devaluing women's peace work as 'accidental activism' and using cultural frameworks such as 'motherhood' for conveniently excluding women from larger public life.

Role of UN

Thanks to the UN, there is now an official emphasizing of the need to recognize women's participation in the peace process. Measures are taken to ensure gender sensitive justice. It is now addressing the specific needs and concerns of women refugees and displaced persons, and increased participation of women in peace building and conflict preventions activities. UN Resolution 1325 on Women's Role in Peace Building and Security, passed in October 2001, links gender equality to global security and acknowledges the importance of women's voices in building lasting peace. It is the first resolution ever passed by the

Security Council that specifically addresses the impact of war on women, and women's contribution to conflict resolution and sustainable peace. UN Security Council Resolution 1325 on 'Women, Peace and Security', adopted in October 2000, stresses the importance of participation and full involvement of women in all efforts for the maintenance and promotion of peace and security, and the need to increase their role in decision-making with regard to conflict prevention and resolution.

The central objective of UN Security Council Resolution 1325 is to mainstream gender at every level of policy and action in peace-building and reconstruction. But does that solve the problem of political, social and economic exclusion during the pre and post conflict stages? Not that UN is unaware of it. The report of the Secretary- General of the United Nations on the theme "Peace: Women and the Peace Process", points out that women have historically been at the forefront of peace movements. It documents their courageous and unflagging efforts to end war through the channels available to them, which have been mostly non-governmental. The report also notes that women, as peace researchers, generally take a holistic approach to peace, based on the assumption that real peace requires the elimination of all forms of oppression and discrimination. This approach is particularly well suited to deal with the interconnected problems of this age. However, the report sadly also notes, "Women are virtually absent from the peace at the official level". Women's concerns, knowledge and experiences have not been sufficiently used at the negotiating table to solve regional as well as global conflicts. Hence, although the UN Security Council Resolution 1325 on 'Women, Peace and Security' is a path-breaking endorsement of women's inclusion in the peace process, their role is yet to be acknowledged effectively (Anderline 2000; Porter 2003). Who are these women, where are they and do they make any difference in the decision making and conflict resolution or reconstruction within the UN system or outside?

Peace Building and Conflict Resolution: A New Approach

Has it ever been thought that the refugee, displaced and migrant women can also display strength, endurance and resourcefulness and can contribute positively either to the countries of resettlement or to their countries of origin on their returns in one or the other forms? Often

- Exchange of experiences in peace initiatives, visits, collaborations and peace studies should be encouraged.

Women and Peace-Building

Peace-building involves a long term effort requiring the transformation of society based on justice, education, poverty alleviation and, most importantly, the abandonment of deeply rooted prejudices. In the current societies, conquest and aggression have lost their credibility as means of solving conflict related problems. On the other hand, diplomacy, networking, cooperation, intuitive power and capacity to link institutions to rational processes are gaining importance. It is believed that women naturally possess these qualities and hence, the number of women admitted into centers of decision-making and judgment are gradually increasing. Fresh perspectives and enlightening consultation involving women is spreading across a new moral and psychological climate with better dynamics and mechanisms for problem-solving and conflict resolution. It is crucial to have women at the peace table as it marks the beginning. Women would have invariably demonstrated their resourcefulness in innumerable ways through conflict mitigation processes prior to the talks over the table. Availing their services during the crucial times of conflict and ignoring them during the peace talks might leave the peace and conflict resolution task incomplete. Hence following the activity of conflict mitigation, women should be encouraged to participate in the peace talks and voice their opinions in shaping new legislative structures of government and social institutions. Since post conflict peace arrangements are open to different situations, the consequences of it to women also differ considerably. Hence, their voices should be mobilized and canalized during the peace talks across the table if women's concerns need more attention and priority. It is believed that a lasting peace cannot be established in any negotiations without the participation of women and inclusion of gender perspectives in the peace process. Women's concerns, knowledge and experiences need to be sufficiently used at the negotiating table.

Involuntary resistance does exist despite rational arguments for including women in decision-making. Exclusion of women from important consultations is indeed deeply ingrained in most cultures and hence change is unlikely without a conscious and deliberate effort

- Information on women, peace and their activities should be disseminated through internet and other medium so that right information is accessible to women leaders who are spread and scattered in the remote corners of the globe.
- Provide training to women so that they can effectively participate in peace process and reconstruction. It shall include gender awareness, human rights law training etc.
- Increase in the recruitment of women in government and non-government organizations. Ensure security of women and children in conflict zones.
- International Organizations like UNHCR and the UN system which is responsible for refugees and other conflict affected populations must provide effective programmes which include income generation, training and education etc. Women refugees should be included in the decision making process, international peace missions and peace exchanges.
- Women's Peace Groups and organizations should be involved and their inputs considered in key peace conferences at all levels.
- A gender oriented budget analysis of post conflict reconstruction is to be ensured so that women are benefited directly from resources mobilized through donors.
- Efforts should be made to ensure that the traditional mechanisms used by women for conflict resolution and peace building is supported, restored and institutionalized.
- Gender sensitive spaces leading to policies should be created so that women are brought to the forefront in all arenas, namely, economic, political, social and legal spheres.
- International network of women, peace and security organizations should be maintained. Lobby with the international organizations and non-government women's organizations on issues related to nuclear disarmament and peace process should be maintained.

they are treated as unwanted mass and as a burden the society unable to get rid off. What is required is a systematic support system which shall canalize their resources and enable them to govern themselves. For that, they need to be involved appropriately in the decision making process. Their experiences need to be noted while debating upon those aspects which affect them directly. The following can be a new approach towards peace building and conflict resolution.

1. Defining Peace and Security in Human Terms

Peace must be redefined as not merely absence of violence but as a step ahead towards building sustainable societies. A human centered approach towards peace and security includes not just disarmament but also social justice, economic development and democratization. Such a paradigm encourages shift from weapons based security and is directed towards gender based human security. Funds also get redirected from arms to human security and eventually sustainable development. It shall establish new priorities ensuring equal participation of marginalized groups including women.

2. Partnership within Civil Society

Peace is sustainable only if it is locally driven and locally owned. Hence consultation at all levels is required. It includes women's groups and organizations at the community and regional level. It emphasizes on collective action.

3. Mainstreaming Gender Perspective

Efforts should be directed in assessing the implications for women and men in all cases of planned action, policies, programmes in all areas at all levels. It is to ensure that women's as well as men's concerns and experiences are taken into account and both form the integral dimension of the design and implementation of the programme. The goal is towards achieving gender equality and to reduce the perpetuation of gender discrimination. (NGO Working Group, 2004)

4. Other Gender Related Measures (Douglas, 2002)

- Maintain a database of women, peace and security experts and organizations across the world. Documentation is necessary to strengthen and legitimize the role of women in peace process.

to involve them is initiated. In fact, change, even when undertaken voluntarily, is rarely perceived as positive at first and often considered as disturbing and unnecessary. The transition to full equality between the men and women, besides harnessing women's potential to the maximum, is a long evolutionary process which requires education, enduring patience and determination. Bringing women in the mainstream of collective decision making is an ongoing long process and cannot happen overnight. It can be argued that the maintenance and promotion of international peace and security cannot be realized without fully understanding the impact of armed conflict on women. It includes that appropriate measures must be taken to ensure their empowerment and security. Women's participation in the peace process is now an essential necessity and precondition for establishing lasting peace because women bring an alternative perspective to conflict prevention focusing on the grassroots level.

Conclusion

If one closely looks at our everyday lives, one realizes that the most powerful forms of resistance to violence and the most effective tools for peace, equality and democracy are often rooted in our simple everyday lives. It is the mothers and teachers who influence children in the formative years and act as powerful agency and communication tool. To put in a nutshell, women are believed to possess the conventional wisdom as peace educators both in the family and at the community level. While the energy is being tapped dominantly at the family/domestic level and to some extent at the community level, it remains untapped and unexploited at the national and international level. If they are involved in the international politics for conflict settlements, probably, many long drawn global conflicts can be negotiated and world peace restored with more magnanimity.

Frameworks largely confine women as victims and welfare beneficiaries. Minimum effort has been done to explore how relief and reconstruction might help women recover from individual trauma and suffering both by national or international agencies either through policies or programmes. Gender analysis needs to go beyond woman-headed households and war widows. Involvement of women's organizations at all levels is crucial for any exercises dealing with gender, but is missing substantially. International agencies have a role in the dynamics of today's wars as they provide an opportunity for consolidating the empowering spaces for women despite loss. Most of the times women make it to the peace table only because of the support from the International community. Support and assistance from the International agencies have enabled women in acquiring new languages of conflict resolution, capacity building and in strengthening regional and international solidarities. But yet there is a huge gap between the commitments of 1325 and the reality of the situation of women in post conflict situations, which cannot be bridged just by adding gender.

Active and a transparent policy of mainstreaming gender perspective into all policies and programmes is necessary while addressing armed or any other conflicts, so that an analysis on the effects of women is made before final conclusive decisions are taken. Mainstreaming Gender in reconstruction should not be a mechanical exercise, which is followed only as a ritual. Most plans and policies add on gender as a formality and an afterthought. The gender gap cannot be solved by forming a subcommittee on gender or by adding a gender dimension in the final draft. Women, Peace and Development are closely interconnected. The link between Peace and Development is well established, for there shall be no peace without development and no development without peace. Women's role is also decisive not just because they are victimized. Their role for both peace and for development is essential because, no sustainable development can be expected to happen where one half of society is excluded.

References

Anderline, Sanam (2000) "The A-B-C to the UNSC Resolution 1325 on Women Peace and Security", International Alerts, London.

Assembly Debate (2004) Parliamentary Assembly Debate on 23 June 2004, In http://assembly.coe.int/Documents/AdoptedText/ta04/ERESI1385.htm

Azarbaijan-Moghaddam, Sippi (2002) "Report of the EC Rapid Reaction Mechanism Assessment Mission", *Afghan Gender Guidelines*, European Commission, Geneva.

Douglas, Marian (2002) 'Kampala Resolution on Women, Peace and Conflict', Petition to United Nations Security Council, NGOs, & Select U.N. delegations. In http://www.PetitionOnline.com/WmnPeace/petition.html

International Women's Peace Organization (2006) 'Peace, Conflicts and International Women's Human Rights', Internet Workshop at University of Wisconsin-Platteville, In http://www.library.wisc.edu/libraries/womenstudies/peace.htm

Linkages (1995) 'A Multimedia Resource for Environment and Development Policy Makers', http://www.iisd.ca/4wcw/dpa-038.html

Manchanda, Rita (2005) "Women's Agency in Peace Building: Gender Relations in Post-Conflict Reconstruction", *Economic and Political Weekly*, Vol. XL, Nos. 44 and 45 (October-November) pp. 4737-45

Meintjes, Sheila, Anu Pilay and Meredith Turshen, eds. (2001) "The Aftermath: Women in Post-Conflict Transformation", Zed Press, London.

Nag, Sajal (2006) "Six Women and the IRA", *Economic and Political Weekly*, Vol. XLI, No 8, (February-March) pp.699-702.

NGO Working Group (2004) 'No Women, No Peace: The Importance of Women's Participation to Achieve Peace and Security' Report Written by the NGO Working Group for the UN Secretary General's High-Level Panel on Threats, Challenges and Change', In http://www.peacewomen.org/un/ngo/ngopub/NowomenNoPeace.pdf

Porter, Elisabeth (2003) "Women: Political Decision-making and Peace Building", *Global Change Peace and Security*, Vol. 15, No. 3.

Elizabeth and Ellen Johnson Sirleaf (2002) "Women, War and Peace", *The Independent Experts Assessment*, UNIFEM, New York.

8

Structuring Negotiations for Durable Peace

Tania Das & Madhavi Bhasin

A common theme of international discourse in contemporary times is conflict resolution and peace building. From Kosovo in Europe to Kashmir in South Asia; from Darfur in Africa to Arab-Israel in the Middle East; from the ethnic crisis in Sri Lanka to issues of power sharing between Britain and Northern Ireland; from humanitarian challenges in Somalia to international concerns over nuclear proliferation, conflicts, crisis, political discords, national rivalries dominate international news. Following Hobbes's analysis and the realist rationale, the source of this international anarchy can be traced to the characteristics of human nature. But according to psychological reasoning, if the desire for power is inherent in human nature, so is the craving for peace. International politics adequately reflects this duality of human nature as the occurrence of conflicts parallels the desire for peace. From the Dayton Accords to the Lahore Declaration; from Norwegian mediation in Sri Lanka to international treaties like CTBT and NPT; from the Good Friday Accord to the Bonn Agreement, every conflict scenario has witnessed a corresponding peace process. But for ending conflicts, rather than merely managing them, it is imperative to make peace irreversible and durable. Most of the above stated conflicts and subsequent redressal measures have resulted in erratic peace. The present study examines the process of structuring negotiations with the aim of turning erratic peace into an enduring experience.

The paper attempts to make a theoretical contribution to the process of peace building in Northeast India. The region has a distinct character and no generalized approach can resolve the prevailing crisis. Nevertheless certain theoretical insights could help in reviewing the conflict dynamics of the region. The Northeast has witnessed numerous peace accords, some of which have been partially successful while some have miserably failed. These challenges increase the need to explore new alternatives for bringing peace to the region. One of the obvious approaches to peace is open discussion and interaction which can lead to proper negotiations and subsequent peace proposals. The substantive portion of this paper deals with the specifics of the negotiation approach. This approach could be further refined and contextualized to address the challenges to peace and stability, which unfortunately are too numerous in this region. This paper in no way presents a peace plan but merely discusses the essentials of a general peace plan which can be applied to the region. Since the journey towards peace traverses through unknown and challenging terrain, innovation and experimentation are unavoidable. It has been widely acknowledged that conflict resolution requires the engagement of numerous actors, including those in civil society, to re-knit the fabric of society at all levels from grassroots to the political elites. (Fisher 2006: 120) The present paper seeks to discuss a mechanism that facilitates this engagement.

There are two discernibly observable phenomenon in conflicts around the world. One is that the root of every conflict lies in the desire for greater freedom, autonomy or sovereignty either by an ethnic group, a regional group or a state. (Daneil Fisher 2005) Second, the mechanism for bringing peace to conflict situations around the globe is negotiation. Despite the aggression and violence, discussions, deliberations and information exchanges are central to any peace attempt. It is on these foundations of real freedom and open discussion that the peace approach of this paper is based.

Negotiations Dynamics

In essence, negotiation is a creative activity in which the parties involved discover information about each other's needs and interests and come to common decisions on some issue or set of issues. (Hemmer 2006:72) Negotiation includes all cases in which two or more parties are communicating, each for the purpose of influencing the other's decision. Nothing seems to be gained by limiting the concept to formal negotiations taking place at a table, and much to be gained by defining the subject broadly. (Fisher 1991, quoted in Breslin and Rubin 1991:69). Though the concept of negotiation is central to peace making, the fact remains that peace in the real sense is still elusive. This makes re-looking at negotiations vital. A few prerequisites and facts about negotiations need to be reasserted.

In a successful negotiation, everyone wins. The objective should be agreement, not victory. This mantra stands in opposition to the common tactics employed during negotiations in contemporary times. Any negotiation which aims to defeat the other party would not result in durable peace. The desire to negotiate implies the willingness to agree in contrast to the desire to win as exemplified in conflict situations.

Without common interests, there is nothing to negotiate for; without conflict there is nothing to negotiate about. This implies that in every negotiation situation, common interests and conflict are inevitably interlinked. The need for negotiations arises from the existence of conflicts, while the hope in negotiations is sustained by the possibility of discovering common interests. Rather than the issue of divergence, it is the anger, frustration, resentment, mistrust, hostility and a sense of futility that complicate the negotiation process.

Negotiations should focus on interests not positions. The purpose of negotiations is to achieve particular interests and satisfy specific demands. Minor compromises and concessions can help achieve desirable results and hence innovative solutions should not be scarified at the altar of sacrosanct positions. The Negotiation Approach discussed in this paper focuses attention on the process of interaction rather than on the content of the negotiated positions.

A critical element in negotiation is to come to understanding the other party's underlying interests and needs. Negotiations imply interactions between two or more parties. For interactions to be fruitful it is necessary that each side acknowledges the needs and interests of the other side. Without such acknowledgement no discussion can take place and interactions become mere political gimmicks.

Negotiation is a sequence of events, not an incident. Negotiations can succeed only when continuity and diligence of dialogue is maintained. Once negotiations are initiated every event, including disruption of dialogue, forms a part of the ongoing process of negotiated interaction. Incorporating lessons from failed negotiations not only link one stage of negotiations to the other, but also provide a self corrective mechanism. Negotiations need to be approached as an exercise in 'image-restoration' (Friedman 1994:120) by all parties, which requires consistent innovative input.

Negotiations should focus on resolving not merely managing conflict. Negotiations can lead to disastrous results if approached as temporary time buying tactics. Sustained and comprehensive negotiations are vital for understanding, discussing and addressing the root causes of any conflict so as to resolve it rather than merely regulate crisis.

If the above discussed essentials are taken into account, a genuine negotiating mechanism can emerge. The general principles of negotiations need to be contextualized for resolving contemporary conflicts. Given the fact that modern day conflicts are usually ethnic, religious or regional in origin, certain additional concerns figure in ensuring successful negotiations. These issues have been discussed in greater details in the work of R. Fisher and W. Ury. (Fisher and Ury 1983)

Separate people from problems. The structural features of any conflict need to be viewed as distinct from its human components. Although an organic partition of the two is difficult, a minimal degree of separation can be managed and is desirable.

Soft on people and hard on the problem. In an attempt to address a crisis, most of the current peace accords follow rigid and unyielding measures, the implementation of which creates hardships for the common people. The resolution mechanisms worked during negotiations have to target the problems rather than those facing the problem.

Integrative bargaining to replace distributive bargaining. (Burgess 2004) Most negotiations fall out on the issue of dividing the pie or the pay-off. Since resources are usually scarce, optimal utilization warrants creating greater stakes in sharing the pay-off rather than dividing it.

How you approach a negotiation will play a key role in how the negotiation proceeds. The foundation determines the character of the super-structure. Likewise the intentions and ground work leading to actual negotiations would determine the nature of peace. Pre-negotiation stage is critical in terms of determining the actual content of negotiations and subsequent peace plans.

NAN – Meaning and Rationale

Having established the centrality of negotiations in building peace and having reviewed the essentials of a proper negotiation approach, it is vital to work out a viable negotiation mechanism to address various conflicts. The present paper attempts to focus on a critical dimension of negotiations in evolving a theoretical approach for structuring peace. The approach is called the Negotiation About Negotiations Approach – NAN. (Burton 1990) There are several prominent theorists like R. Fisher (1983, 1989), J. Burton (1986), E. Azar (1990) and Galtung (1996) who have referred to different aspects of the negotiation process. Based on the writings of these theorists, conflict dynamics in various crises and Edward E. Azar's study (Azar 1990) on protracted social conflicts, this paper discusses the NAN approach to peace.

For the purpose of conceptual clarity it is important to note that NAN is not negotiation about the problem, but emphasizes on the pre-negotiation dynamics. It is an exercise in suggesting on how to approach the problem rather than outlining the final resolution of the problem. The NAN Approach concentrates on the immediate environmental variables so that actual negotiations can be initiated from a point of convergence. The bargaining space in terms of participants and issues is delimited during the NAN phase. The overt politicization of conflict situations and peace processes has diminished prospects of any positive outcome. NAN allows shifting the focus of attention from the macro political determinants to the micro human demands. In doing so, NAN leans heavily on the support and involvement of Track Two elements in the negotiating process.

The nature of contemporary conflicts and its complexity vindicates the need for a NAN approach. It is an innovation necessitated by circumstances. Most of the conflicts have got frozen in a historical space; NAN helps the respective positions and demands to reconnect to reality. In conflicts where combatants and victims of war are largely civilians, citizen-based peace processes are crucial to healing the deep wounds of the communities and thus finding lasting solutions. A study by Paula Garb and Susan Allen Nan (2006) shows how participants in multiple peace building initiatives systematically negotiated mutually satisfactory arrangements that progressed from information sharing to joint strategizing; several organizations managed to take that cooperation further to share resources and cooperate on joint initiatives and projects.

Harold Suanders (2001) contends that peacemaking cannot focus solely on the negotiation of agreements between representatives, but must involve changing relationships among societies. Thus many other activities need to occur prior to, around and after negotiation in order to secure a lasting and comprehensive peace, particularly in deep-rooted human conflicts where people will not negotiate about their identities, historic grievances, dignity and so on.

The basic idea of NAN is to reverse the current strategy. During the negotiations, political leadership prepares the overall framework and inputs are sought from the local level. In NAN strategy, the framework is fashioned at the local level within which macro-level actors would operate. The greatest potential for preparing societies for peace comes from the grassroots. Peace cannot be imposed but rather must grow from the bottom up. NAN as a bottom up approach aims at four objectives in evolving a peace approach.

- To evolve the underlying consensus in the multiplicity of demands.
- This consensus on the political, economic, strategic, ethnic and religious issues would then emerge as a charter of demands.
- The Charter is presented to the political leadership at different levels.
- Political level consultations have to take cognizance of this charter of demands.

Guidelines for NAN

After having re-looked at negotiations and established the importance of pre-negotiation stage in determining the durability of the peace process, the following guidelines would help in giving practical shape to the NAN Approach.

Hegemonic dialogue is to be replaced with a multilogue: In a hegemonic dialogue the structure and substance of negotiations is pre-determined and rigid. The dialogue process is opened to the various parties having a stake in the resolution of the conflict. An inclusive dialogue process acknowledges plurality, transparency and flexibility, and ensures the sustainability of the peace plan.

Non-Political in Character: The inclusivity of the dialogue tends to de-politicize the process making it an open interaction involving representatives from different regions, ethnic communities, separatist groups, state and national political parties, members of the local police force and armed forces, and international actors. Such interactions can be chaired by a recognized neutral international forum or civil society group at the national or international level. Wider participation expected due to the non-political character of the interaction. For too long has the desire for peace been hostage to the lack of political will. A wide range of intermediaries like a diverse collection of non-governmental organizations working in the humanitarian, development and religious domains, are already engaged in the process of facilitating negotiations. The NAN Approach seeks to increase their involvement at the stage of structuring negotiations rather than merely assisting in implementing it.

Unit of Analysis is the Group: Demands of the regional, religious, ethnic and cultural collectivities should be discussed at the NAN stage. Group is not to be viewed as a competitor to the state. Attempts are made to discuss the insecurities and apprehensions of the group rather than labeling them as illegitimate demands. Identity politics is central to any ethnic conflict and if the other party attempts to overlook this fact, their commitment to a negotiated settlement may dwindle.

Concentrate on the enduring features of the Conflict: Most conflict studies are based on the analysis of immediate events of violence and ceasefire. The real roots of the conflict are contained elsewhere in the unintegrated social and political systems, economic deprivation, technological underdevelopment, communal insecurities. NAN approach focuses on the events of violence as merely the symptoms rather than the causes of the malady.

Emphasis on micro-level actors and their demands: Simple issues of peace and development affect the people in conflict situations the most. Highly political and technical issues of resource sharing, autonomy etc., are rarely the immediate concerns of the real conflict bearers. Socio-economic concerns like minority groups and their demands of organized safeguards, issues of child and women development, youth empowerment and constructive employment emerge as more critical demands. Over-emphasis on macro-level factors has led to politicization of the problem, turning dispute centers into lands of empty promises.

Convergence on the issue of denial of human needs: The NAN strategy is not to seek compromises from one set of concerns over others, but to find convergences. Every regional, ethnic, religious and cultural concern needs to be respected, and deprivation of group rights needs to be viewed and projected as denial of human rights. Divergence needs to be tackled by working on Habermas's insights on disagreement as both threat and remedy.

NAN and Real Conflicts

It is interesting to see how NAN performs when applied to real conflict situations. Though the approach may sound too ambitious various peace attempts contain certain elements of the NAN approach. There are numerous examples where either NAN has been ignored or partially applied to result in fragile peace. Similarly, certain peace attempts owe success largely to the decisions made during the NAN phase.

The Sudan conflict demonstrates that any consensus on basic principles makes the road to peace a little smoother. The Declaration of Principles signed in 1994 between the Sudan Peoples Liberation Movement and the Government of Sudan helped in clarifying the claims and plans of each side. Resolution of the Indo-China boundary dispute according to many is making no headway. But the fact is that both countries are working on an agreement on the principles guiding the resolution of the dispute, which characterizes the NAN approach. Rather than rushing into unworkable agreements, NAN allows concerned parties to freely interact for arriving at certain agreeable principles. Most of the features of the Good Friday Agreement are drawn from the vigorous civil society interactions and the ensuing reports. The Jan Andolan in Nepal is an example of how convergence in civil society can ensure rapprochement among the macro level leadership. The peoples' uprising in June 2006 forced the Seven Party Alliance and Maoists to come together and work for a durable political resolution of the internal crisis. Though the peace process in Nepal is still continuing, NAN has given it a good start. NAN is merely the first stage in the peace process; it prepares the groundwork for actual negotiations to take place.

The Innovative Problem Solving Workshop employed in the Peru-Ecuador (Kaufman and Sosnowski 2005: 98) peace process, clearly highlights the degree to which the civil society can contribute to peace making. Herbert Kelman (1995) maintained that the 1990-93 continuing workshop helped to lay the foundation for the Oslo Accord. In US sessions of the Secretary's Open Forum (State 2002:101) are held under the auspices of the Department of State since September 2002 to encourage popular discussion on various issues in foreign affairs, including global peace building. Dialogue processes have contributed to the official pre-negotiation efforts, helping to build the legitimacy and/or support for official negotiations to take place, as in the dialogues between representatives of the ANC and influential white South Africans that were organized by the South African leaders in the period leading up to official negotiations. (Lieberfeld 2002: 29)

NAN is also susceptible to misuse in certain cases to stall the peace process. The Norwegian mediation in Sri Lanka has facilitated the NAN phase between Tamil and Sinhala fractions. But there appears to be a stalemate at the NAN stage. There is no urgency for charting a peace plan and implementing it with sincerity. Hence graduating the NAN to the phase of actual negotiation is imperative.

Another very important area concerning international peace is the issue of international involvement in crisis situations. We have the most vivid examples of Bosnia, Afghanistan and Iraq among others. These regions are still facing several challenges in terms of establishing durable peace – ethno-religious co-existence, unsatisfactory power-sharing arrangements, problems of economic development, stability and security after the international forces withdraw.

For such situations an international forum for durable conflict resolution can be created. The idea of this forum draws inspiration from John Burton's Human Needs Model (Burton 1990) and conflict transformation approach of Folger (Folger 1993) and Lederach (Lederach 2003). The basic aim of the forum in every case is to create the 'humanitarian space' – a space of freedom in which we are free to evaluate needs, free to monitor the distribution and use of relief goods, free to have a dialogue with people. To create such a space the humanitarian agencies will have to assume pseudo-diplomatic functions, which would further ensure space for the politico-strategic variables to operate with least friction. The forum can comprise of the following structures.

Permanent Wing: Officials from agencies like UNHCR, UNOCHA, ICRC, WFP, WHO, MSF, Human Rights Watch, Amnesty International – will form the permanent arm of the forum. All areas experiencing or threatened by any major crisis will be reviewed by the wing and for handling the political areas of the crisis, the following wings will be constituted. Depending on the nature and geographical location of the crisis, the constituents of these wings will change.

Diplomatic Wing: Representatives from the international community, which will include countries with direct interests and facilitating countries. Personnel from the humanitarian agencies will also be included to ensure that the whole process is not solely dominated by political concerns of some selected countries. Representatives of the donor agencies and countries can be actively involved in the discussions of the wing, where their concerns regarding accountability of the projects can be addressed. The basic task of the wing will be to work out an ad hoc engagement to restore order within the concerned country and utilize the resource wealth of the country in a mutually beneficial manner.

Military Wing: This wing will consist of forces drawn from countries willing to contribute to the peacemaking efforts under an international command. The peacekeeping role is redefined to provide defensive cover for humanitarian assistance programmes, apart from observing the ceasefire. The forum can over a period of time create an autonomous defense wing comprising of personnel drawn from guerilla and paramilitary forces of areas where conflict resolution is underway. A special reorientation programme will have to be designed and followed by the permanent wing for suitably preparing the forces for the required tasks. This would gradually reduce the dependence on individual states for contributing to the protection force and will help to stabilize the peace process by gradually inducting disbanded guerilla and paramilitary forces.

Reconstruction and Rehabilitation Wing: This would include the donor and Humanitarian agencies along with private companies' consortium. Reconstruction of public utilities like roads, schools, hospitals, water and food supplies can be given to interested consortium of private companies, with a revenue sharing agreement with their respective governments. The priority areas and necessary plans are to be prepared jointly by these consortiums and humanitarian agencies. These plans will be submitted to the donor agencies for seeking necessary financial assistance. Responsibility for ensuring the completion of the projects will be shared by all wings of the Forum.

Concerned Party Wing: The country facing a conflict needs to be substantially represented on the Forum to comprehend the ground situation and communicate possible solutions. Based on the specificities of the conflict and available strategies, an ad hoc arrangement will be proposed by the other wings, to which the parties will have to respond with their suggestions. Through negotiations and bargaining, a roadmap will be evolved, which will be implemented through guarantees by each country represented on the forum.

The example of Bosnia-Herzegovina highlights the costs of neglecting the NAN phase. The Dayton Accord was essential for stopping the ensuing violence. But Dayton did not, and some may argue could not, involve an input from the real conflict bearers. One of the enduring problems of peace in Bosnia-Herzegovina is the difficulty in getting the Bosnians to face up to their problems and contribute to the resolutions. Expert analyses hold that unless solutions grow indigenously out of the political culture of Bosnia, they are unlikely to be respected by the population, once the international community leaves. People who have not contributed to the solution can abdicate the responsibility for its failure. The Dayton Accords have failed in the essential task of creating a political community that takes responsibility for resolving its own problems, which is perhaps the most damming evidence that a peace, with a life and logic of its own, has not been created in Bosnia-Herzegovina. Once Dayton had established conditions of relative peace, the NAN approach could help to work out possible contours of durable peace.

NAN is necessary not only in particular conflict situations, but is also vital for the general conduct of international relations. Negotiations and treaties on issues like non-proliferation (NPT, CTBT), environmental protection (Kyoto Proposals) and economic interests (WTO negotiations) have failed in achieving the desired objectives primarily because the NAN phase has been ignored.

NAN- A Rational Approach to Durable Peace

The above examples clearly highlight the flexibility and adaptability of NAN. Essentials of the approach can be applied in several conflicts, ranging from intra-state ethnic differences to inter-state boundary disputes. NAN even holds promise of emerging as a more acceptable pre-emptive mechanism to tackle conflicts. The flexibility of the approach is drawn from the fact that it is a dialogue promoting approach rather than a rigid problem-solving mechanism.

While activating the NAN strategy, it needs to be reasserted that this is not a solution to actual or potential crisis, but merely a mechanism to approach the crisis. To turn this mechanism into a solution generating platform, participation of the non-political elements is essential. At the onset of the paper, it was stated that the desire for greater autonomy or freedom lies at the root of all conflicts. Autonomy literally means empowerment. NAN empowers the conflict units by enabling them have their space in the structure negotiations. Hence NAN guarantees autonomy in the true sense of the term and thereby addressing the basic cause of every conflict. And the durability of peace generated by the NAN approach rests on this fact.

Acknowledgements

Prof. Omprakash Mishra's guidance and Dr. Tania Dass's involvement were crucial in writing this paper. Due acknowledgement needs to be given to my parents, especially my mother, for helping me to conceptualize and write this paper.

References

Azar, Edward E. and Rick Ayre (1990) *The Management of Protracted Social Conflict: Theory and Cases*, Dartmouth Press, Brookfield, VT.

Burgess, Heidi, (2004) "Negotiation Strategies: Beyond Intractability", In *Conflict Research Consortium*, Guy Burgess and Heidi Burgess, eds., University of Colorado, Boulder, Posted: January 2004, http://www.beyondintractability.org/essay/negotiation strategies/

Burton, J. (1990) *Conflict: Human Needs Theory*, Macmillan, London.

Burton, John and Frank Dukes, (1990) *Conflict: Resolution and Prevention*, St. Martin's Press, New York.

Burton, John W. (1993) "Conflict Resolution as a Political Philosophy", In *Conflict Resolution Theory and Practice: Integration and Application*, Dennis J. D. Sandole and Hugo van der Merwe, eds., Manchester University Press, New York, pp. 55-64.

Burton, John, (1986) "The History of International Conflict Resolution", In *International Conflict Resolution: Theory and Practice*, Edward E. Azar and John W. Burton, eds. Boulder, L. Rienner, p. 40-55.

Fisher, J. Ronald & W. Ury, (1983) *Getting To Yes: Negotiating Agreement Without Giving*, Penguin Books, New York.

Fisher, J. Ronald (1989) "Pre-negotiation Problem-solving Discussions: Enhancing the Potential for Successful Negotiation", In *Getting to the Table*, J.G. Stein eds., Johns Hopkins University Press, London, pp. 206-238

Fisher, J. Ronald (2006) "Coordination between Track Two and Track One: Diplomacy in Successful Ceases of Pre-negotiation", *International Negotiation*, Vol. 11, p.66.

Fisher, J. Ronald and Daneil, Shapiro (2005) *Beyond Reason: Using Emotion As You Negotiate*, Viking/Penguin, New York.

Folger, J.P. (1993) *Working Through Conflict: Strategies for Relationships, Groups, and Organizations*, Harper Collins College Publishers, New York.

Friedman, A. Raymond (1994) *Front Stage, Back Stage: The dramatic Structure of Labor Negotiations*, MIT Press, Cambridge.

Galtung, Johan (1996) *Peace by Peaceful Means: Peace and Conflict,*

Development and Civilization, Sage Publications, London.

Garb Paula, Nan A. Susan (2006) "Negotiating in a Coordinated Network of Citizen Peacebuilding Initiatives in the Georgian-Abkhaz Peace Process", *International Negotiation*, Vol.11, p. 7-35.

Kaufman, Edy & Saul Sosnowski (2005) "The Peru-Ecuador Peace Process: The Contribution of Track Teo Diplomacy", In *Paving the Way: Contributions of Interactive Conflict resolution to Peacemaking*, Ronald Fisher, ed., Lexington Books, Lanham, p. 175-201.

Kelman, Herbert (1995) "Contributions of an Unofficial Conflict Resolution effort to the Israeli-Palestinian Breakthrough", *Negotiation Journal*, Vol. 11, p. 11-27.

Lederach, John Paul & Michelle Maiese, "Conflict Transformation", In *Beyond Intractability*, Guy Burgess and Heidi Burgess, eds., Conflict Research Consortium, University of Colorado, Boulder, Posted: October 2003. Available online: http://www.beyondintractability.org/essay/transformation/

Lieberfeld (2002) "Evaluating the Contributions of Track Two Diplomacy to Conflict Termination in South Africa, 1989-1990", *Journal of Peace Research*, Vol.39, No.3, pp.355-372.

9

Economic Policy Making in a Terrorist Economy

Dipankar Sengupta

Introduction: What is a Terrorist Economy?

It was Ajai Sahni who defined the term Terrorist Economy (TE) to describe the economy of a region afflicted by terrorism for an 'adequate' period of time, taking cognizance of certain common features that these regions possess, which are uniquely and indeed inexorably produced by the activities of terrorist organisations.

Sahni's definition (which we follow) and contribution, which has received far less recognition than it deserves, defines a TE by critiquing theories that contend that it is economic neglect and lack of development that leads to terrorism in the first place and reversing this trend by stepping up investment and introducing development programmes will lead to the roll back of terrorism.

However, as Sahni points out this programme of development has proved to be non-implementable in normal circumstances due to State incapacity as well as leakages (of up to 85 per cent of spent funds). Additionally he points out that should it succeed or promise to do so, it will attract terrorist attention because the terrorists would not like any programme that turns the population away from them. As if that were not all, much of these funds actually end up in the coffers of the militants themselves. Most importantly, in the long run, state investment does not prevent the flight of private capital from the affected areas.

Sahni contends that it is useful to study Terrorist Groups as Organised Crime Groups with one difference. He contends that Terrorist Groups differ from Organised Crime Groups insofar as they are ideologically motivated and that the overthrow of the state remains a goal. However, it is also contended that over time the profit motive becomes more important.

Although Sahni specifically looks at India's Northeast before describing a TE, it may be argued that of late Jammu and Kashmir too has followed a similar trajectory in this respect. The Northeast, it must be remembered, is a region that is marked by centralised decision-making (as indeed are most parts of India). They are also affected by Terrorism which has caused the respective state governments to shrink in effectiveness (but amazingly as he points out, not budgetarily). In this region, Terrorist Groups are increasingly showing a tendency to maximise profits, relegating the stated political goal on a back burner. It is also increasingly apparent that in this state, collusion cannot be ruled out.

According to Sahni, the TE has the following features:

- The TE is a complex economy with the illegal underground economy and legal above ground economy intermeshed so that isolated attacks on obvious targets affect the legal sectors as well.
- It chokes legitimate and productive investment as it is based on extortion which cuts into the profits of legitimate entrepreneurs.
- The TE is an evolving entity which has to innovate to prevent leakages from its own as it grows.
- It has a tendency to substitute the state in the provision of certain services (especially those that depend on force applied).

Why Does a TE Exist?

While Sahni's description and isolation of the features of a TE economy may be adequate, it does not explain why a TE exists. It does not explain the change in the Terrorist Groups' shift in objective functions or, for that matter, state complicity. This is an important gap that must be filled if there is to be a relevant discussion on policy making in a TE.

Here, an attempt to provide a rationale for the actions of the Terrorist Groups as well as the state is provided. The aim of such a 'rational' behaviour, a stable outcome, is the existence of an equilibrium as described by Sahni.

What is the objective of the Terrorist Groups that operate on Indian soil? By and large, their main objective is the separation of the region they claim to represent from the Indian Union. A subsidiary objective is the collection of the treasure that is required for the pursuance of the first. However, of late, the subsidiary objective is fast replacing the first as the primary goal. At any given time, the terrorist group in question tries to do both. Indeed, it cannot concentrate on one objective alone. Should the group choose to concentrate on 'Liberation' alone, it would provoke a strong response which might break its back. Should it concentrate on acquiring treasure alone (to the neglect of its ideological objective), it may acquire the reputation of a totally mercenary outfit, lose sympathizers and mass base, and thus gain enemies. In such circumstances, the terrorists can no longer be the 'fish' where peasants are the 'water.' Thus the terrorist group chooses to mix the strategies; there are operations that are aimed at acquiring loot, which do not provoke state response, as these are considered criminal activities that do not have the same priority to them as secessionist activities do. But there are also costly operations that bring no financial remuneration but are political in nature. These are to assure the faithful that the 'cause lives' and ensures that the 'water' remains for them to swim in. The relative ease with which finance is acquired through extortion over time makes the subsidiary objective the *de facto* prime one.

As for the state agencies, their prime task is to ensure the unity and integrity of India. Enforcement of law and order comes second. An all-out war on terrorist groups is likely to be long-drawn and bloody with reports of real and imagined Human Rights violations, putting the state on the back foot. On the other hand, organised extortion which relies more on fear of violence than actual violence itself is condoned as the primary objective of the state is obtained with little overt violence.

Thus the equilibrium observed more often than not is little overt violence but one where extortion is common and marked by periodic acts of political violence. Existing businesses may stay but new businesses do not come in.

Why Do Government Policies Fail in Such Economies?

Given the perverse nature of the equilibrium described above, prolonged economic stagnation coupled with increasing popular alienation is the only logical outcome. As the people find it safer to express frustration with the state than with the extorting terrorist groups, it is the state that is compelled to act.

When the state designs an economic package, it is along certain predictable lines. It generally announces a package that contains some mega-projects; some projects are geared to improving infrastructure; some are commercial projects that will provide jobs for the youth of that particular state. Arguably, such measures have never worked. The reasons of such failures are because of the very nature of the TE.

When the state spends on infrastructure, it does so with the help of contractors who are considered fair game for militants for extortion. The reputations of these contractors who are rich are never very high and their extortion by the terrorist groups is not considered as objectionable as the extortion of a small businessman would be. Thus one of the effects of plans aimed at boosting infrastructure is to fill the coffers of terrorist groups regardless of its effects on infrastructure. The main aim of spending on infrastructure is to make investment more profitable and draw in fresh investment. This is unlikely to happen in a TE as businessmen would like to set up businesses in a more secure environment. Indeed, post liberalization, with the scrapping of the license-permit Raj and with a host of states trying to attract investments, this is the more likely outcome.

The setting up of commercial enterprises by the state generally does not boost employment directly. Indeed, if they are related to the extraction and refinement of mineral resources, they are likely to be capital intensive and create very little employment. They are likely to attract charges of plundering the states' wealth. Thus much money is spent with little employment being created. This does nothing to reduce the feeling of alienation and consequently does not make life for the terrorist groups harder. The problem remains as intractable as before. How then should the State respond in such circumstances?

The Consequences of a Plebiscitary Democracy

Before putting forward mechanism designs for effective economic policy in a TE, it would not be out of place to analyse why a section of the populace take recourse to militancy or more importantly, why a substantial section of the populace harbour sympathies towards militants when grievances can be redressed through elections. The gravitation of the latter section towards sympathy with a form of resistance which is fundamentally undemocratic is a paradox in a democratic system, where technically the operation of one-man-one-vote in a parliamentary democracy should see to it that all shades of opinion are represented in both the Parliament and State Assemblies.

This phenomenon ceases to be puzzling when it is realised that mere representation does not necessarily lead to action on issues of interest close to *all* sections of the population. Indeed before 1991, India's polity was of a type where much of the Nation's administrative power and resources was concentrated in the Central government. The party that ruled the Centre set an upper bar on the conditions that governed the lives of all of India's citizens. It was practically impossible for any constituent unit of the polity (let alone a small section of the people) to improve upon Central government performance. The constituent units did not have the power or resources to even attempt such a task. Thus even the existence of a talented and enterprising pool of people, receptive and indeed capable of innovative ideas, could not do much in this milieu. *Their ideas would be implemented only if they caught the attention of a powerful figure at the Centre.* Consequently, even technological breakthroughs would be associated with politicians, and not seen as market induced (as the market was circumscribed). Thus computerisation in India was associated with Rajiv Gandhi, the telecommunications revolution with Rajiv Gandhi and Satyendranath (Sam) Pitroda, Operation Flood (that boosted milk production) with Verghese Kurien, etc. All of them were either State-sponsored or had the backing of the State. Without State backing, they would simply not get off the ground. Thus even while India was formally a democracy, functionally power was concentrated in the hands of the very few who were elected.

The liberalization of the Indian economy ended the Centre's monopoly over licensing. But where infrastructure was concerned, it transferred plebiscitary politics to the State capitals. Thus where crucial services like electricity and water was concerned, it was the State government alone that would decide what was to be done. If dedicated NGOs or a group of persons were fortunate enough to be close to the State government, their ideas would be given a hearing. But actual action and the ground, and indeed the right to initiate action, (some States have insisted) were the State government's alone. Thus although formally a democracy, the Indian State has disempowered the very citizens whose exercise of the franchise legitimize it! It is not surprising that sooner or later a group of citizens (not necessarily constituting a majority in any area) may be persuaded to withdraw from the process of participating in elections and support non-democratic means to achieve their goals as formal democracy ceases to reflect popular sentiment in any meaningful fashion.

Indeed, it may even turn out to be the case that local action can deliver local public goods only by defying the state ostensibly run by democratically elected representatives. It is in this context that the success of the *Tarun Bharat Sangh* (TBS) has to be measured and analysed. The TBS, set up by Magsaysay Award winner, Rajendra Singh, with the help of the villagers of Kaonta Bhaontala (district Alwar), constructed the first check dam in 1985. In 1986, they constructed a *johad* (a traditional crescent shaped pond) at the source of the River Arvari, which had become a seasonal rivulet. Other villages too followed suit constructing *johads* in the other catchment areas of the Arvari. When the number of ponds touched 375, the Arvari that had almost ceased to exist, revived and from 1994 became a perennially flowing river. What TBS has accomplished is a vindication of the Nurkse-Vakil-Brahmanand thesis, that in a labour abundant economy like India, labour combined with very little capital can bring about a remarkable economic transformation. The economic impact can be gauged for the effect of the investment made by the villagers of Neembi. On an investment of Rs 50,000/- to build two check dams, Neembi produces vegetables and milk worth Rs 3 crores. This is not the kind of capital-output ratio that can be easily ignored especially by States who are financially constrained. The TBS, a grassroots organization set up in Rajasthan by Rajendra Singh, transformed an area designated as a 'dark zone' into a water abundant area with a thriving agriculture reversing the drain of labour into the cities. Indeed he also revived the once-dead River Arvari over the vociferous objections of the officials of the Rajasthan State government. Indeed, had it not been for the organized protests of the beneficiaries of the TBS's activities, the check dams constructed by the organization would have been demolished, the vast improvement in the lives of the people that has taken place not withstanding. Unlike Sam Pitroda *vis-à-vis* Rajiv Gandhi, clearly TBS did not have the ear of the Chief Ministers of Rajasthan and in a sense the *legality* of TBS's actions as opposed to their appropriate nature remained suspect.

What is eminently clear is that there must be an institution that incorporates social entrepreneurs in its functioning and uses their talents, rather than have such organizations/persons work outside the system and often against it while attempting to do something constructive. Such an institution obviously cannot be a 'distant' one buffeted by a host of 'societies' and NGOs, spurious or otherwise, all claiming to have ideas that will revolutionise life. Such an institution will perforce have to be local and numerous. The Panchayat is no doubt one of the institutions that fulfill this criterion. Social entrepreneurs and activists will be able to interact with a tier of the government, capable of putting their ideas to work. Indeed, they may even choose to run for office to occupy one of these institutions as the number of voters to be convinced is low and thus election expenses low. Thus innovation will stand a greater chance of legitimacy and State support than under a centralized government. The implications for innovative labour-intensive and environmentally friendly social capital formation are profound. If the success of the TBS is replicated nationwide with State institutions reinforcing local initiatives rather than suffocating them, the implications for economic growth are obvious. However as of now, things stand very differently. The Indian State which is effectively still centralized is unable to incorporate men and ideas and talent which could enable to provide it public goods at the lowest possible cost. Today, NGOs with proven track record as well as dubious ones jostle for State attention and funds at the Centre and State level. Effectiveness of action is not necessarily a criterion for survival; contacts are. A democracy in this form is not likely to reduce alienation as it does not necessarily give space to local knowledge. As we will argue later, this is not only bad politics, it is also bad economics.

Towards an Appropriate Policy Design: Involving the Passive 'Citizen'

It is clear that an appropriate policy design has to take cognisance of the features of the TE. It also has to take into account the nature of the state that is in charge of implementing this 'package'. Additionally, it has to take into account the reasons why such an economy survives. It is only then a viable plan of action may be designed.

A close look into Sahni's model of the TE makes it clear that there exists a player who is conspicuous by his silence. This is the citizen. This *per se* is not a shortcoming in Sahni' model. Given India's record of dirigisme and centralisation, this is reasonable. However, given the fact that India has now embarked on a programme of liberalization, where the private sector is increasingly being encouraged to invest in all areas but a few (generally related to defence), a rethinking of the role of the 'passive citizen' becomes necessary. Secondly, with the passage of the Seventy-second and the Seventy-third Constitutional Amendment Acts that grant constitutional status to the third tier of government, the possibility of the citizen acquiring a more active role even in the provision of public goods cannot be discounted. This is important because an appropriate economic policy geared towards a TE must be two-pronged. One has to deal with the provision of public goods; the other with steps that directly promote economic growth. Both aspects of the strategy must involve the player, 'citizen' who is passive in Sahni's model.

(a) *The Provision for Public Goods*

The pitfalls of centralised infrastructural projects have already been detailed at length. Clearly, this is not an approach that can work and has to be replaced or certainly re-thought. This however does not solve the problem of inadequate infrastructure in terrorist-infested economies. For example, it is common knowledge that poor roads and irregular supply of water during dry seasons is one of the many problems in such economies that inhibit economic growth and development.

For the provision of such goods, a centralised stem of governance/ implementation is distinctively unsuited. This is because, many infrastructural requirements are locality specific; designing or budgeting for them in Delhi or even the state capital is impracticable and is likely to lead to failure. This is especially true for watershed projects.

The failure is likely to be two-fold:

I. Project objectives are not likely to be met.

II. A large proportion of the funds sanctioned for the project ends up in the hands of terrorist groups who extort the implementing contractors.

An alternative method of project implementation is to involve local self-governments, Panchayats, Municipalities and Zilla Parishads in the planning and implementation of such projects.

There are a number of reasons as to why these bodies (especially Panchayats) may succeed where the state and central governments have failed.

(a) When the Panchayats execute a project, extorting the panchayat by terrorists will be counterproductive, as such an act would be seen as extorting the populace. This is because while extorting a contractor may have social sanction (as contractors have a poor image), extorting the panchayat is likely to be seen as a direct extortion of the village community. While the Government Contractor is a distant person, the panchayat is not. Terrorist groups would risk alienation and would thus 'drain the water in which they swim'. Thus the chances of terrorist groups receiving funds from government expenditure on infrastructure would be reduced.

(b) The involvement of villagers through the Gram Sabha in planning the project increases participatory planning and decision-making which in turn reduces the feeling of alienation from the State.

(c) Most importantly, as the experience of Gujarat has shown vis-a-vis Andhra Pradesh, especially in the case of rain-water harvesting, participatory planning and implementation has been far superior to a centralised approach that relies on contractors.

Thus this approach by conferring the role of planner-implementer on the targeted beneficiaries of planning themselves has the potential of reducing costs, preventing extortion, increasing effectiveness as well as reducing the degree of alienation of the people by enhancing participatory decision-making. It is to be noted, that in the context of the TE, giving autonomy to the regions to solve the problem of terrorism is no solution at all. *Such a step transfers centralised decision making from New Delhi to the respective state capital without any appreciable reduction in the psychological distance between the ruler and the ruled.* Such a step only ensures that while the *responsibility* of reducing alienation remains *de facto* with Delhi, it loses the *power* to do anything about it.

What is the economic argument for decentralization? A case for decentralization may be made not only on the principle of subsidiarity but allied to it on the grounds on which von Hayek defended the market econ omy vis-à-vis the planned economy. In so far as one of the roles of the State is to provide public goods like infrastructure where externalities are involved, a theory may be advanced. It must be recognized that most economies are not homogenous entities. There is a wide variation among various regions and localities within regions. (This is particularly true for many of the states afflicted by militancy.) Consequently, economic infrastructure that has to be created is not always standardized or uniform. Planning for infrastructure in a non-uniform environment, especially when local economic activity is affected by local factors, requires the collection of relevant data – available locally – and then processing this data into information. Ideally, it should be this information that is the basis of planning for certain kinds of infrastructure. This is especially true for agriculture and a host of agro-industries. To that extent infrastructure required to support that industry/economic activity will be peculiar to the locality as its nature and quantum will depend on local conditions. Thus, that portion of infrastructure will be best planned, executed and managed by the members of the locality itself. The reasons are simple. The members of the locality or their representatives, being first hand observers of local conditions, should know the best way to create an appropriate support of local infrastructure and should be able to do so in the most economical manner. Indeed, for projects relating to watershed management, local self-governing bodies can mobilise free labour (by suitable innovation as regards distribution of benefits) from its citizens, which in the context of South Asia usually means unutilised labour.

If, on the other hand, the Central or State government is entrusted with the responsibility of providing all infrastructural requirements, then it has to collect information from all the localities, aggregate this information and process it to arrive at a plan to provide infrastructural support. This is obviously a monumental task and one that is not easily accomplished. Secondly, in the process of aggregating information, it is likely that some information of value will be lost. To that extent the plan created will be *faulty/sub-optimal*. Thirdly, given the magnitude of this exercise, it is also likely that the *lag* between the perception of the problem and action will be larger. Fourthly the possibility is that the link between local public good requirement and a local solution will be broken. While local demands will be aggregated, the solution that is proposed will be a centralised one. Take the case of the construction of a multi-purpose irrigation dam to cater to the needs of a large number of people spread over a large area distributed into various localities. This solution, while at times the only and perhaps the best solution, may not always be so. For one, the capital costs of such projects are very high. Secondly, they can take a long time to complete. Thirdly, it has a tendency to submerge the most fertile areas and thus the most populated areas and displace a section of people 'for the greater common good.' However, in the absence of effective decentralization, the solution like the one above will be the only solution. Before discussing the effect of the redistribution of powers, a look at the public goods requirements of the Indian economy integrating with the global economy is useful.

This is not to say that Panchayati Raj Institutions do not have their problems. Indeed charges of nepotism and mismanagement of funds have been leveled against such bodies. However, if given the fact that the Panchayat committee members as well as the Sarpanch living among the villagers, and if regular meetings of the Gram Sabha are ensured, then nepotism will draw public anger, which will be targeted at persons responsible and identifiable, not at the nameless faceless bureaucrat or MLA identified with the state. Taking the former to task is also easier than holding the latter to account. Moreover, a supervisory role by the District Commissioner that ensures that rules are followed but does not interfere in planning or implementation can reduce the chances of Panchayati nepotism. All in all, decentralised governance that calls for grassroots participation has a better chance of success in providing local public goods than centralised implementation from Delhi or the state capital. It is also less likely to be targeted by the terrorist groups for fear of popular alienation.

Promotion of Economic Growth

While the effective provision of public goods, especially infrastructural capital, is extremely important, the aim of this investment is to make commercial/private investment attractive and profitable. Thus the most important component of an economic package is thus the commercially productive investment as this is the only provider of sustainable and productive employment.

The problem with the TE is that it drives away (or at the very least fails to attract) commercial capital. This (as we have seen) is because the 'taxes' collected by terrorist groups tend to add to costs, eating away at the profitability of private enterprises. In most cases, such enterprises are owned by 'outsiders', that is, persons originating from other states and there is sufficient social sanction for the terrorists to extort such enterprises. The larger the business, the larger is the profit and greater is the emotional distance of the proprietor from the people of the locality where his plants are located. As the proprietor is seen to be part of an exploitative class, their extortion by the 'boys' who are fighting for the region is at least not vigorously opposed. This is especially true for businesses whose linkages with the domestic economy are very low (i.e. tea in Assam). It is clear that in such cases private investors from outside the state will step in. Nor is the local business class up to doing the needful.

Can public commercial enterprises fill in this gap? It must be remembered that commercial public sector units (PSUs) do exist terrorist-infected states like Assam. These PSUs are not looked by the population at large as providing employment; they are seen as exploitative projects that extract and process the wealth of the state (oil in this case) for use by the rest of the country without adequate recompense to the state. In any case the inter-linkages with the rest of the economy are extremely limited and as the technology utilised is capital-intensive in nature, not much employment generation is achieved.

The question is, how does one make his way out of this *cul de sac*? Again, we have to take cognisance of the fact that the terrorist group targets businessmen because the latter are generally outsiders, psychologically distanced from the people and whose operations are shrouded in mystery, lending credence to charges/suspicions of dishonesty. Targeting such a class meets the objective of collecting/ acquiring treasure without keeping intact that base which enables the terrorist to swim in water. Thus any policy of intervention must ensure that the beneficiaries possess as few characteristics of the existing business class as possible.

Thus preferably, the sectors so chosen must be labour-intensive in nature that do not call for much by way of supporting infrastructure. Specifically for the Northeast as also Jammu and Kashmir, sectors like horticulture and floriculture must be targeted. Such sectors call for widespread participation by farmers. Targeting such a large group of beneficiaries by the terrorists is self defeating as it alienates the very people whose help (even if unwillingly given) is vital for survival.

Processing flowers for the export market is again a labour intensive job which can be done through cooperatives run by locals or alternatively by local businessmen. Targeting either again affects the fortunes of a large number of farmers as well as that of a person/institution who is and seen to be a local boy. Thus targeting such persons by terrorists would certainly lead to alienation of the locals from the terrorists. Similarly sabotage of deliveries, especially if delivered by farmers themselves to the collection centres, is likely to have a similar reaction. What the state needs to coordinate is the collection of flowers and their export to the global flower markets. The latter is not exposed to terrorist attacks. The former is done in coordination with farmers.

Where horticulture is concerned, processing fruits has to be carried out on commercial lines. While the technology for diffused production exists, the marketing of such products has to be carried along modern commercial lines. NERAMAC (full form) has been set up with a view to exploit the fruit growing potential of the Northeast. Unlike tea and petroleum, the growth of this sector, given the obvious inter-linkages, increases employment as well as income. Indeed given the low cost of raw materials in this region, NERMAC is able to market its product at about 50-60 per cent of the price for similar goods from other brands like DABUR and KISSAN. However, it is also clear that even given the clear price differential, NERAMAC has not yet been able to gain visible shelf space as compared to the other brands. There is little doubt that an alternative route via which cooperatives negotiate with established brands for marketing must be explored.

Such strategies which are participatory in nature and seek to diffuse entrepreneurship rather than concentrate resources in capital intensive projects whose linkages to the rest of the economy is negligible, should be stressed. Given the nature of the TE, such strategies have sufficient versatility to maneuver around the minefields that abound.

Strategies that are participatory insure themselves from attack of terrorists because they involve the very people that the terrorists do not want to alienate. This is not something that conventional policies implemented by the state have done. It is to be noted that decentralisation of power confined to transfer of power from centre to the states has little to do with this strategy. What is being referred to here is gram swaraj and the attendant responsibilities that come with it.

Conclusion

The mere presence of formal democracy with all its attendant features like universal adult franchise cannot temper feelings of alienation especially when such a system does not allow participation. Sustained neglect of local opinion as well as disregard of local knowledge, which is almost inevitable in a centralised polity, delegitimises democracy. Certainly in a region that is heterogeneous, it cannot be expected to fulfill its economic functions as a provider of public goods efficiently. Using such an administrative structure to administer 'economic packages' usually leads to the evolution of a system that bribes militant groups to inaction punctuated by sporadic 'incidents'. Neither Economic Development nor Participatory Democracy receives a fillip. Thus a peace of sorts is maintained till a more puritanical militant group evolves and receives supports of sort from a section of the population whose alienation from the State has not been tempered. Thus it is not surprising that in some regions a second cycle of violence is being experienced.

Section III

Peace: Issues and Strategies in Northeast India

10

State Formation, Nation-building and Aspects of Peace in Northeast India

A C Sinha

Peace may be seen as lack of violence and not as denial of conflict. Peace is also an inseparable ingredient of consensus building for an open society, which permits formal difference of opinions. Democracy, which was defined by Abraham Lincoln as the 'government of the people, for the people and by the people', cannot be conceived without a civic society. How does one conceive a civic society? A civic society is one, which is based on consensus of views on socially important issues among the citizens, who consciously decide to abjure violence for settling differences among themselves. In this way, peace, civic society and social consensus are significant ingredients of any democratic dispensation. No doubt, there is a variety of democracy; but in spite of all difference of opinions on its content, operation and forms of governance, it takes care of the maximum interests of the largest number of the citizens of the state.

Northeast India, formerly known as the British Assam, got its present identity after 1947, when the British Indian Empire was divided into Indian Union and Pakistan. The region, tugged into the eastern-most corner of the country and bedeviled with a series of problems, developed an enclave mentality and invariably found itself pleading for operation of the normal rules of the Republic, which are elsewhere granted as a matter of routine. Why is it so? Some of us, who spend decades of active lives serving in Northeast India, are puzzled to apathy and stereotype on the region found elsewhere in the country. I for myself have been asking an obvious question: 'why do the violence, conflict, insurgency and denial of civic rights in Northeast region not create an instant national concern?' Without blaming any body, one potential source of the answer may be identified with that of the uneven growth of civic society and nation-building mechanism in the country.

Nation-building is the resolution of the polity to shape the destiny of its citizens in the image of a commitment made by the national leadership. It may be in the form of welfare measures for the citizens, providing the basic necessities of life, diversifying the economy through time bound planned development of the resources, taming the rivers through dams, building steel plants, shipyards, harbours, machine making factories and a host of other visible signs of reconstruction. It may as well have some ingredients of image building devices such as a national airline, national flag, carrier shipping lines, an imposing architecture for seating its legislature and headquarters of the head of the state / government. The nation-builders send the message to the masses suggestive of their sense of purpose, direction of policy and capacity of resources. Normally, nation-building refers to reconstructing the polity with a purpose within a given time frame and accordingly the objectives of the nation-building exercise may change from time to time.

State formation is a historical process through which a polity transforms itself into a state with its various distinct functions with a distinct monopoly of physical coercion of its citizens in certain conditions. Though there are a number of claimed theories for the origin of state, social evolution, theory of coercion and conquest, theory of association throw possible light on the evolution of the state as a universal institution. However, all scholars agree that generation of economic surplus for maintaining a standing army, a functioning bureaucracy and building of a capital/ urban centre is the necessary condition in almost all the cases. And these considerations amply make clear how ecologically favoured locations such as Nile valley in Egypt, Hwan Ho in China, Mohanjodaro and Harappa in the Indus valley and Euphrates and Tigris valley in Babylon gave birth to not only the early civilizations, but also the organized states. The state boundaries depended on the might of the rulers and thus they kept on changing in course of time all through human history. There have been great empires, great rulers, and mighty conquers in the past in the different parts of the world, whose exploits make rich folklore of the human heritage. Though at least some of them inspire the peoples in different parts of the world, it is difficult and futile to identify and draw the boundaries of those past states as living reality of modern life.

Nation-states came into being in Europe after renaissance at the end of the medieval period of their history as a reaction to the supremacy of the papacy. Many of such newly emerged states sent voyages of geographical discoveries, took advantage of scientific and technological inventions and established great modern empires all over the world, turning many of the traditional societies into their colonies. Two Great Wars in the twentieth century changed the imperial map of the world and many of the past colonies declared their independence from the European powers. Indian Union was one of the early members of the newly independent comity of nations. The social reality of India turned it consciously into a federation of nationalities with a unitary constitution, which provides the basis for federating units' inter-relations on a democratic basis. In this way, India is not a nation-state on typical European model, but national state, in which nations together constitute the Indian Union.

The paper briefly examines the historical process through which regional entities of Northeast formed the states in the past and what happened to them in course of time. Secondly, it tries to identify aspects of nation-building, which impinge on the region and comment on the socio-political scene in the region. Thirdly, an effort has been made to understand the prevailing conditions of conflict and violence in the region as an uneven process of consensus building for a regional civil society. Peace in itself may be desirable, but it cannot be attained in the absence of consensus building among the regional communities, which may pave the way for building a civil society essential for a democratic polity. The author believes that violence emerges, when efforts of consensus building are denied a chance and thus, push the regional societies away from possibility of being a civil society. In other words, perpetrators of violence in an open society such as India, either do not believe in its efficacy, or are guided by their stark petty considerations and selfish motives.

State Formation in and Ethnic Groups of Northeast India

A number of political philosophers wrote on the origin of state and developed a number of hypotheses as to how communities turned in to structured states. The study of early state formation has a problem of primary and secondary formations. Early states have been termed as the pristine ones and secondary states were termed as the derivatives of some or other primary states. However, Henry J M Claessen and Peter Skalnik believed that state as an ancient institution "gives expression to the existing relations in a society and to ideas pertaining to power, authority, force, justice, property and many other phenomena" (Claessen & Skalnik 1978). Frederick Engels found the state as a later development, as in his formulation, "the state…has not existed from all eternity. There have been societies, which managed without it, which had no notion of the state or state power. At a definite stage of economic development, which necessarily involved the cleavage of society in to classes, the state became a necessity because of this cleavage" (Engels 1972). Furthermore, based on the stages of development of the various societies, the states have been categorized into (i) Early and (ii) Modern ones. While early states were found to be institutionally simple, pre-capitalist and non-industrialized, the modern ones are complex, bureaucratic, developed and industrialized. After F Engel's classic work, Sripad A Dange studied early Indian formation through his famous work, *India: Through Savagery to Barbarism*.

Historians inform us that Magadh was the earliest mighty empire in India. Chandra Gupta Maurya not only succeeded to the throne of Magadh, but also defeated Greek ruler, Salucus, a successor of Alexander the Great. From Maurayan rulers to Guptas kingdom of Magadh saw consolidation of the empire from Himalayan ranges beyond Vindhyan ranges from Afghanistan (Gandhar) to Pragjyotisa (Assam) and from the Arabian seas and Bay of Bengal. Thereafter, there were ups and downs, but there were a number of States, strong and weak, big and small, in the various parts of India all through ancient period to the medieval age of the Indian history. First, it was the Kushanas, followed by the Afghans, and then the Mughals, the migrants or invading armies from the North West corner of India, who turned out to be the rulers of better parts of India invariably based in Delhi. The Great Mughals ruled India for better than two hundred years and consolidated their empire from Afghanistan to Deccan and Bengal to Baluchistan. It was a period of glory, wealth, luxury, power, prosperity and all-round development. In course of time, internal contradictions emerged and the empire declined leading to the emergence of the Marathas, the Nizam, the Awadh, Hyder Ali and others. In this confused situation, the British Empire came on scene and projected itself as the successor to the Great Mughals. A number of historians have written on that and we need not go into the details of it.

Coming to the Northeast region, it was the Ahoms, who crossed the Patkoi ranges and established their kingdom in upper Assam in the twelfth century A D. Since then a number of Indo-Burman, Sino-Indic and Indo-Tibetan speaking communities moved to the various parts of the region. These communities were at different stages of their socio-economic development at that time and their myths of migration and origin state a rich tapestry of human heritage. Naturally, some of them got evolved into state systems in course of time. In recent times, Surajit Sinha wrote his much acclaimed paper on Rajputization among the Bhumij of Chotanagpur, on the western border of Bengal (Sinha 1962), which set a new trend of analyzing polities among the preliterate communities. Some two decades after his major work on the Bhumij, Sinha initiated a seminal exercise on polity formation and state system on about half a dozen communities of Northeast region (Sinha 1987). Among more than two hundred ethnic groups of the region, only about half a dozen communities had state systems in the past: Meiteis, Ahoms, Jaintia, Koch-Rajbanshis, Dimasas, Cacharis, Bhotias. In all the cases discussed on the occasion, two reasons emerged supreme as catalyst for state formation: (i) coagulation of lineage or clan-based units of one or more ethnic groups, or/ and (ii) conquest of segmentary tribes by larger principalities or states (Sinha 1987: xviii). Based on the studies presented in workshop, Sinha developed a three-fold typology of the regional polities: (i) small chieftainships such as Mizos, (ii) evolved chieftainships like Khasi Syiems, (iii) archaic sovereign states such as Ahoms, Jaintias, Meiteis, Dimasa and Bhotias of Sikkim (Sinha 1987: xvii). It is pertinent to note that many of the regional communities remained in the classical pre-state stage of their social and economic development up to the beginning of the nineteenth century, when the British emerged on the political horizon of the region as arbitrators of political destiny.

This brief and hurried survey gives certain lessons for us to keep in mind. Firstly, every age has its legitimate political systems in various parts of the present day Indian Union as elsewhere. Secondly, the state boundaries have been fluctuating and there is no fixity of territorial limits of a state in time and space. Thirdly, there has been evolution in case of certain communities from statelessness to state systems, while in case of others, there have been cases of devolution, when states lost political power and the communities got incorporated as subjects/ citizens of some other states. Fourthly, human society is a dynamic entity; it not only evolves itself, but also migrates from one location to another because of a variety of reasons leading to plurality of the communities at strategically favoured regions. Lastly, taking lead from the first point above, Indian Union came into being on 15 August, 1947 as successor of the British colonial power and it legitimately inherited the territories enshrined in the Indian Constitution.

Nation-building Efforts among the Newly Emerged Developing Countries

We have noted how the Second World War became a catalyst for the emergence of new nations, which aspired to evolve institutions, amenities, and over-all development of resources with a view to providing better quality of life to their recently liberated citizens. The problem was that the resources, human and material, were limited and urgent commitments to impoverished masses were daunting. There were two models of development easily available in the 1950s: market driven capitalist mode of production followed by the Western Democratic countries and their colonies, and the state-controlled socialistic planned economic restructuring of revolutionary Socialist blocks of the countries. It was a difficult choice for most the new nations, as they lacked resources, skills, administrative acumen and leadership. Moreover, those at the helm of affairs of these nations had made commitment to their peoples that once the hated colonial rulers would be driven away, all their problems would be solved within no time and they would have a life of comfort and prosperity. But the reality turned out to be harsh in especially war ravaged post-1945 years. In such a situation, India made a conscious choice to adopt revised Soviet model of planned economic development, in which State controlled market driven capitalist mode of production as a part of Five Years Plans. Very soon, many of the third world countries adopted different variants of the socialistic mode of planned economy and got themselves busy in building national resources in terms of institutions, amenities and services.

With a view to building a strong and new nation in many of the countries, special privileges of the elite were abolished; land tenure was reoriented; social engineering was attempted and people's voices were heard before taking far reaching decisions affecting them. New capitals were built; factories were installed; ports, airports, cities, and other such amenities were created; agricultural and industrial production was proposed to be increased in a pre-fixed short period of time. In brief, an outlook of newness, dynamism, capacity building and serving the national cause was instilled as the mantra of the new establishment. The new leaders of new nations were in a hurry, so to say, to show and prove to the world that they were capable of bringing prosperity, development and happiness to their peoples. But age-old impediments to these efforts were many and at times they proved to be stronger than that of the forces of the new dynamism. Thus, committed goals were occasionally not met leading to diffidence and frustration. Apart from traditional vested interests of religious obscurantism and feudal privileges, a variety of corrupting elements also got opportunities to sabotage the on-going march to future. Naturally, criticisms, and at times, quite uncharitableones, were leveled and the entire efforts of nation building were ridiculed. In frustration, some of the newly emerged nations turned authoritarian; further giving gist to the criticism of their known or unknown enemies. The vested interest in the form of opponents of change and former colonial elements were as if waiting in the wings to find faults with the entire exercise.

Social scientists were quick to provide appraisal to this new experiment under way in such a massive and comprehensive way. For example, Karl Deutsch studied the routes of assimilation and mobilization in the post-World War I Czechoslovakia and Finland, a non-sovereign state of Scotland, a new nation-state of the Third World, India (Deusch 1963). However, the most significant attempt to conceptualize the phenomenon of state formation and nation-building was the series of studies of political transformation organized by Gabriel Almond –Lucien W Pye Committee of the American Social Science Research Council (Almond & Coleman, 1960 and others). These studies were mainly concerned with the newly emerged polities of the 'Third world' such as Burma, Ghana, India, Iran, Nigeria, Pakistan, Ceylon, Turkey, etc. They tried to identify crucial variables in a generic process of change from the traditional polity to the modern 'bureaucratic – participant' state, though the idea of such a participant nation-state was European in origin. These studies failed to provide comparable experiences of nation building in Europe and the Third World countries.

Then in the 1960s, a series of studies were made in which varied experiences of nation building in Europe and other parts of the world were compared. In this series of studies, mention may be made of Richard Benedix's (Benedix 1964) comparisons of nation-building experiences of Germany, Russia, India and Japan. Holt and Turner's work on England and Japan, France and China (Holt and Turner 1966) and Barrington Moore's analysis of the economic bases of political transformation in England, France, Germany, Russia, United States of America, Japan, China and India. (Moore 1966) Karl Deutsch and his colleague at the universities of Yale and Harvard took up another dimension of and built up computer archival data on the new as well as the old polities.

By early 1970s, a relatively vast literature was piled up and it was thought desirable to assess the conceptual contributions to the understanding of genesis and growth of the polities of the world. In such an effort, Stein Rokkan (Rokkan 1971) identified the imbalances in the ranges of the cases and variables in the studies of the polities under the heads, (i) the large nation bias, (ii) the whole nation bias, and (iii) the economic growth bias. Further, he emphasized the need for comparability of nation building experiences across the continents. He also identified six 'crisis of development' such as penetration, integration, participation, identity, legitimacy and distribution as issues, challenges and policy options in course of nation building. Similarly, Kothari reviewed the literature on nation building under three heads: (i) social mobilization theory, (ii) centre and periphery and (iii) modernization as the favorite themes of the Western academicians.

(Kothari 1971). These Western biases were criticized by the academicians of the Third World, and rightly so. All these resulted in the publication of a significant work on State Formation and Nation Building edited by S N Eisenstadt and Stein Rokkan in 1973.

One learns from the above that nation-building is both an effort to reorient the national governance on a participatory basis, in which citizens willing to contribute and play a positive role in shaping the national policies, and a process through which various amenities, assets and services are created for the wellbeing of the nation state at large. This was considered imperative in the aftermath of newly emerged states in the 1950s, when the colonial powers withdrew from the scene, leaving behind their impoverished and exploited colonies to fend for themselves under trying conditions. The newly independent states were proud inheritors of rich historical traditions and had promised their citizens a new dawn of prosperity in freedom, but resources, expertise and experience were so limited at their disposal that they had planned for cherished goals. Many of them had visions for a bright future, but they were also handicapped by the hostile international atmosphere. Those were the days of 'cold war' in which external support was always provided at a political price, which many of the new nations were unwilling to pay. In this background, their visions, commitments, priorities, policies, and in short, their nation building efforts were implemented in a lop-sided manner leading to regional imbalance even within the nation states. Meanwhile, aspirations of the people were rising exponentially without reference to the nation building endeavours. Ill-effects of lop sided nation building are invariably expressed by the civil society as a mechanism of corrective democracy.

Civil Society and Democracy

Civil society as opposed to primordial ethnic entities is considered an essential ingredient of a functioning and vibrant democratic system. Century's back, the social philosopher, Adam Ferguson, wrote an 'Essay on History of Civil Society' in 1767, in which he treated it as a system of interrelated institutions. Since then, there is a considerable literature on the theme of civil society. As a representative source, the *International Encyclopedia of Social Sciences* finds the term used in five different meanings:

(a.) The term civil society can imply a recognition of general obligation of citizenship and thus legitimacy of the existing legal order as a society as a whole; pains taken to limit defiance to a particular legal clause or policy, and/ or avoid violence, may be construed as an affirmation of general citizenship duties.

(b.) Civil can be taken to refer to the opposite of 'military' in a broad sense. The customary stress on non-violence may be construed to signify either: (a) a recognition of the state's claim to monopoly with respect to all physical violence, or (b) a rejection of all physical violence as illegal or morally wrong under all circumstances regardless of purpose.

(c.) Civil can refer to opposite of 'uncivil' or 'uncivilized'.

(d.) 'Civil' can suggest that the objective of obedience is to institute changes in the political system, affecting not only one individual's or group's liberties, but the liberties of all the citizens". (*International Encyclopedia of Social Sciences*, Vol. 2: 473-474)

In this context, among the increasing corpus of literature on civil society, mention must be made of volume seven of 'themes in Indian sociology' series of publications. (Jayaram 2005). The volume was edited by N Jayaraman, the editor of the *Sociological Bulletin* and it contains as many as a dozen articles on the theme. In view of D N Dhanagare "(t)he most significant feature of civil society... is that there must be self-policing and modularity, and above all the pursuit of disinterested and individually sanctioned virtues, which are the most essential bases of democracy and civil society". (Dhanagare 2005: 63) In Indian conditions, P K B Nayar draws certain pre-requisites: a political system with a neutral state and liberal democratic setup; an economic system guaranteeing economic justice to all citizens; and a sociocultural system based on universalistic values. (Nayar 2005: 133) Nayar's prerequisites of the civil society appear to be more in the nature of ideal types than based on empirical situations. In every day life, one finds a binary existence between the state and civil society, either one versus the other or one is paired against the other. And for that, there is a background of this development. It so happened that during the past communist regimes in Europe, some of the intellectuals felt that the idea of civil society was a programmed one of building independent forms of social life from the below, free from state tutelage. However, the conviction became widespread that this independence of society should be an integral feature of democracy. Jayaram pleads that setting aside the binary opposition between the state and civil society, we see other dimensions of relationship between the two such as an intermediary group between the two. (Jayaram 2005: 21) For the time being, I shall go with the most liberal definition of democracy with the plea that this may not be the ideal form of the governance; still it is the least evil among all the known forms of government.

Nation-Building Efforts in India's Northeast

We have noted above that nation building refers to both the efforts initiated by the states to evolve institutions and infrastructure for an assumed national prosperity. However, some historical points need to be noted before under-taking such an exercise for the region. The British began administering their Indian colonies from Bengal Presidency of Calcutta, Madras Presidency in port city of Madras and Bombay Presidency from port city of Bombay on Arabian Sea and further vanquished territories were added to them turning them in course of time hugely cumbersome entities. These Presidencies turned out not only territorially unwieldy, but also multilingual in terms of human multitude. The All Indian National Congress (AICC), when it was in the vanguard of the freedom movement, had made a commitment to the nation that once they would come to power, they would institute linguistic states as the units of independent India. And thus, naturally, major regional languages became the basis for formation of the new provinces such as Andhra, Orissa and so on after State Reorganization Commission gave its report in 1956. The Assamese speaking people of Assam perhaps without realizing the implications that their state was not monolingual such as Bengal or Tamilnadu, decided to declare Assamese as the state language, which was seen as a problem of communication among the many of the Hills communities. Secondly, the British bureaucrats since 1928 tacitly began to work on a plan to give an impression that the hill districts and the plains parts of the province of Assam were so different that they would not work together in an administrative unit once the British withdrew from India. Its culmination may be seen in Sir Robert Reid's Coupland Plan to carve out a Crown Colony from Garo Hills to Upper Burma and from present day Arunachal to Arakan Hills on Bay of Bengal. Wisdom prevailed on all the sections concerned and this plan was not carried through ultimately. Thirdly, in the confused scenario of the 1940s, the Christian Missionaries had created an impression that the Muslims were getting a separate country of Pakistan and the rest of India would be governed by the Hindus. Hence, the hills tribes, who were neither of the two, would have a difficult future in Hindu dominated province of Assam in India. Thus, many of the hill communities became restive immediately after independence.

The national government of free India was luckily aware of these implications and thus, they framed the Indian Constitution in such a way that the Northeast tribesmen were given an autonomous status through the enactment of Sixth schedule. Moreover, the national leaders were careful to the sensitivities of the various cultural entities of the region. To understand this, one has to read Prime Minister J L Nehru's Secret Note to the Chief Ministers of the various provinces after his visit to the Northeastern frontier Areas in October, 1952. He pleaded through this letter how historically and culturally unique Manipur and Tripura were and why they should not be integrated to the province of Assam and why these two units should have representative governments of their own. (Secret: A Note by the Prime Minister on his Tour of the North-Eastern Frontier areas in October 1952) Nehru also tried to take the Assam Chief Minister, B R Medhi, in confidence on an already complicated Naga Issue. (Secret & Personal, No. 1116-PMH/56: 1956) Furthermore, in the aftermath of the Second World War with the rising prices all over, it was expected that the state would start industries for creating jobs for unemployed youth in the region, the public in Assam, specially the students, went on an agitation for establishing an oil refinery for which crude oil was drilled in the state. Nehru wrote to Fasl Ali, the Governor of Assam, why it was not possible to establish such an industry in Assam, as Defence Chiefs of the time refused to undertake security of such a heavy industry in the then hostile international environment surrounded by East Pakistan, China and the unsettled Burma. (Top Secret/No. 459-PMO/57: 1957) It is another matter that a small refinery was set up in course of time, but the state got the impression that they get nothing from the Centre without an agitation. Broad gauge railways, national highways, bridge over the mighty river Brahmputra and other establishments were created. Of late, a number of academic institutions of repute have been opened in the region. Now a decision has been taken that all the states in the region will have a centrally funded university within their limits.

The tragedy was that while Assam was trying to consolidate itself institutionally, its own hill communities and the Central government were evolving plans for its dismemberment. The State Reorganization Commission recommended language, geographical location and historical antecedents as the criterion for creation of federating states in Indian Union. Bulk of the states was created on linguistic basis. However, Maharashtra and Punjab remained bilingual, which were divided within a few years on linguistic ground. Manipur was permitted to remain outside Assam on the plea of its historical uniqueness. Bengali speaking Tripura was not merged with another Bengali speaking West Bengal because of the geographical distance between the two. State of Nagaland was the first in India, which was created in 1963, on ethnic basis out of Naga Hills District and Tuensang Frontier Tract. This set a trend for the other hill districts of Assam which went on agitation demanding for separate states of their own. Ultimately, Meghalaya, Mizoram and Arunachal Pradesh were carved out of Assam as separate states in course of time. Of late, this logic has been further extended by creating Jharkhand and Chhatisgarh.

Most of these frontier states are small states in terms of their territories, population and revenue. They are located on topographically difficult mountainous region. They lack basic infrastructure. They have a subsistence level of agriculture and there is hardly any industry worth the name. In such a situation, primary and tertiary (service) sectors of the economy are the major employers in these states. These are the states, which have a higher literacy rate and educational amenities are of traditional type in which graduate degrees are awarded for general subjects and graduates are normally not exposed to an expertise, which enables them for skilled jobs. Consequently, the state governments are the biggest employers in these states, still states cannot employ every educated unemployed person. And thus, there is a built-in unrest in these states, as the system of governance is always constrained in trying to win legitimacy by offering non-existent jobs to potential trouble shooters. Apart from apprehensions in the minds of hill men, there was a massive human migration from across the border of the then East Pakistan and now Banladesh to the Brahmaputra valley in particular and the region in general, creating a reasonable apprehension in the psyche of the people. The regional youth hailing from relatively small ethnic groups find India overcrowded, complex, callous and even hostile to their aspirations. Ever since the demise of Gopi Nath Bordoloi and B P Chaliha, there has been no regional leader of stature and concern, who could fire up the regional imagination and inspire confidence among the youth. Furthermore, in an open and democratic system such as ours, it takes time to build up a consensus on issues of national importance. By the time it is done, genuine demands made by a small articulate social segment of society at one time, can turn into a potential source of political upheaval at another. A former politician-cum-academic has rightly come to conclude: "...the inordinate delay spanning over two decades on the part of the Union Government had drastically reduced the amount of good-will of the people which it should normally have been able to enjoy had it not been for such undue delay or for drifting policy". (Pakem 1993:120). Then it was an easy way to build up unrest leading to insurgency in Nagaland, Mizoram, Manipur, Assam and elsewhere in the region.

Civil Society and Constituency of Peace in Northeast

I have mentioned above that compared to others, the states in Northeast India are relatively small in size, territorially and demographically. Moreover, there has been uneven pace of nation building endeavour in the country in general and in the Northeast region in particular. India consciously adopted a democratic style of governance for its multi-ethnic society. However, because of the historical reasons, class and civil society emerged elsewhere in India much earlier and societies developed a shock absorbing capacity within it and civil society could tolerate the variety of disagreements and still work for a common good of the people at large. The story is slightly different in the region. To begin with, in case one takes the type of administrative and political development in India from the beginning of the British rule, the British rule came to Assam almost a century after it came to Bengal. Then they had different rules for the administration of the hills and the plains of Assam. Apart from Inner Line Regulation of 1873, separating Arunachal, Mizoram and Nagaland from the rest of the region, almost the entire hill region was administered by the Governor of the province calling them 'Excluded or Partially Excluded Districts'. To aggravate the situation still further, between the hills and the plains, these hill districts were apportioned to the various Christian Missionaries for evangelical and educational purposes, while in the plains the colonial administration itself established such institutions. Consequently two sets of development took place: white color jobs, an emergent middle class, a variety of occupations, various political institutions and the rudiment of political parties etc., took routes in the plains districts of Assam on the one hand, and on the another, the hill districts were not only denied of such developments, but were deliberately kept under tutelage of the specially selected army or police service Political Officers' paternalistic rule along with the scholar-administrator ICS officers. In such a situation, the public space was very much controlled by the British administrative machinery in the hill districts and it was they who used to speak effectively for the hills communities by and large and their voice was audible and also heard, where and when it mattered most.

Once the British were forced to withdraw from the Indian scene, there was chaos, uncertainty, worries among the hills communities, and lack of a clear contingency plan among the new rulers. Whatever the limited infrastructure they had, were all either dismantled or damaged or reduced to non-functional ones because of the division of India into two warring countries, India and Pakistan. Food scarcity was further aggravated by the communal clashes. The former political agitators, now occupying the chairs as the rulers, lacked expertise to tackle complex problems of administration. Moreover, they had their own bias and prejudice, at the same time; their political parties (National Political Parties) did not have presence in the hill districts by and large. Apprehensions, prejudice, inexperience, lack of resources, limited infrastructure and non-existent guidance in the event of contingency created a lot of complications and misunderstanding among the people of the region in the late 1940s and early 1950s. In this confused situation, the Nagas reportedly declared their independence even before Indian independence and were threatening to take to arms for the sake of independence. In such a situation, there was no possibility of existence or formation of a civil society; what came in its place were the ethnic associations, which began to play political roles. And within the years to come, a series of insurgent groups emerged operating from various parts of the region. The British trained civil police was found ineffective to tackle these trying situations and the new rulers sent in the armed forces to help the non-existent / non-functional administration in the region. Thus, it was no more a civil strife but it turned out to be a civil divide.

The irony of the fate was that ex-agitators, now new rulers, were pleading for peace in society so that a democratic beginning could be made. And elections were held for the state assembly and federal parliament, once the Indian Constitution was approved in 1950. This did create a level of legitimacy and lull in the violent political acts, but it also created heightened expectations and urge for achieving something spectacular. Very soon, the hills turned out to be unsettled even outside Naga Hills. Sane elements from among the local ethnic groups and church leaders came forward and pleaded for giving a chance to peace. This went almost unheard in an environment of the sound of the guns and peace remains illusive in the region today. But generations have suffered and today's children are not sure whether they will have a different path than the violence. But then the appeals for peace are made more frequently and more and more fervently. Will there be a dawn of peace in the region?

What are they fighting for? A series of insurgents' objective has been their 'liberation' from India. Is the Indian Union an empire, a dictator's regime, a totalitarian state, a theocracy, a monarchy, a feudal kingdom? Is it ruled by an army general, or autocrat, or an oligarchy or a cartel of financiers? India is a democratic republic, run on the rules framed as per provisions of Indian Constitution. It is one of the few open societies, where democracy is practiced since India gained her independence. So these disserters are fighting for what, what their objectives, and who suffers from the atrocities committed by the rebels? A columnist in a respectable news Journal from Chennai wrote on 26th January, 2007:

> This (ULFA's attack in the third week of January, 2007 on the migrant Hindi- speaking labour in Upper Assam) may be the final war, in which the enemy is the citizenry of the country. It has no weapons and no intension other than to earn some sort of living.

> But that may provide casus bell; seeking to work is very well but where it is sought is crucial. If it is the state of Assam and the citizen is not born Assamese, and then it means he is not seeking work there, he is seeking war against the State of Assam. At least, this is what the United Liberation Front of Asom (ULFA) obviously believes and would like us to believe. It considers mere fact that Biharis work in Assam, or go there to look for work, and what better enemy could it have than the unarmed labourers, who would not know what to do with semi-automatic rifle any more than they would with a variable energy cyclotron. It means they, the brave ULFA warriors, are in danger of being injured, let alone killed. And in this war they will obviously win every encounter. (Ghose 2007: 107)

The Indian Union is a democratic state, run by the elected representatives of the bonafide Indian electorate. It has an honoured position among the comity of the nations. The Indians and aliens, who act against the established law, will be dealt with by the appropriate law enforcing authorities as per the criminal law of the state. Those who wage war against the Indian state will have to confront the defenders of the Indian state, the Indian armed forces. But what happens to those unarmed common citizens, who are subjected to untold misery? Is there any way for them to be heard? And why do people take to arms? Why do they rebel? And there are many more questions, which beg at least some answers. Do we have some? No doubt, the constituency of peace has the maximum stake holders. And peace has different shades of meaning also.* Peace does not necessarily mean end of all the conflicts. Similarly, perhaps, here we may not be interested in individuals' peace, which is an 'undisturbed state of mind'. Here, we endeavour to secure a lasting peace, which will mean "freedom from public disturbances or disorder; public security; and law and order."

One point needs to be mentioned for the sake of the legal and constitutional pundits. When the states were created on ethnic basis

---

* *Oxford University Dictionary* defines peace as: 1. free from war or civil strife; 2. a treaty or agreement to end war; 3. freedom from public disturbances or disorder; public security; law and order; 4. freedom from disagreement or quarrels; harmony; control; 5. an undisturbed state of mind; absence of mental conflict, serenity; 6. calm, quiet, tranquil.

such as Nagaland, Meghalaya and others, the migrants from other states (linguistic, ethnic, religious minorities) who also have constitutional safeguards – do they have any right of citizenship or is it the reign of terror of majority local ethnic group, which will prevail? In other words, does it mean that, say in Meghalaya, the basic constitutional rights of those not from Meghalaya will have no validity? Whom will they turn to when their very physical existence is being threatened? Can we think aloud on such possibilities? And such incidents have been happening quite frequently.

It is perhaps time for thinking aloud on the constitutional framework of the country. Rajya Sabha, the upper chamber of the Indian parliament, is also reflective of the demographic size of the federating states, some thing like the Lok Sabha, the lower house of the parliament, for which members are elected by the electorate. In this way, Rajya Sabha is a smaller version of the Lok Sabha, demographically speaking. May be all states should be given equal representation in the Rajya Sabha to inculcate a semblance of equality among the federating Indian states of the Union. Similarly, the small states do not have upper chamber of state legislature. In such a situation, can we think of having, say, a legally binding Community Consultative Body? This body should continue to exist as a permanent body with periodically retiring members, who represent linguistic, religious and ethnic minorities, occupational and professional bodies (such as lawyers, doctors, teachers), NGOs, artists, craftsmen, men of letters, and any group of citizens, who are otherwise not represented in the system of governance. The idea is not to shackle the existing legislative procedure and to minimize the legitimacy of the exalted position of the people's representatives, but to enhance the legitimacy of the democratic system in the eyes of all its citizens. Now we have the Right to Information, which may enable us to pin point the sore points in the system conveniently; this proposal has a potential in which every modest citizen may see himself/herself as a part and parcel of the political system. May be this will give boost to the civil society on a broader basis. May be, these new actors on the political platform, who otherwise avoid taking part in the political process, would provide some new input without threatening or minimizing the significance of the existing process of governance. Perhaps this may strengthen the constituency of peace, which is the precursor of the nation-building endeavour at another level. There are many new schemes initiated by the Central government. Some niche will have to be found among them for these unrepresented segments of the people. In this way, state formation, nation-building, civil rights and peace will not remain isolated as concepts and will not be seen as distinct processes; rather, these all will proceed in unison in one direction towards peace, prosperity and welfare of all.

References

Almond, G A and J S Coleman (1960) *Politics of Developing Areas*, Princeton University Press, Princeton.

Benedix, R (1964) *Nation Building and Citizenship*, Willey Publishing House, New York.

Binder, J and J Coleman (1971) *Crisis and Sequences in Political Development*, Princeton University Press, Princeton.

Claessen, Henry J M and P Skalnik (1978) *The Early State*, Mouton Publishers, the Hague.

Coleman, J S (1965) *Education and Political Development,* Princeton University Press, Princeton.

Deusch, Karl (1963) *Nationalism and Communication*, M I T Press, New York.

Dhanagare, D N (2005) *Contextualizing a Discourse*, In N Jayaram, *On Civil Society: Issues and Perspectives*, Sage Publications, New Delhi.

Eisenstadt, S N and Stein Rokkan (1973) *Building States and Nations,* Vols. 2, Sage Publications, London.

Engels, F (1972) *Origin of Family, Property and the State*, Progress Publishing House, Moscow.

Ghose, B. (2007) "A Case for Compassion?" *Frontline,* vol. 24, No.1, January 26, pp.

Holt and Turner (1966) *Political Development across the States*, incomplete reference.

International Encyclopedia of Social Sciences, Vol. 2, The Macmillan Company and the Free Press, pp 473-74.

Jayaram, N (2005) *On Civil Society: Issues and Perspectives*, Sage Publications, New Delhi.

Kothari, Rajani (1971) "Variations and Uniformities in Nation Building", *International Social Science Journal*, Vol 23.

La Palambara, J and M Wiener (1966) *Political Parties and Political Development*, Princeton University Press, Princeton.

La-Palombara, J (1967) *Bureaucracy and Political Development*, Princeton University Press, Princeton.

Moore, Barrington Jr, (1966), *Social Origin of Dictatorship and Democracy*, Beacon Press, Boston.

Nayar, P K B (2005) *Lessons from India*, In N Jayaram, *On Civil Society: Issues and Perspectives*, Sage Publications, New Delhi.

Pakem, B (1993) 'Nationality Question in the Hill Areas of North-East India', In *Regionalism in India*, By B Pakem, ed., Har-Anand Publication, New Delhi.

Pye, L W (1963) *Communication and National Development*, Princeton University Press, Princeton.

Pye, L W and Sidney Verba (1965) *Political Development and Political Culture*, Princeton University Press, Princeton.

Rokkan, Stein (1971) "Nation Building", *Current Sociology*, Vol.19.

Secret & Personal, No. 1116-PMH/56, Letter from the Prime Minister to Shri B R Medhi, Chief Minister, Assam, Shillong, May 13, 1956.

Secret: A Note by the Prime Minister on his Tour of the North-Eastern Frontier Areas in October, October 29, 1952, To the Chief Ministers of States.

Sinha, S C (1962) "State Formation and Rajput: Myth in Tribal Central India", *Man in India*, Vol.42, No.1, pp.35-80.

Sinha, S C (1987) *Tribal Polities and State Systems in Pre-Colonial Eastern and North Eastern India*, K P Bagchi & Co., Calcutta.

Tilly, C (1973) *Formation of National States in Western Europe*, Princeton University Press, Princeton.

Top Secret/No. 459-PMO/57, Letter from the Prime Minister to Shri Fasl Ali, Governor of Assam, Shillong.

Ward, R E and D D Rustow (1964) *Formation of Nation States in Western Europe*, Princeton University Press, Princeton.

11

Unrest and Prospects of Peace in Assam

Walter Fernandes

The prospects of peace in Assam looked somewhat bright two years ago. The Union Government (GOI) was keeping an open mind on a dialogue with the United National Liberation Front of Assam (ULFA) that had issued a manifesto which could function as its starting point. Problems began immediately after it and culminated in the killing of some Biharis in Upper Assam in January 2007. The prospect of peace has thus receded for the time being. So ways have to be found for reviving it. In an attempt to support this search, the present paper will analyse some recent events and look at the challenges ahead on the road to a solution. The assumption in this attempt is that one cannot begin by polarising the issues or by attributing the situation to a single cause. Its complexity has to be understood.

Steps towards Peace

One can begin to study this complexity with the ULFA manifesto of 2005 because it was an outcome of several moves before it. It brought together the concerns that the struggles beginning with the Assam Movement of 1979-85 had expressed over the years. It had somewhat clear statements on the economy but its political statements remained vague, probably intentionally so. It spoke of the nation of Assam ready to deal with the nation of India as well as other nations within Assam. It mentioned sovereignty but not independence. The socialist Assamese nation would have the overall control of the economy, especially tea, because the State produces fifty-six per cent of India's tea but the industry is controlled from Kolkata. Thus, for the first time a militant outfit had spelt out its political as well as economic thinking. It is true that the political issues remained vague and the socialism on which the economy was to be built belonged to the 1980s but it was adequate as a starting point. The Central Government responded positively to the possibility of talks without committing itself fully. ULFA formed the people's consultative group (PCG) as a think tank to assist it in the parleys.

There have been other turning points before it in the movement towards a dialogue in the region, the best known being the July 2004 bare body demonstration of 12 women in Imphal, demanding action against the security persons who allegedly raped and killed Manorama Devi. They also demanded repeal of the Armed Forces Special Powers Act (AFSPA) that provides legal justification to such acts. The armed forces are trained to deal with the enemy. Internally they can at best be peace-keepers and use their guns against the militants but they do not have the background required for a search for peace with justice. (Mukerjee 2005) As a result, a law of this type runs the risk of legitimising repression and intensifying enmity. Equally important was the July 2005 blockade of the highway by the Naga groups that paralysed Manipur. (Hazarika 2005). The Centre had till then viewed the unrest mainly as a law and order problem that could be controlled through the AFSPA. These events showed it that the problem is deeper. So it appointed a committee to study the AFSPA and a second one to inquire into the death of Manorama. (*The Telegraph,* 12th July 2005).

This response gave some hope of an end to militant violence and to repression by the security forces. Both of them are central to militarisation by which one does not mean the security forces alone but the vicious circle of violence and counter-violence that loses sight of the objective for which insurgency or counter-insurgency began. When a struggle continues for a long time, violence becomes an end in itself and retribution is turned into a virtue. Economic and political vested interests develop around it and hardliners sideline the moderates. Human rights are ignored and those who demand adherence to them are viewed as criminals, not as facilitators of peace. As polarisation sets in, people get reconciled to violence as a way of life. Hope of a peaceful solution recedes. (Barbora 2005: 80-86).

That is what seems to be happening in the Northeast. After giving some hope of a solution, GOI has kept under wraps the reports of the committees on AFSPA and on Manorama's killing. A national daily put the former on its website. The Committee recommends its repeal and modification of other laws to ensure security but the Centre has initiated no action on it till now and has not made a beginning in dealing with the causes of unrest. Another reason for the failure of the talks seems to be that dialogue is only with the militant groups. At the end of the negotiations, the State often concedes some demands of the militants without necessarily dealing with the causes of the unrest. Besides, dialogue is with one of the militant groups. The other factions retaliate by raising their demands and making lasting peace difficult to attain. (Jacob 2004) For example, the Bodo Accord was signed with the Bodo Liberation Tigers (BLT) to the exclusion of the National Democratic Front of Bodoland. In Nagaland negotiations are continuing with the NSCN (I-M). The NSCN-K that is excluded makes counter-demands. Such limited interaction runs the risk of ignoring the major issues leading to militancy.

Moreover, by opening a dialogue with the militant groups alone, the Centre can give a wrong message to the youth in this region of a high level of education and massive unemployment. The Assam Economic Survey speaks of some 17 lakh persons in the live registers of its 40 employment exchanges. The problem is more serious than that because the rural unemployed cannot approach the employment exchange easily. So one can easily put the unemployment backlog in Assam at 30 lakhs and in the Northeast as a whole at 40 lakhs or 25 percent of its active workforce. After the Bodo Accord, the BLT cadres were rehabilitated with a job. Also the surrendered ULFA cadres (SULFA) were offered a job or small tea gardens. In the context of high unemployment, this solution can motivate the unemployed to join the outfits and then surrender. One does not state that the youth join them only for a job. One only speaks of the process that has the potential to displace the objective of the struggle and close the vicious circle of violence. A possible way out of it is to treat the civil society as a crucial component in the dialogue. (Chutia 2002)

The Assam Struggles

Some present ULFA as purely secessionist or terrorist and others as a nationalist struggle that deserves support. There has thus been polarisation around it as well as around the Assam Movement of 1979-85 which is central to an understanding of later struggles. That movement too had moderates and hardliners both among its participants and the public and polarisation at times as a 1980-81 debate in the form of a series of articles and letters in *The Economic and Political Weekly* (Published in book form as Ahmed (ed) 2006) brings out. Sanjib Baruah justified it as a nationalist struggle while Hiren Gohain considered it anti-Left chauvinism or fascism while Amalendu Guha viewed it as nationalism that had become chauvinistic. Gail Omvedt thought of it as an economic problem alone while Tilottama Mishra situated it within a colonial perspective.

Though externally anti-foreigner in reality, the movement had these and more components. There was resentment against foreigners taking up jobs but also the issues of sub-nationalism and identity were strong. One section took sub-nationalism to a chauvinistic extreme. Some even gave it a communal turn. Though initially it was both against the Nepali and Bangladeshi foreigners, slowly the Nepali and Bangladeshi Hindus as well as Biharis were forgotten and focus shifted to the Bangladeshi Muslims. Thus, even the identity issue ran the risk of getting a communal colour or turning chauvinistic. Not surprisingly, its most decisive moment was the 1983 Nellie Massacre. (Rafiabadi 2002: 9-11). Against the moderate view of Assam that could accommodate many communities, the hardliners gave it an exclusively Assamese or even Hindu identity. The latter seem to have got the upper hand as seen in the fact that though most ethnic groups joined the movement, the 1985 Accord referred only to the ethnic Assamese. That laid the foundation for more conflicts like the one for Bodoland. (Das 1994: 37-38).

The movement also had an economic component of resentment against outsiders who controlled its economy but did not invest in the productive employment generating secondary sector. In 1996 the Northeast had 166 major and medium industries, 118 of them in Assam (D'Souza 1999: 14) against 374 in "industrially backward" Orissa. (Fernandes and Asif 1997: 59) According to a news item (*The Assam Tribune,* Sept. 28, 2006), 42 units in Assam may be declared sick. That continues the past trend. The number of sick units, including small scale, rose from 5,686 in 1985 to 11,448 in 1994. (Bhattacharya 1998: 2) The feeling of neglect existed already in the 1960s. The reality seemed to substantiate it as well as the feeling of outsiders taking away scarce jobs. For example, the Centre viewed the region only from a security perspective and shifted the refinery for oil produced in Assam to Barauni in Bihar for fear that it would not be able to defend it against China. Even in the 1960s only 27 per cent of the staff of the few industries built in Assam were locals. (Chattopadhyay 1990: 101)

Centre and Periphery

This economic failure is one of the components of the feeling of an attack on the Assamese identity. Assam resented what it viewed as the domination of the Hindi region but found it difficult to deal with its own minorities. As a result, three new States were carved out of it between 1963 and 1972. The ethnic Assamese resented it but it also brought the double centre-periphery issue to the fore. On one side Assam was the periphery of the Centre. On the other, the minorities in the State felt that the ethnic Assamese considered themselves its centre. The rest were its periphery. (Sen 1992).

At the national level, the colonial view of the Northeast being a buffer zone against Burma and China continued to some extent after 1947. For example, a member of the Constituent Assembly is reported to have demanded immediate assimilation of the Mongoloid ethnic groups for fear that they would join Burma. The leaders of the region resented such distrust because many of them had supported the freedom struggle and were searching for a post-independence autonomous existence within India that could protect their identity. (Sanyu 1996: 131-134) However, most national leaders identified unity with uniformity and cultural homogenisation. They knew only an Aryan India that could extend to the Dravidians but not the Mongoloid stock. A pluralist India and autonomy were foreign to their concept of a centralised administration. As a result, even those leaders of the Northeast who wanted autonomy within India felt that on one side the central leaders did not understand their identity demands and on the other they got no benefits of the British regime. So they remained ambiguous. That gave control of the movements to those who demanded independence. For many years even after 1947 most national leaders failed to understand the aspirations of the Northeast. When realisation dawned on a few of them of the need to make compromises, accords were signed with the Naga and Mizo that recognised their identity by allowing their civil affairs to be run under their customary laws. (Fernandes 2005a: 94-95)

Thus, most struggles for political autonomy are also for the recognition of their identity and cultural decentralisation and against the homogenising trend of "one State one nation" and the tendency "to take the degree of Aryanisation as the measure of Indianisation." (Datta 1990: 41) From the rejection of this trend which they viewed as an effort of "mainland" India to submerge their identity, homogenise cultures and monopolise their livelihood is born sub-nationalism that takes the form of a demand for sovereignty by which most mean cultural, economic and political autonomy. (Das 1994: 3-6) Since this interaction conditions much of their history, the three steps of defending their livelihood, protecting their identity and propounding a sub-nationalism specific to a cultural and ethnic group merge into one.

Immigrants added to the problem. Many in Assam felt that the Centre was at best passive on the immigration issue and was at worst, encouraging it. As stated above, focus has been on the Bagladeshi Muslims, whom the colonial regime encouraged from the 1920s to migrate to Assam. The 2001 census indicates that the Biharis and Nepalis who came to the State later are probably 60 percent of the estimated 40 lakh immigrants in Assam. The Bengali speaking Muslims are around 17 lakhs. (Fernandes 2005b: 3238) Most Muslims live in western and southern Assam while Upper Assam, especiallyy Tinsukia, the second commercial capital after Guwahati, has a big Hindi-speaking population.

The Assamese view the growing number of immigrants as an attack on their identity and a threat to their economy because they encroach on their land, also do low paid jobs as construction workers, rickshaw pullers and others that the local people do not take up easily. (Baruah 2005: 38-39) Most ethnic conflicts are around land. In the context of high unemployment, it is easy to view the immigrants as competitors for jobs. The Bengali speaking persons become the target in western and southern Assam while the Biharis are the main target in Karbi Anglong and Upper Assam. Resentment is primarily against those who control their economy and devalue their culture. But it is not easy to attack them because they are powerful and also pay "taxes" to the militants. As a result, the poorest among the immigrants become its victims.

Double Domination and the ULFA Manifesto

Centralisation exists also in the region in the form of what its minorities consider non-tribal domination. Tribals are a majority in the Hill States of Arunachal Pradesh, Meghalaya, Mizoram and Nagaland but non-tribals dominate the populous plains, the ethnic Assamese in Assam, the Meiteis in Manipur and the Bengalis in Tripura. This unequal power relationship has led to conflicts between the locally subaltern and dominant communities because India has political but not social democracy. (Barman 2005: 61-63) The Mizo and Boro struggles are cases of reaction to locally dominant groups.

From the early twentieth century, the Bodos competed with and emulated the Assamese and formed new organisations with the hope of making progress in education and joining the administration. In the 1930s they formed associations such as the *Bodo Chhatra Sammilani* in order to encourage Bodo education and welfare and to standardise their language. Indebtedness and land alienation that they considered their major problems did not decline even after the Notified Areas Act was amended in 1947 to prevent these evils. They felt that the bureaucracy was not implementing it seriously and asked for political autonomy in order to take control of their resources. In the Constituent Assembly, they asked for the safeguards available to the Hill tribes. But the Assam Congress leader Gopinath Bordoloi who headed the Constituent Assembly Committee on this issue contended that the Plains Tribes were being assimilated with the rest of the population and could not be granted the Sixth Schedule. The climax came when they were all but ignored in the Assam Accord. That led to the Bodo movement (Roy 1995: 41-45) from which emerged the Bodo Territorial Council in 2003.

We do not need to go into all the struggles other than to say that the Mizo story too is similar. One can only add that it makes the manifesto meaningful because it deals with the centre-periphery dynamics. On one side it makes a distinction between the State and the nation and on the other, it keeps the issue of sovereignty vague. It speaks of the nation of Assam dealing with the nation of India on one side and the nations within the territory of Assam on the other. Thus it takes the nation as a people and the State as a legal entity. (Das 1994: 9-12) By recognising Assam as the homeland of many groups, whose identity has to be respected, it deals with a major cause of ethnic conflicts that is not exclusively religious or cultural or economic or political but combine these and more components into one. It also shows the possibility of a common economy for all and tries to take the dialogue beyond the militant-State level by forming a People's Consultative Group (PCG) that includes members of the civil society.

The Hardliner Reaction

This is the moderate approach. Hardliners exist both in the militant and the Central camps. As a result, problems began immediately after it. Within weeks came the army crackdown on ULFA in a wildlife sanctuary in Dibrugarh district. The PCG intervened to stop it in an effort to push the talks forward. An explosion attributed to ULFA killed several children at Dhemaji on August 15, 2005. Within 24 hours the person who allegedly planted the bomb was killed in an encounter. There has been a spate of explosions in Guwahati and elsewhere. They climaxed in the killing of Biharis in the Tinsukia and Dibrugarh districts in January 2007. These events have two commonalities. Firstly, the official spokespersons invariably attribute the explosions to ULFA but produce no proof. Those supposedly responsible for them have not been brought to trial. The security forces have not explained how they identified the person who allegedly planted the bomb at Dhemaji when they were unable to prevent the killing of children. Secondly, with each event the possibility of a dialogue recedes. (Bhat 2004)

That a link probably exists between the two is better understood if one realises that neither GOI nor ULFA are monolithic but have both elements that are more-or-less open to a dialogue and hardliners who oppose it. Many political leaders of the present Central Government seem to keep an open mind but one dare not say the same about the security forces, the Defence Ministry and those from "mainland" India who control the economy. Besides, some think that the Centre is not fully aware of the situation in the Northeast and goes by the advice of some persons who have an interest in conflicts. (Yadav 2001) That can strengthen the hands of the hard liners who have many allies in the region.

ULFA too has both moderates and hardliners. The difference between them is not merely in strategy but also of ideology and in the understanding of sovereignty and autonomy. The hardliners in ULFA veer towards independence and those in the "official camp" demand centralisation in the region that they consider a buffer zone which the Centre should control fully for national security and protect its territory. This thinking often extends to culture and goes against the very concept of an Assamese identity that is central to the cause that ULFA represents. The hard liners may take it to the other extreme and speak of a break from India. While the Assamese masses do not support violence and the cause of culture, identity and an autonomous economy has near universal support among them. The identity issue can mobilise them since they feel dominated by the Hindi-speaking region. An attack on it can result in their alienation. (Nag 2005: 114-116)

The hardliners on both sides are wary of a dialogue. Besides, a long drawn conflict creates its own vested interests. Some analysts think that the security forces have a major interest in the arms and drug trade and that many security operations were meant to forestall a dialogue. Some even feel that they engineer some explosions. Those who control the economy want to continue their presence and an autonomous economy is a threat to them. Some extortionist groups use the militant banner and many militant leaders see their social or political power being eroded by prospects of peace. (Fernandes 2007) Many attacks that have stalled the peace process have to be situated within these dynamics. None considers the ULFA hardliners innocent. Most attribute the latest killings to them possibly in reaction to a "plebiscite" on "sovereignty" conducted by an agency unknown till then. It claimed to have polled 2,50,000 Assamese, 95 per cent of whom opposed sovereignty. The newspapers that have no sympathy for the cause of autonomy identified sovereignty with independence and presented ULFA as isolated from the Assamese public. The killings that came two days later seem to be the hardliners' way of telling the world that they cannot be taken for granted. The target too was clear. Assam has a problem of immigrants. The killings were in Upper Assam where most of them are Hindi-speaking, not Bengalis.

The resentment against the immigrants may also explain the ambiguity in the reaction to the killings. Most condemned them but a *bandh* was called by the Bihari dominated Assam Bhojpuri Association, not by the All Assam Students' Union. It was observed mainly on the highways and in the Bengali speaking Barak Valley in southern Assam that has a big immigrant population. But the reaction of the political and security forces is unambiguous. The fundamentalist forces alleged that the killings were a conspiracy to turn Assam into a Muslim majority State by sending Hindus away. An English daily asked the ULFA why it was attacking Hindu Biharis, not the Muslim Bangladeshi. It forgot that Upper Assam does not have many Muslim immigrants. The overall reaction of the political parties and State bodies was to demand retribution with no talk of a search for peace based on justice.

The events also legitimised the thinking that identified sovereignty with independence. Dr Indira Raison Goswami, a key person facilitating a dialogue declared at a press conference that she did not support sovereignty. The killings have also provided the security forces the legitimacy required to take charge of the region. The Bihar Regiment has been brought to Upper Assam. During the next few months one can expect every Assamese village to feel threatened. Fear will result in resentment and that gives more sympathisers to the cause of the ULFA. Most such "converts" will be hardliners.

The Role of the Civil Society

Thus, the prospects of peace have receded. That throws up a challenge to the civil society. Only a dialogue between the State and the militant outfits cannot solve the problem. The civil society has to be involved in it, firstly by creating a link between the opposing sides. In so doing it can learn from the action of ULFA in setting up the PCG to assist it as a think tank. ULFA needs PCG because most of its cadres with a political understanding of the issues were killed in the Bhutan Operation. So one has to situate its actions in this context and acknowledge that it has its shortcomings. So without extending total support to ULFA one can find ways of supporting the processes that can lead to peace. The outfit represents the socio-economic and political aspirations of the people of Assam but most of them do not support violence. It shows that, only armed reaction cannot solve the problem and dialogue cannot be restricted to the militants and the State but has to include other social forces. (Mishra 2005: 90-92) Unless a political process is re-started, the national security issue will dominate. Protection of the territory will get priority over people's security. Resentment may grow and violence may follow.

In order to break this vicious circle through a political process, the civil society has to take the initiative of identifying issues that lead to conflicts and of searching for a solution to them. The first step may be to deal with the identity and autonomy issues. It may begin with the Mainland-Assam dynamics and come to an understanding of the type of autonomy that is viable. But it has to go beyond the ethnic Assamese to the remaining nations within its territory. It also involves looking at issues such as the economy, culture and other issues that have a bearing on identity. It is important to have an open debate on what sovereignty and self-determination mean in this context. Talking to all the communities living in Assam can provide it the clarity of focus required to solve the ethnic problem and can help the dialogue also in the remaining States of the region. For this effort to succeed, it is important to recognise that, just as the central leaders have not paid adequate attention to pluralism in India, many in Assam have not recognised the diversity within its territory. Crucial to the future of Assam and of peace with justice is the recognition of the fact that, many nations make this State and that ethnic conflicts are also an offshoot of resentment against this domination and their solution has to be integral to the dialogue. (Bhattacharjee 2003). No single community, however numerous it is, can impose itself on the rest.

In other words, civil society has to help all the communities to look at their own histories not in isolation but together with that of all the groups of the State, even the region. It will show, for example that most Hill Tribes ran their affairs according to their customary laws in the colonial age. (Srikanth 2006) Since the Brahmaputra plains were needed for land, for tea and oil, autonomy was all but non-existent there. As a result, Assam has not always recognised autonomy that is crucial to the identity of the tribes as actions such as the 1960 Official Languages Act indicate. Today the debate on the name of Assam or Asom tends to betray a similar trend about the exclusive rights of the ethnic Assamese. Taking the debate beyond one community to all the nations within Assam can also take the parleys beyond ULFA and the State to other militant groups in Assam and turn into a composite dialogue between all the militant groups and function as a springboard for a common dialogue with the Centre.

The Land Issue

While supporting a movement forward, one cannot ignore the economic issue either. Underdevelopment is one of the causes of the unrest. (Masih 2003) Besides, land is a basic issue and most conflicts in the region are around it. An important cause of anti-immigrant stand of many groups is land encroachment though language and cultural differences too play an important role. In order to find a solution one has to begin with the legal ambiguity around common land that makes encroachment easy in the Northeast, especially in its tribal areas. Most tribes of Assam and the rest of the Northeast run their civil affairs according to their community-based customary law but the land laws are individual-based and treat what does not have a *patta* as State property that can be appropriated without the consent of the community, whose sustenance it has been for centuries. Such imposition of the individual-based formal law on their community-based customary law often results in land alienation.

Among its examples is a recent study on development-induced displacement in Assam during the period 1947-2000. It showed that the official files acknowledge that 3,91,772.9 acres of land have been used for development projects including refugee rehabilitation, environment protection, defence, transport, water resources, industries and others. But the reality is at least 1401184.8 acres have been used for this purpose. (Fernandes and Bharali 2006: 77) The files account for around 4.5 lakh persons displaced (DP) or otherwise deprived of their sustenance (PAP) by these projects when the reality is a minimum of 19 lakhs. (ibid: 107) Thus, more than 10 lakh acres that are the livelihood of over 15 lakh persons are not accounted for because the law does not recognise community ownership. In the eyes of the State, those who have inhabited them for centuries before the colonial law was enacted are encroachers.

The caste-tribe of more than 50 per cent of the DP/PAPs could not be identified but the fact that, 36,000 acres in the char areas have been used for environment protection indicates that most of their 100,000 DP/PAPs are fish workers, 68 per cent of whom live below the poverty line. Official records exist on 16,297.9 acres of private land acquired for refugee rehabilitation, when the reality is at least 350,000 acres used for this purpose, around 95 per cent of it mostly trial common land. One cannot oppose the humanitarian effort of refugee rehabilitation but some 500,000 internal refugees were made in Assam, most of them tribal, in order to resettle external refugees. Similar information comes out of data on major dams, industries and other sectors. That explains why more than 50 per cent of the 19 lakh DP/PAPs are tribals who are 12.49 per cent of the State's population.

Also studies on immigration show that the land laws are basic to their influx. Of importance to those who lose their land to the immigrants is not their origin or religion but the fact that, they occupy the CPRs that are the tribal livelihood and the centre of their economy, culture and identity. Whether they are from Bangladesh, Bihar or Nepal, the push factors are poverty and the feudal system in their area of origin. Most of them are landless agricultural labourers but land reforms have not been implemented in their feudal regions. Their low wages and poverty push them out of their region. (Majumdar 2002: 107-108). The pull factor is the fertile land in the Northeast and the legal system that allows them to encroach on community land, since the law recognises only individual ownership. The disjunction between the formal and informal systems makes it easy for them to encroach on the CPRs and cultivate them. Being agricultural labourers, they are familiar with cultivation techniques that they use on that land and prosper.

Another pull factor is cheap labour that many in the region need. We shall not dwell on it further but shall focus on land laws because most conflicts in the Northeast are around this resource. The October 2005 Karbi-Dimasa conflict was probably engineered by "a third party", (Civil Society Mission 2006) but the Karbi-Pnar and Karbi-Kuki conflicts were around land, so were the April 2003 Dimasa-Hmar conflict. It began when the Hmars, threatened with displacement by the Tipaimukh dam went to the Barak Valley and to NC Hills in search of land. (*The Telegraph,* April 23, 2003) Also the Bodo-Adivasi conflict is mainly around land. So the problem is less with the refugees or immigrants than with the legal system that treats people's centuries-old livelihood as State property and allows them to occupy it and later claim it for themselves. Its dependants have no right over their livelihood.

Civil society organizations have to help the State to face the situation of injustice caused by the laws that deprive the tribals and other subalterns of their right to their livelihood. In so doing one has to acknowledge that the immigrants who are already in the State cannot be deported. Assam has become the home of most of them and a large number of them were born in the State. They cannot be sent away without bloodshed. At this stage one can only remove the causes that encourage more immigration. A solution to this issue begins with the recognition that both the local people and the immigrants have a right to a life with dignity enshrined in Article 21 of the Constitution. In the present situation of Assam, an important component of this right is security of tenure. The legal system has to be changed to provide it. Besides, a new autonomous economy has to be envisaged that can protect the rights of the local people as well as of past immigrants. The civil society has to get involved in this long search.

Conclusion

In the context of the recent killings in Upper Assam, the present paper has attempted an analysis of the social, political and economic situation resulting in conflicts. Some militants outfits demand self-determination or sovereignty that the hardliners among them interpret as independence. But most others understand them as autonomy all of whose details are yet to be worked out. Economic autonomy has been better defined than the political components. These issues have to be clarified in order to support a dialogue that can lead to peace with justice. That cannot be achieved if the dialogue is held only between the militant outfits and the State. Such an approach can at best stop armed violence but cannot solve the social, political and economic problems leading to the conflict. A way forward can be found if the civil society gets involved in it. ULFA has taken a step towards it through its Manifesto and by choosing some civil society persons to facilitate the dialogue. It can facilitate the search.

The civil society has to get involved in it without taking sides between the actors. It may agree with the issues that one or the other side raises but has to do it without aligning itself with them. In identifying areas of division and possible solutions, they cannot limit themselves to any one of the issues such as economic, political or cultural. It has to find a way of bringing all of them together. In this effort it has also to face the fact of the Centre-periphery within Assam and has to deal with all the nations that form Assam. The civil society can thus assist the dialogue in two stages. The first is between the various communities of Assam. The second is all of them together dialoguing with the Indian State. That can be a major step in dealing with the divisive issues and giving priority to the regional and local identity which is based on a combination of economic, social, political and cultural factors.

References

Ahmed, Abu Nasar Saied, ed. (2006) *Nationality Question in Assam: The EPW 1980-81 Debate*, Akansha Publishing House, New Delhi.

Barbora, Sanjay (2005) "Peace: Some Concerns and Considerations," In Imdad Hussain, ed., *The Guwahati Declaration and the Road to Peace in Assam*, Akansha Publishing House, New Delhi, pp. 79-88.

Barman, Hemanta (2005) "Ethnic Unrest," In Imdad Hussain, ed., *op. cit.*, pp. 57-70.

Baruah, Apurba K. (2005) "Roots of Conflict," in Imdad Hussain, ed., *op. cit.*, pp. 32-56.

Bhat, Anil (2004) "To Act or Not to Act," *The Statesman*, December 25.

Bhattacharjee, Tarun (2003) "Ethnic Conflict an Ominous Trend," *The Meghalaya Guardian*, December 17.

Bhattacharyya, Hiranya Kumar (1998) *Economic Development of Assam*, APH Publishing Corporations, New Delhi.

Chattopadhyay, Dilip Kumar (1990) *History of the Assamese Movement Since 1947*, Minerva, Calcutta.

Chutia, Ramchandra (2002) "Insurgency and Its Flame in the Northeast," *The Northeast Times*, April 19.

Civil Society Mission (2006) *An Independent Fact-Finding Team's Report on Conflict and Violence in Karbi Anglong and North Cachar Hills*, Civil Society Mission for Peace in Karbi and Cachar Hills, New Delhi.

D'Souza, Alphonsus (1999) *North East India*, Kohima Jesuit Region, Jakhama (mimeo).

Das, Samir Kumar (1994) *ULFA: United Liberation Front of Assam: A Political Analysis*, Ajanta Publications, Delhi.

Datta, Brijendranath (1990) "Ethnicity, Nationalism and Sub-Nationalism, with Special Reference to North-East India", In D. Pakem, ed., *Nationality, Ethnicity and Cultural Identity in North-East India*, Omsons Publications, New Delhi, pp. 36-44.

Fernandes, Walter (2005a) "Reservations and Social Change: The Case of the Northeast," In Stephanie Tawa Lama-Rewal, ed., *Electoral Reservations, Political Representation and Social Change in India A Comparative Perspective*, Manohar Book Centre and Centre de Sciences Humaines, Delhi, pp. 83-104.

Fernandes, Walter (2005b) 'IMDT Act and Immigration in North Eastern India', *Economic and Political Weekly*, 40 (n. 30), pp. 3237-3240.

Fernandes, Walter (2007) "Hawks Descend on Assam," *Himal Southasian*, February 1.

Fernandes, Walter and Gita Bharali (2006) *Development-Induced Displacement in Assam 1947-2000: A Quantitative and Qualitative Study of Its Extent and Nature*, North Eastern Social Research Centre, Guwahati (mimeo).

Fernandes, Walter and Mohammed Asif (1997) *Development-Induced Displacement and Rehabilitation in Orissa, 1951 to 1995: A Database on its Extent and Nature*, Indian Social Institute, New Delhi: (mimeo).

Hazarika, Sanjoy (2005) "Manipur's Unending Tragedy," *The Statesman*, August 6.

Jacob, Malsawmi (2004) "Rearing Frankenstein's Monster," *The Assam Tribune*, January 23.

Majumdar, Anindiyo J. (2002) "Human Movement and the Nation State: Dimensions of an Indian Crisis in its North-Eastern Region," In Joshua Thomas, ed., *Dimensions of Displaced People in North-East India*, Regency Publications, New Delhi, pp. 91-101.

Masih, Manorama (2003) "Impact of Insurgency on NE," *The Assam Tribune*, June 19.

Mishra, Udayon (2005) "Shrinking Democratic Space and the Role of Civil Society," In Imdad Hussain, ed., Op. cit. pp. 89-104.

Mukerjee, J. R. (2005) "Armed Forces Special Powers Act in the Northeast," *The Statesman*, March 15.

Nag, Sajal (2005) "Peace and Cultural Space," In Imdad Hussain, ed., *op. cit.* pp. 111-118.

Rafiabadi, H. N. (1998) *Assam: From Agitation to Accord*, Genuine Publications and Media, New Delhi.

Roy, Ajay (1995) *The Boro Imbroglio*, Spectrum Publishers, Guwahati.

Sanyu, Visier (1996) *A History of Nagas and Nagaland: Dynamics of Traditional Village Formation*, Commonwealth Publishers, New Delhi.

Sen, Sipra (1992) *Tribes of Mizoram: Description, Ethnology and Bibliography*, Gyan Publishing House, New Delhi.

Srikanth, H. (2006) "British Colonialism and the Hill Tribes of Composite Assam," *Man and Society: A Journal of North East Studies*, 3 (Spring), pp. 79-116.

Yadav, Yogendra (2001) "The Three Word Trick," *The Telegraph*, August 18.

12

From Victims to Actors in Peace Building

Anuradha Dutta

Survival of the fittest is the reality that guides every living being on earth, even more so every man and woman in the world today. Leaving men folk apart, in most parts of the world today even women seldom have the resources to actively organize themselves or the time to think of anything else than their daily survival. As a result women get caught in endless circles where lack of time, money and self reliance make changes impossible. From time immemorial most societies have been characterized by traditional and patriarchal values that accentuate the belief that women are incapable of taking part in any decision making process. There is structured inequality, and men are not aware of their oppressive nature. The general assumption of tribal women being in an egalitarian society has also been proved incorrect. How does then one view security of women in this non-egalitarian society?

From the feminist perspective, the world security system would attempt to include all people and all nations based on the notion of kinship extended to the entire human family. Security also means individual well being and personal safety in various social relationships, including the family. Women's access to land, educational reforms and other circumstances of development are indicators to measure welfare of a society. Feminist conceptions of peace are extended to the conditions of social justice, economic equity and ecological balance. Thus women must have a space to provide their own contribution and intervention. Security is definable and perceivable also in terms of peace. The goal of peace can very well be enhanced by the feminist agenda committed to the rejection of coercive power in human interaction. Women, making intervention for peace look upon themselves as custodians of society and their political role is marked as an extension of the social role. Thus the process of building sustainable peace goes way beyond deactivating the situation of armed conflict.

Peace building seeks to prevent, reduce, transform, and help people recover from violence in all forms, even structural violence, which is but yet to lead to massive civil unrest. There are four categories of peace building, including efforts to (i) wage conflict nonviolently through activism and advocacy; (ii) reduce direct violence through peacekeeping, relief aid, and legal systems; (iii) transform relationships through dialogue, mediation, negotiation, and trauma healing; and (iv) build capacity through training and education, development, military conversion and research. Women play important roles in each of the four categories of peace building. Women are particularly vulnerable during and after conflict but the situation also create a unique opportunity for women to take part in 'creating new societies from the ruins of the old'. However, women's identity as victims often obscures the important roles they play in the peace building processes. Does this apply to the fate of womenfolk all over the world? Here we need to look for a holistic picture of world societies in time and space.

Despite this growing awareness about the role of women, inclusion of women in peace efforts is still not a norm. In many areas of the world it is found that women have the capacity for both violence and peace. Democratization is directly and positively correlated with conflict resolution or prevention because socio-economic development is directly and positively correlated with participatory democracy. Thus democratization and socio-economic and sustainable development are necessary prerequisites for the resolution or prevention of deep rooted conflict. With this principle women's groups assert that the values of empathy and building community can contribute significantly to a discourse on peace and security that is based on coexistence and cooperation. Socialization process in many cultures helps women to avoid violence. It is, therefore, important to bring their qualities of peace building to the forefront. It is interesting to analyse how the same women group who are victims of state violence like molestation, rape and even killing later take up the responsibility of reconstructing the society. But when one looks back it is found that in the histories of these movements, contribution of these women are seldom recorded.

Women's Variegated Negotiation with Conflict: Capacity to Emerge as Agents of Social Transformation

Marked by sorrow, women in fact are identified with sorrow. But, is this the only facet of women? Certainly not. Beyond sorrow, there are many facets of women – citizens, combatants, producers of soldiers, heads of households, prostitutes, political leaders at local and national level, countless emerge. Why are then women identified only with sorrow? Do all these facets (and many more), other than sorrow get due recognition? They do, but in space and time which is countable. In the contemporary times in conflict ridden societies research has proved that women have not only proved to be extremely creative in developing survival mechanism but they have also established that they can also play any role in arm conflict resolution.

In situation of conflict women's bodies become the terrain that wars are fought on. Women's language of resistance gets eroded in their cultural space of being. And then, violent conflicts open up for women, spheres predominantly controlled by men. As the security forces and armed groups spread institutional terror, not only the evil society gets suppressed, the public spheres of men also collapse. Violent conflict blurs the division between the private sphere of the family and the public sphere of men. Women's engagements in everyday violence lead them to think of issues of security, peace, conflict, management and transformation. But it has been found that women's activism grounded in the informal space of politics does get undervalued and marginalised, more so with women who are victims of political violence, physical violence and economic violence. Why women post conflict are marginalised?

Women's activism is obscured by the fact that women's language of support and resistance flow from their cultural expression, especially of being disempowered – women have never been strong enough in the classic rallies and speech variety politics. As Bennet et all state, "Many women perceived conflict as something entirely outside their control, a struggle for power at a level beyond their reach. But they recognised the effort that has to be made by every individual to rebuild society after conflict". Women's specific concerns are shaped by their obligation which they have in the family and community and by prevailing cultural conceptualisation of gender role and relationship. The structural and situational factors play a decisive role in defining the motivation as well as the constraints on women's involvement as social actors in the political process toward sustainable peace.

It is always that domestic activism challenges the conventional notion of the public and private sphere. But this has not stopped women from being actors in public yet private sphere. As Paula Banerjee states, "Women denied space in public sphere creatively expanded informal political space to negotiate and transform conflict". Women form survival strategies, build dialogue, co-existence and reconciliation at the grassroots. But they never get a seat in the negotiating table. One must recognise the new perspective and untapped experiences of women in promoting non-violent ways of dealing with differences. But it is not so. In fact, impact of violence on women is gendered. Their response is gendered. Their notion of praxis of peace bias is gendered.

The thinking is no different world over. Northeast India too resembles similarities in this respect. In the words of Paula Banerjee, "The reality of state verses community conflict in Northeast India is a male reality". But there are attempts. The UN War Report 1995 states, "The work of peace has also been identified by women as unique opportunity to become organised. This can be helpful may contribute both to counteracting dominant stereo type of the 'ethnic other'". There are cases where women have succeeded in breaking the gendered barrier to a certain extent and reaching out. The Naga man and women fought together. As agents of social transformation, the Naga women's initiatives show the scope and limits of transcending the public-private divide to legitimize a measure of authority in the public sphere of formal politics. Women in Nagaland not only face new challenges today but also have inherited responsibilities in the post-conflict period and finally in the social transformation occurring in the post-conflict context. Even going beyond this, it must be realised that post conflict context opens up opportunities which should not be missed by women to strengthen and enhance democratic governance. And hence determination is necessary to make women's historical invisibility visible.

But it is unfortunate that for the voice of the women negotiating conflict women's question in democratic struggle remain unresolved.

It is difficult to bring women together. There may be two reasons for this – (a) the leaders of ethnic groups control the response of women in their communities. Identity politics has fractured a possibly artificial women's movement; (b) women are not just passionate enough for representing.the community identity.

In the light of the above discussions and considering the time and space constraint, in this article, I stick myself to an analysis of women's identity 'from victims to actors in peace building process' in Assam with special reference to the Bodo women.

From Victims to Actors in Peace Building: The Bodo Women

As activists and advocates for peace, women "wage conflict non-violently" but they hardly find a space in writings. This is true even in Northeast India. As Paula Banerjee remarks, "Ethnic movements were presented from male point of view. It is also to be noted that regional media on the whole does not give much space to these demand movements thus most of the incidents were projected from one perspective. Most of the works analysing intra-state conflicts in the Northeast do not deal with women's engagement in it." Nevertheless, in different movements of Northeast India beginning from the Assam movement to the Bodoland movement, the participation of large number of women in non-violent ways was visible.

Security is a wide concept, which as already mentioned, considers the issue of individual dignity, water security, food security, humane governance and environmental security. Similarly positive peace includes social justice, gender equity, active co-existence, economic equality and ecological security. Thus to achieve sustainable peace and democracy in post-conflict societies is a great challenge for us. Democratic society and even civil society with strong social capital are not sufficient for maintaining peace. Civil society is a network of relationships among the state, market and the private family of individuals which has manifested into a whole different set of organizations in the cultural, religious and social spheres. These same interests could go against each other producing conflict and also could be used to reduce the level of conflict. The civil society can also mediate between the state and the citizens or monitor corporate interest. In case of the Bodoland movement, women supported the Bodo youth without questioning them. But their method of support was a non-violent one. Women got involved in various activities acting as messengers, carrying messages from one person to another and from one place to another, and also lending a hand in relief works. Did the Bodo women play the role of the support soldiers by providing food, health care etc., to those fighting for Bodoland? Women's activities for peace are often labeled 'voluntary', 'charitable' or 'social' even though they have a political impact. This may be the reason for not focusing on the activities of the Bodo women's organisation during the Bodo agitation. It was found that the role of the Naga Mothers' Association was limited to making appeals to the government and insurgent groups to shun violence and come to the negotiating table. The Bodo women group in comparison was guided by the students' group. They played their role as friends and mothers. Young Bodo girls were even fascinated to join the rank and file of the insurgent groups and thus become a part of violence. We find a few of these women cadres in the Designated Camps of the National Democratic Front of Bodoland (NDFB) today. Why did they join the armed movement? Was it because the composition of the Bodo students' organisations proved that there was no space for females in them, and so the young girls were desperate to participate in the alternative way of negotiation?

Rita Manchanda, the human right expert, comments that the Naga women are – (a) managing survival, (b) mitigating violence, and in the end (c) building ceasefire in the peace process. But she adds that even this is not being recognized. We can say the same about the Bodo women, who (a) supported the youth whole heartedly in the identity movement of the Bodos, (b) protested the illegal activities of the state actors, and are (c) building peace by reconstructing the society today. But these contributions of the Bodo women have been ignored. This may be because women here are more used to listening and more used to compromise. This is, however, a universal phenomenon and so the resolution 1325 has been adopted which recognises that war affect men and women separately. The resolution demands involvement of more women in the peace making process. As women constitute half of the civil society they can as well contribute for conflict management. An attempt here is made to examine the role of the All Bodo Women's Welfare Federation (ABWWF) in such a situation.

Women from Northeast India have been organizing themselves for peace in different ways. The Bodo women, in spite of being the victims of violence once, are working for sustainable peace today. These women in particular were strong supporters of the movement for identity in the Bodoland areas organised by the students under the leadership of Upendra Brahma. The Bodo women organized under the banner of the All Assam Tribal Women's Welfare Federation (AATWWF) joined the movement for the adoption of the Roman Script way back in 1974. Most of these women belonged to a tender age group, most of whom were school or college going students. As Upendra Brahma sought participation and help of boys and girls from local colleges and schools, many girls participated on equal footing with the boys. The Bodo women leaders were more or less socialized through this movement which was non-violent in nature.

Looking into the history of the AATWWF, it was formed at the initiative of Upendra Brahma, Sansuma K. Bwismithiary, Subhas Basumatari and Deorah D. Basumatary, student leaders belonging to the All Bodo Students' Union (ABSU). According to the Constitution of AATWWF, "It is considered expedient to form a federation of womenfolk belonging to all tribal groups of entire Assam to unite themselves in a common platform through mutual understandings, fighting for ensuring right and justice of the tribal women in the sphere of socio-economic, political, educational, cultural and for emancipation of themselves from socio-domestic drudgery and thereby enabling themselves in rendering services to the promotion of welfare and preservation of the indigenous self-identity of tribal groups living in Assam". For the first six years that followed, the AATWWF had no independent programme. It was under the sway of the student body, the ABSU.

But eventually the ABSU movement, i.e. the movement for an independent Bodoland, established a military wing to conduct an armed struggle. It also wanted to train the womenfolk in arms. So from 1989 onwards, some women did join the armed wing but they were not sent for direct action. The AATWWF was not in favour of this decision. The AATWWF changed its nomenclature to All Bodo Women's Welfare Federation (ABWWF) in 1993. As the ABSU could not reach the nooks and corners of Bodoland, they took the help of women's groups to mobilise people in support of the movement. The AATWWF members even accompanied Upendra Brahma when he went around different parts of Kokrajhar. Gradually, Pramila Rani Brahma (present MLA and Minister, Government of Assam) and Malati Rani Narzary, founder President and Secretary started to associate themselves and participate in various phases of the Bodo movement.

They were encouraged to form their own organization. One of the reasons was to protest against the atrocities committed to the Bodo women during these movements by the Assam Police. As victims, they suffered enormously. Some of these incidents of assault on women are given below:

- September 19, 1989: Five Bodo women, including a minor, gang raped at Bhumka in Kokrajhar district by the police.
- May 1, 1991: 11 Bodo women including six minor girls raped by Assam Police at Bagmara in Barpeta district.
- November 25, 2004: Rijuli Basumatary of Belguri Forest Village, Sarfanguri Police Station, ganged raped and murdered by miscreants.
- December 31, 2004: Five elderly Bodo women gang raped by army at Ultapani and one at Shiva temple.
- April 15, 2005: Nani Basumatary and Anjula Basumatary of Choto Gendholoi gang raped and murdered.
- December 23, 2005: Three students shot dead by Haryana Police at Salakati and Five college girls molested by Haryana Reserve Police in the running Brahmaputra Express.

Thus, under the direction of the student leaders, the Bodo women organized themselves. It was not smooth everywhere. But members of the AATWWF had remarkable contribution toward organizing the people during the movement. Moreover, when there was rift between the ABSU and Plains Tribal Council of Assam (PTCA), they tried to act as the mediator.

During the movement when police personnel and army men raided the villages, women were asked to stay in groups and train themselves to take the necessary steps. Thus as a result of this organised group, the ABSU could establish close relationship with common people and this strengthened their movement. Most of the members of the AATWWF were related to the ABSU members. During the movement though women were victims of violence nevertheless they performed activities like addressing the public to make them aware of the demands of the ABSU, worked as rapporteurs, and participated in the meetings held by the ABSU. In fact, the history of the Bodo movement is full of stories of the courage and commitment of these women.

In January 1988, a number of women of Bhumka area were raped. The AATWWF members immediately took steps and punished the guilty though the government tried to suppress it. During those times there were a number of other incidents like arresting innocent people by the police on no solid grounds whatsoever. Each case of illegal arrest was taken care of by the women's group. In June 1990, almost one thousand women gathered in Mushalpur and Barbori police stations for release of eight innocent villagers. In one such incident when people rushed to the police station, the police opened fire and killed two women. Thus the history of the Bodo movement is the 'history of the young men and women together'. Student leaders took care to train the women in different aspects like nursing for the need of those involved in the movement.

During the movement, political organisations at the village level became defunct. The common people approached the ABSU and AATWWF members for solution to any problems. It is interesting to observe how this organization helped many women from being victims of polygamy. They organized seminars discussing mainly the role of women in the movement for identity. Thus with a good networking the Bodo women were sensitized about the need of the Bodo movement. During the period from 1987 to 1995, ATWWF organized a number of conferences. And in almost all of these conferences the theme was training of women for the benefit of the society. On the whole these women's organizations explained the programme of the ABSU to the people from time to time, convincing people about their demands. They also taught people to remain alert about army and police raids. They approached people to help the ABSU and ABSU VF with food and shelter. Thus this group of women activists had unique characteristics. They as victims also protested against frequent police and army raids in the villages and arrest of innocent people. The Bodo women's group has had a very good networking in every nooks and corners of the different Bodo dominated areas. The result of which can be seen even today with the kind of activities taken up by the ABWWF. Though the Bodo women found no place on the negotiation table, they established their own space by playing a very constructive role. They never had the patronage of the state, nor was the civil society favourable to them. Apart from the peace initiatives, ABWWF works for social regeneration. The ABWWF has set up an orphanage for children affected by conflict. Under the leadership of Pramila Rani Brahma and Kanan Basumatari, the children are being trained with care to be self sufficient. Thus once victims, these women are contributing a lot for positive peace as agents of social transformation.

Another Bodo women's group is the Bodo Women's Justice Forum which was constituted in 1993. This group supports the growth of self-government and takes up cases to be presented before the national and international communities. Anjali Daimary is the present Secretary of the Forum. The Forum recently had organized protests against the killing of Dainis (so called Witches). Golapi Basumatari, the founder Secretary of this organization, was gunned down along with her friends when trying to organize the Assamese-Bodo dialogue on peace in December 1996.

It is seen that at the negotiating table even these agents of social transformation have failed to find a space. It is only the male representatives of armed groups who have found a place. Women have participated only as observers. Women are achievers in healing at local levels. The Bodo women in spite of being so active in the Bodo movement have not been a part of the formal peace process. Sustainability of peace process in many ways depends on local level involvement and initiative. There must be efforts to reconcile and to develop new non-violent means to voice local concern and settle emerging disputes. It is always a continuous process. At this level new relationships of trust and solidarity must emerge. But the ABWWF did not develop; rather it has failed to develop. There are many facets of women's existence - from powerless victims to dangerous soldiers to resourceful refugees and powerful actors. The Naga Mothers'

Association criticised violence but the ABWWF did not. The Bodo Women Joint Forum though tried to reconcile with different groups like the Naga Mothers' Association, it however, failed to continue.

Post-reconciliation also, ABWWF has failed in finding for itself a political space. In the election to the Bodoland Territorial Council (BTC), the Bodoland People's Progressive Front (BPPF) which was formed in April 2005 was divided in May. One faction comprised the BLT leaders and surrendered cadres, while the All Bodo Students' Union (ABSU) who took the lead in formation of the BPPF comprised the other faction. In Kokrajhar, several leaders of the disbanded militant outfit filed nominations against the BPPF President Rabiram Narzary. The BTC Chief Hangrama Mahillary supported former comrade Manoj Kumar Brahma. Though initially the ABWWF, a key player in Bodo politics lent its support to the new party BPPF, it withdrew from the party as not a single woman candidate was nominated. The influential women's body extended support to the former BLT leader instead, who stood as the rebel candidate against the official BPPF candidates.

Women are important actors of peace because of their experience. But women like men are also individuals in their own rights and shaped by the values of the society in which they live. Women also have been and are trained as militants inducted into different insurgent groups operating in Northeast India – whether it is the United Liberation Front of Assam (ULFA), National Democratic Front of Bodoland (NDFB), or the Adivasi militant groups. The inherent 'peaceful' nature with which women are identified with is in fact a misconception. They are not 'peaceful by nature' but traditions cast women and men in completely separate roles. In almost all conflicts men go to the front while the women maintain the social life. During times of peace, women go back to their previous positions. The experience gained by women during 'war and conflict' are usually ignored. A recent visit to two designated camps set up separately for male and female cadres of the insurgent group NDFB, which is under ceasefire with the Government of India echoes this very reality. The male cadres in their uniform seem to be enjoying a comfortable life while the women cadres in their traditional dresses seem to be controlled by the patriarchal structure.

Thus, it is seen that groups who have a broader definition of peace are more successful. As stated by Kumari Jayewardene, "Women movement do not occur in vacuum, they correspond to and to some extent are determined by the wider social movement of which they form a part". The Bodo women have proved it right. Women want to achieve their goal by peaceful means. For them 'peace is not mere absence of conflict' but it is much more than that. Women working under ABWWF realize that today the 'new states' formulate rights and obligations in ways that strengthen the masculinity of the public sphere and feminity of the private sphere. These women by making 'peace' women's work, and approaching peacemaking as a part of their traditional role have arrogated for themselves some space for intervention into the political realm where society has traditionally denied them 'other entry power'. The success of any organization will depend on trying to navigate through these complexities.

References

Chaudhuri, S. Sen. (2004). *The Bodo Movement and Women's Participation.* Delhi: Mittal Publications.

Banerjee, P. (2002). *Women's Intervention for Peace in North East.* South Asia Partnership Canada.

Schirch, L. and M. Sewak. 2004. "Women: Using the Gender Lens" in *People Building Peace II: Successful Stories of Civil Society*, P van Tongeren, M. Brenk, M. Hellema and J. Verhoeven, eds. London: Lynne Rienner Publishers, pp. 97-146.

Bennett, O., Bexley, Jo., and Kitty Warnock (eds). 1995. *Arms to Fight, Arms to Protect: Women Speak Out About Conflict.* Panos.

Contribution of Bodo Women Towards Peace Process. 2006. Workshop conducted by Peace Studies, OKDISCD, Guwahati. Kokrajhar, August 20.

13

Peace in a Dialogue: The Tripura Perspective

Chandrika Basu Majumder

The state of Tripura, a land-locked hilly state in the Northeastern India, is surrounded on the north, west and south by Bangladesh. It is accessible to the rest of the country only through the Cachar District of Assam and Aizawl district of Mizoram in the East. With an area of 10,492 Sq. Km i.e. only 0.32 percent of the total geographical area of India, Tripura is the third smallest State in India. It has 856 kms long international boundary with Bangladesh, which is 84.08 per cent of the total perimeter of the state. On the other hand, boundaries with Assam and Mizoram are only 53 Kms and 109 Kms respectively.

The state is an admixture of races and culture as there were contacts between various ethnic groups in the resultant process of migration and settlement. The State of Tripura in North-East India has been experiencing the brunt of insurgency problem from the very last part of nineteen eighties. The century long enriched tradition of having cordial relationship of mutual trust and goodwill amidst tribal and non-tribal communities is at stake. Tripura has been continuously beleaguered by socio-economic problems since independence. It is one of the worst affected areas of countries by the partition of India. Because of the inadequate Central Government attention and failure in the past to exploit the natural resources and creation of infrastructural facilities led to growing unemployment and resentment among a section of the youth. The border with Bangladesh is open, porous and on the eastern side, extremely inhospitable in terms of terrain. This facilitates smuggling, border crime, infiltration and free movement of extremists to their hideouts in a neighbouring country where the extremists have safe hideouts and training grounds for militants from the North-Eastern region, including Tripura.

Demography

The total population of Tripura, as per 2001 census (provisional), is 31,91,168 (16,36,138 males and 15,55,030 females). Tripura is the home of 0.33 per cent of India's population and the State accounts for 0.32 per cent of the total area of the country. The State is inhabited by 19 tribal communities who occupy 30.95 percent of the total population. The density of population in Tripura has been found to be increasing with each successive census. In 1911, the density of population was only 35 persons per sq. km. In 1951, it rose to 62, whereas in 1961 it stood at 109. The density of population, which was 196 persons per sq. km in 1981, has gone up to 263 persons per sq. km in 1991. As per 2001 census the density of population is 304 per sq. km. Although the density of population of Tripura has been increasing at a very fast pace, it is below the national average. Tripura registered a phenomenal growth of population during the last century. The total population of the state was 2,29,613 in 1911. Since then, in a period of 90 years, the population increased to 31,91,168. During this period the population increased by 13.92 times. After independence of India and merger of Tripura with the Indian Union, the tribal people of Tripura faced with the new challenge of being minority in the state due to major influx of population from the then East Pakistan who were victims of Partition.

SENKRAK

In 1947 'Seng- Krak' was formed by a group of tribal people who were fully against the influx of refugees. The movement was started as a reaction to settling down of nontribal refugees in the Tribal Reserve Forest Areas. SENKRAK activists launched a large number of violent attacks on Government officials also. This movement was however, controlled in 1968.

In 1967, a younger section of the tribal organized themselves under the banner of 'Tripura Upajati Juba Samiti'. The four demands put forward by TUJS were:

1. Restoration of tribal lands transferred to non-tribal since 1960
2. Formation of an Autonomous District Council for the tribal community of Tripura
3. Reservation of Government jobs for the tribal
4. Recognition of KokBorok as State Language and a medium of instruction and introduction of Roman Script of this language.

Since 1967 TUJS has been launching democratic movements in support of tribal demands. But its younger group went underground and formed a secret organization named' Tripura National Volunteer Force' which adopted militant line of action

Tripura National Volunteers (TNV) / ATPLO

Mr. B.K. Hrangkhawal, a young tribal leader of 'Tripura Upajati Juba Samity', a regional party for the tribal, formed an underground organisation styled as "Tripura National Volunteers (TNV)" on 10th November, 1978 with a design to conduct insurgent activities in collaboration with the Mizo National Front (MNF) of Mizoram. There were wide spread communal riots in the State in June, 1980 when a large number of people from two ethnic communities lost their lives. Sri B.K. Hrangkhwal was arrested in June, 1980 and lodged in jail. On his release from jail in Dee, 1980, he announced dissolution of TNV.

But, some followers of TNV led by Mr. Binanda Jamatia formed another extremist group styled as "All Tripura People's Liberation Organization (ATPLO) on 12th Dec, 1980 at Thangnan, Mayani Reserve Forest, Bangladesh. In 1981 Mr. Chuni Koloi broke away from A TPLO led by Binanda Jamatia. Mr. Jamatia arranged kidnapping of Mr. Hrangkhwal and his wife, Mrs. Linda Hrangkhwal from their house at Kamalacharra, under Ambassa Police Station on 13th Aug. 1982, suspecting his support to Chuni Koloi. Hrangkhwals were kept confined in Thangnan camp under guard.

On 3rd Sept, 1982 Chuni Koloi and his followers raided Manu Police Station and looted a huge number of arms and ammunitions. The faction led by Chuni Koloi, after becoming stronger than the faction led by Mr. Jamatia, attacked ATPLO Camp at Thangnan and rescued Mr B.K. Hrangkhwal from captivity. Many ATPLO members surrendered to Chuni Koloi. On 10th Nov. 1982, TNV was revived with B.K.Hrangkhwal as its President. Binanda Jamatia and his supporters took shelter in South Tripura. Later, in response to a call of Mr. Nripen Chakrabarty, the then Chief Minister, Mr. Binanda Jamatia & his followers surrendered before the State Government on 23rd July, 1983. The ATPLO became defunct. TNV activists continued their attacks with renewed vigour and intensity. Their attacks were directed to killing non-tribal and security personnel and looting of arms and ammunitions which continued till 1988. On 12-08-1988 a Tripartite Accord was signed by the Government of India, State Government of Tripura and the TNV. In all 447 TNV activists led by Mr. B.K. Hrangkhwal surrendered before the Government with arms and ammunitions.

Tripura Resurrection Army (TRA)

Mr. Dhananjoy Reang, who had been Vice-President of the TNV and President of the NLFT, formed TRA on 11th Feb, 1994 following an attack on him by a splinter group of NLFT in his hideout in CHT, Bangladesh on 10th July, 1993 as per direction of Bishwamohan Debbarma and Joshua Debbarma. However, Dhananjoy Reang could manage to escape with a quantity of arms & some of his followers. This outfit could not sustain itself for long and finally surrendered to the Government of Tripura on 5th Feb, 1997. Mr. Dhananjoy Reang and his followers have declared total dissolution of the gang.

Other Gangs

A large number of small groups of extremists having link with either NLFT or ATTF came into existence and perished. Those having link with NLFT were - Tripura National Liberation Front (TNLF), Tripura Tribal Volunteer Force (TTVF), All Tripura Volunteer Force (ATVF), Social Democratic Front of Tripura (SDFT), Tripura Tribal Democratic Force (TTDF), All Tripura Volunteer Association (ATVA), Tripura Tribal Action Committee Force (TTACF), Tripura Humkurai Sepoy (THS), All Tripura Security Armed Force (ATSAF), Liberation of Tripura Tribal Force (LTTF), Tripura Regimental Force (TRF), All Tripura Bharat Suraksha Force (ATBSF), (Source: Tripura Police)

Harmony between the tribal and the non-tribal has been excellent for a long time despite large-scale migration of the non-tribal. But during the later half of 1970s, organised tribal militancy started spreading roots in the State. Strong feelings of social and economic deprivation and insecurity combined with communal feeling and ambition for political power deposited in the minds of a section of tribal youths. These feelings mixed with adventurism and aids from foreign agencies got stronger in the later part of '70s. As a result, the untoward ethnic riots took place in June 1980 when each other & large-scale arson killed more than 1300 tribal and non-tribal and damage of properties also took place. The great tribal uprisings of 1980 was accompanied by large scale devastations and killings of hundreds of men and women by the TNV Extremists.

Prof J. Ganchoudhury described the situation in his book entitled A *Political History of Tripura* as under:

> "The flame of fire spread very rapidly from village to village burning thousands of houses and huts, cattle and crops. Numerous villages were laid waste. Lakhs of People were rendered homeless. Properties, both movable and immovable worth several crores were destroyed, damaged, burnt, looted and captured. Hundreds were murdered. Women were raped. All contemptible crimes in human history were committed. Both the communities were affected".

Gan Choudhury,J. A Political History of Tripura, New Delhi,1995, p. 64

Present Phase of Insurgency

The present phase of insurgency started in 1989. It is dominated mainly by two groups namely National Liberation Front of Tripura (NLFT) and All Tripura Tiger Force (ATTF). Both the groups are armed with sophisticated weapons, well trained and have links with other North Eastern insurgent groups. The Government of India has declared both these groups as unlawful under the Unlawful Activities (Prevention) Act, 1967, on the proposal of the State Government.

National Liberation Front of Tripura

Origin

National Liberation Front of Tripura (NLFT) was formed on 12th

March, 1989 with some of the disgruntled TNV returnees led by Mr. Dhananjoy Reang, the former Vice President of TNV. The group declared its existence by attacking Tainani Out Post under R.K. Pur PS, South Tripura District on 11-12-1991. Mr. Dhananjoy Reang, later being expelled from the NLFT , formed his own group - TRA .

Main Demands

The main objective of the NLFT is to establish an 'Independent' Tripura through an armed struggle.

Other demands are:

(i) Liberation from 'neo- colonialism'

(ii) Instilling consciousness against exploitation,

(iii) Furtherance of indigenous culture.

The main strategy to achieve its objectives is:

(a) Extortion, b) attack on non-tribal, c) ambushes on Security Forces, d) Kidnapping of innocent civilians.

NLFT has also set up number of camps in a neighboring country.

Split in NLFT

NLFT faced disintegration alongwith ethnic line on 03-02-2001. Some senior leaders like Mr. Joshua Debbarma and Mr. Nayanbashi Jamatia were expelled from the NLFT as an outcome of their differences with Mr. Bishwamohan Debbarma and his followers.

Internal bickering within NLFT and its political wing has led to a spate of violent intermittent clashes in Bangladesh as well as inside the State. The causes of split were mainly:- a) reluctance of the Central Executive Committee(CEC) of NLFT led by Mr. Bishwamohan Debbarma to nominate Mr. Joshua Debbarma as the King of 'Tripura Kingdom', b) misappropriation of fund by some leaders, c) lavish lifestyles of senior leaders, d) forcing Christianity on the tribal. This split has lowered the morale of both the factions of NLFT. Many NLFT cadres surrendered with arms and ammunition to the State Government. NLFT (Nayanbashi Jamatia faction) has strength of about 125 hardcore. It also possesses some sophisticated arms and ammunitions with which they had deserted the main group. (Source: Tripura State Police)

All Tripura Tiger Force

Origin

All Tripura Tiger Force was initially established as All Tripura Tiger Force on 11th July 1990. Differences had cropped up between the leaders of ATTF namely Mr. Ranjit Debbarma and Mr. Lalit Debbarma on the issue of signing a 'Memorandum of Settlement' with the Government of Tripura and surrender of its cadres. Mr. Lalit Debbarma and his followers signed the 'Memorandum of Settlement' on 23-08-1993. 1633 All Tripura Tribal Force militants surrendered to the Government. Mr. Ranjit Debbarma and his followers did not surrender and continued terrorist activities with the same name, viz. "All Tripura Tiger Force". In volume 1 dated 11-07-1994 of 'Chaba', mouthpiece of All Tripura Tiger Force, ATTF claimed that the change of symbol of the Organisation and substitution of the word 'Tribal' with 'Tiger' were made in 1992 by Mr. Ranjit Debbarma in accordance with a decision of the Central Committee of ATTF.

Main Demands

(i.) Expulsion of all foreigners who entered Tripura after 1956

(ii.) Restoration of land to tribal under "Tripura Land Revenue and Land Reforms Act" 1960

(iii.) Removal of names of migrants who entered Tripura after 1956 from electoral roll ATTF has also set up a number of camps in a neighboring country.

Situation in the State of Tripura

Insurgency Situation in the State

There has been significant improvement in the insurgency situation of the State. The statistics enclosed highlights improvement which is being sustained during the year 2004. Some of highlights are as follows:

- Against the monthly average of 16.7 extremist incident in the year 2004 we have 25.92 in 2003 showing the complete reduction in the number of incidents committed by the insurgents.

- Comparative study of Extremists related incidents upto November 2006:
- During the year 2004 an average of 7 persons was kidnapped per month whereas during the year 2003 the monthly average stands as 25 with a phenomenal decrease.

Comparative study of Civilian Persons Killed by Extremists upto November 2006:

- The killings of Civilians by the extremists which stood at 25 per month during the year 2003 has come down to 6.33 per month in the year 2004.

Comparative study of persons kidnapped by extremists upto November 2006:

- The arrest of Hard Core extremists which was 14.08 per month has now increased to 17 per month.
- The arrest of harbourers during the year 2000 was 73 whereas in the year 2001 it has been increased to 513.
- The number of force personnel killed was increased from 1.3 per month in the year 2000 to 2.5 per month in the year 2001 which is due to 2 major ambush in which large number of force personnel killed.
- The number of encounters which was 3.8 per month in the year 2000 remains at 4.91 per month in the year 2001. (Source: Tripura Police)

NLFT & ATTF are antagonist i.e. antagonistic to each other for gaining supremacy over the tribal areas. As a result, several violent clashes between these groups have taken place. These two groups have a common aim to the oust non-tribal, from the Autonomous District Council area and its fringes. To implement this plan, these groups raid localities where non-tribal traders are predominant & carry out mindless killing and large-scale arson for creating scare among non-tribal. These groups also kidnap innocent civilians and sometimes kill them brutally even after extorting hefty amount of ransom. All such acts are unethical and brutal violation of human rights.

The internal security scenario had taken a dangerous turn with the building up of mass resistance by the affected non-tribal community and emergence of United Bengali Liberation Front (UBLF), a parochial extremist organization, on 1st August, 1999. UBLF started retaliating by kidnapping tribal, extortion, arson, exploding crude bombs and killing innocent tribal. With the arrest of Mr. Biplab Das, self-styled President of UBLF, there has been a breakthrough in curbing down the activities of UBLF.

Our effort for containing militancy in the State has started yielding some positive results. In February 1997, 19 Police Station areas were declared disturbed. Subsequently, the areas of 6 more Police Stations and parts of six Police Station areas, were declared as disturbed, within the purview of the Armed Forces (Special Powers) Act, 1958. Security forces have fought back the militants and other criminal elements in a forceful but legal way in the recent past. There have been many encounters leading to the killing or the arrest of extremists, recovery of large number of weapons, rescue of kidnapped persons and tracking down of many criminals involved in harboring and providing logistic support to the unlawful militants. The effort of Security forces has also resulted in reduction in number of kidnappings and controlling the ethnic unrest.

The Effect of Militancy

As the militant groups have been carrying out their offensive mainly in the hilly areas, the tribal populace is mainly in the receiving end. The helpless and hapless tribal has been put to such a complicated and difficult situation which they could not even dream of. The tribals of Tripura are overwhelmingly rural people. According to 1991 census, 98.35% of the total tribal population of the State lives in hilly areas. The percentage of urban population is microscopic though it has been increasing considerably in the recent years. The remaining urban tribal populations are spread over the other Districts, Sub-Divisional and Block Headquarters.

The worst victim of this rural militancy is the young tribal generation, which is being deprived of education, health care and other facilities. They are also being grown up in a hostile atmosphere of fratricide. The Tea and Rubber plantations had instilled a new spirit to the Jhumias (shifting cultivators) for their livelihood, which attracted investment over the years. Government spent millions of rupees for rehabilitation of the Jhumias through these plantations and associated schemes. But atrocity of militant groups has almost disturbed these endeavours. Besides, the directives of the extremist groups to the tribal to cast vote as per their direction have caused adverse impact on the socioeconomic and political situation in the State.

Though according to 2001 Census Report about 70 % population of Tripura are literate a large section of children have little or no access to schools- mainly due to threat of violence by armed militants. The Tripura State Government admitted (In the winter session of legislative assembly) that 28 primary schools in the rural areas were partly closed while seven others were shut completely.

Most fall under the jurisdiction of Tripura Tribal Areas Autonomous District Council (TTAADC) In other interior areas, the teachers are unwilling to travel due to the looming threat of militant attacks. Their fears are not out of place; as 242 teachers have died in extremist attacks. (Source: The Hindu, Sunday 8th August 2004) Reports also say that in many schools, teachers send proxies to engage the class. In this arrangement, the" proxy teacher" receives a share of the salary according to mutually agreed terms. However, neither the parties involved nor any official records admit the existence of the "proxy teacher" practice.

Incidence of Surrender

Having realized the futility of armed struggle, 39 extremists of ATTF and NLFT (BM) have approached the Police in the last couple of months. On 30-10-04 the Director General of Police, Tripura at the headquarters, Agartala, has accepted their formal surrender. Out of 39 extremists 14 are from ATTF (Group Leader Paban Debbarma) and 25 from NLFT (BM) (Group Leader Jaba Mohan Jamatia). They have also deposited 14 arms (04-AK- Rifles, 05-SLRs, 02-9mm carbines, 02- FM Revolvers, 01- CM Gun, 03Grenades, 21- Magazines and 999- Rounds. Laying down of Arms by NLFT (Nayan basi).

Comparative Statement of the Extremist Related Incidents up to November 2006

Name of incident	*1999*	*2000*	*2001*	*2002*	*2003*	*2004*	*2005*	*2006*
The total no. of extremist related incidents	367	445	85	196	311	200	105	94
The total no. of civilian persons killed by the extremists	227	149	107	135	203	81	30	13
The total no. of persons kidnapped by the extremists	389	476	134	145	194	90	62	38
The total no. of persons released by the extremists	241	202	76	63	72	35	36	31
Killed after kidnapping	28	15	8	15	24	12	0	2
The total no. of kidnapped persons untraced so far	120	254	57	63	124	72	32	6
The Arrest of hardcore extremists	111	157	169	57	133	100	68	70
Brought for interrogation	361	687	449	283	506	265	287	151
The arrest of harbourers/collaborators	498	876	513	258	633	356	276	138
No. of service weapon recovered	20	21	22	64	116	83	67	64
No. of force personnel killed	46	16	31	42	38	41	8	14
No. of extremists killed	19	46	44	31	62	59	22	26
No. of encounters	42	91	59	50	89	84	53	56

In pursuance of the Memorandum of Settlement (MOS) signed between the Government of India, the Government of Tripura and the National Liberation Front of Tripura (Nayan Bashi) on December 17, 2004 at New Delhi, NLFT (NB) has formally laid down arms and returned to the mainstream. 10 senior leaders and 128 cadres along with 14 weapons, 15 magazines and 493 rounds of ammunition have presented themselves before His Excellency, the Governor of Tripura.

The NLFT (NB) leaders and cadres took an oath to abide by the Constitution of India after laying down the arms. His Excellency, the Governor and the other speakers welcomed the NLFT (NB) surrenderees to join the mainstream and be partners in the overall development of the state. Buchuk Borok, SS Senior Vice President of NLFT (NB) sought the help of the people of Tripura in their effort to join the mainstream.

Laying Down of Arms by NLFT & A TTF on September 02, 2005

A significant improvement in the prospect of peace and prosperity in state of Tripura is in the offing as more and more number of underground cadres of National Liberation Front of Tripura (NLFT) and All Tripura Tribal Force (ATTF) defied the dictates of their leaders and surrendered. The yearning for peace among the disillusioned cadres and leaders of these outfits was so strong that in Dhalai District alone, more than 20 cadres of dreaded NLFT - Biswamohan faction returned to the mainstream with a large cache of weapons.

On Sept, 2, 2005 86 cadres (NLFT- Biswamohan faction-56, ATTF-30) formally laid down their arms in a simple ceremony being held in A.D. Nagar Police lines, Agartala. The returnees took an oath of allegiance to the Constitution of India in future and to Eschew violence in all forms.

The state police headed by the Director General of police Sri G.M. Srivastava and Security Force personnel deployed in the counter-insurgency grid in the state identified these developments as 'a combination of twin factors of sustained and concerted anti -militancy operations involving the state and paramilitary force as well as Assam Rifles and the frustration that has set in the ranks and file of the militants due to internal dissension, inability of the militants to extort money at will and a massive disparity in the living standards of the cadres and leaders of the militant groups especially in their camps in Bangladesh.' Return of such a large number of cadres, especially after surrender of 322 cadres in 2004, which had included coming over ground of a majority of NLFT -BM leadership under Mantu Kolai and Kamini Debbarma in May 2004 and an entire faction of NLFT after a 8 month long ceasefire in Dec-2004 was a reflection of the attrition within the groups and a deep sense of frustration.

The MHA (Ministry of Home Affairs) has formulated a new surrender - cum rehabilitation package, which provides for sufficient incentives to the returnees to start a normal life. With all possible help from the state government, successful rehabilitation of these militants would be ensured.

From 1998 to May, 2005 Total (Seven Hundred fifty eight insurgents of NLFT faction and 114 insurgents of ATTF have surrendered. Besides these two major terrorist groups, till recently another faction of NLFT namely Nayanbashi faction was active in some pockets of the state. However, following a tripartite agreement in December, 2004 involving Govt of Tripura, Government of India and representative of the NLFT faction most of the cadres have surrendered but Nayanbashi who didn't agree to the terms of surrender fled away.

Another group namely Borok National Council of Tripura (BNCT) was active in the State till mid 2003. After this their cadre surrendered and the outfit is no longer active.

Surrender Ceremony of 2nd January, 2006

33 Militants of different out fits have decided to abjure violence, bid farewell to arms and finally laid down the arms to Shri G.M. Sribastava, IPS, Director General of Police, Tripura on 2nd January, 2006 at 1200 hrs at Police HQs in a simple ceremony. Many high officials of CPOs and State Police were present to witness the ceremony. Of 33 surrendered militants, 24 are of "National Liberation Front of Twipra" (NLFT) Biswamohan group) while eight are of "All Tiger Force" (ATTF) and one (women cadre) is of" National Liberation Front of Twipra" (NLFT) (Jashua group). She is Smt Sadhana Deb Barma, wife of Jogendra Deb Barma. The ultras deposited AK Rifles- 05 Nos, SLR- 04 Nos. Pistols /Revolvers -04 Nos, Hand Grenade -10

Nos, Rounds-817 Nos, Magazine-27 Nos and Country made gun-03 Nos.

The extremists who surrendered on 02-01-2006 took Oath of Secrecy and solemnly affirmed their allegiance to the Constitution of India and promised to live in the society as peace-loving citizens of India and to a bide by all Rules and Regulations established by laws. The Security Forces are resolved to further intensify their anti-militancy operations to establish an era of peace and ensure development, especially in the interior areas. At the same time return of such a large number of cadres is a strong message to the remaining militants living a difficult jungle life and chasing an inherently flawed dream of a So-called Independent Tripura outside the ambit of the Indian Constitution to follow suit and join the national mainstream.

Observations

It seems that Tripura is curving out a story in the troubled setting of India's Northeast as the comparative figure of violence reveals that the counter-insurgency strategy of Tripura police has left militants in disarray. This achievement is remarkable in view of the fact that as much as 856 kilometers of its boundary of 1,018 kilometers (84.04) percent in total lie along the porous international border with Bangladesh and much of this is inaccessible local forest terrain.

Reasons for surrender: On the basis of the statement submitted by the Extremists and the available documents the following grounds are identified as the major factors of recent occurrence of surrender by the militants:

1. Frustration of extremists lives (No food, no sleep, insecurity of life).

2. Extensive mobilization of forces all over Tripura, movements have been restricted and unable to collect extortion from villagers. Now, about six hundred camps are active within the State. The militants are deterred by the Police Force.

3. *Construction of Border Fencing.* The regular patrolling by the Border Security Force in the Bordering areas are bound to restrict the free movement of militants to the other side after doing operation here,

4. Acute financial crisis.

5. Ill-treatment of bosses / loss of confidence in the leadership.

6. They have failed to believe the ideology of freedom through armed struggle

7. Forceful conversion. Jamatiya Hada (a major group of tribes in Tripura) has started relentless struggle against the forceful conversion and creating social pressure among the members of the community to adhere to its religious practice.

8. Lack of support of local population. It seems that over ground political support base has also become weak.

9. Above all the uncertain and turmoil political situation of Bangladesh are also not congenial for acting as heaven for the insurgents.

Because of the above reasons the extremist cadres became very frustrated and have surrendered. According to them more extremists are likely to surrender in the near future. The surrendered extremists have decided to abide by the Constitution of India and lead a peaceful life.

The ethnic strife began in Tripura with tribal believing that the immigrant people had displaced it from its land and occupation. The situation turned aggravated due to neglect of successive governments and dearth of opportunity in want of establishment of socioeconomic structure to meet the growing needs of the people. Recently, the surrendered Militants have expressed their resentment against State Administration for failure of proper implementation of rehabilitation scheme ensured in the Memorandum of Settlement. On 22nd January, 2007 the leaders of the surrendered militants met the Chief Secretary of Tripura and complained that the package scheme of Rs 55 crores has not been introduced. The Chief Secretary has ensured them that very soon it will be carried out. (Source: *Dainik Sambad,* the Bengali Daily in the State, 25th January, 2007)

The State Administration, led by the Chief Minister, Manik Sarkar, has taken several steps to empower the local bodies so that the benefits of development reach every village, however remote. The recommendation of Dinesh Singh Committee is being implemented.

The youth should rethink before joining hands with the militants. Restoration of alienated tribal lands is being undertaken and provisions relating to these have been made stricter. The cut-off date of 25th March, 1971 for identification and pushback of foreigners is also being enforced. The State Government has taken up broadcasting programming in local languages on Radio & TV and the opening of a channel of All India Radio in Kokborak, the main tribal language in the State. Kokborok is also taught as a language in the tribal areas at the school level. In addition, different policies have been taken and are under consideration to create more economic and employment opportunities for the tribal youth. These are in the form of opening of international border for trade and transit, permitting forest based development through viable schemes of small scale rubber and tea plantations and support for gas based industries in the state and expeditious implementation of the Prime Minister's development package for the North-East. Three vocational Training Centre are fully working (Two in South District and One in North District) to give vocational training to the surrendered extremists of the State.

The attempts to enable the living standards of the tribal population to be improved are to go hand in hand with the need to lessen the extremist elements. This is being attempted through steps targeted at bringing them back to the mainstream of democratic policy. State Government had appealed several times to the misguided elements to give up the path of violence and join the mainstream. In response to the calls, several listed extremists submitted offers of unconditional or conditional surrender. Time and again the Chief Minister of Tripura brought into notice the issue of shelter of different extremist Groups in our neighbouring country Bangladesh identifying the location of sixteen camps there. So the responsibilities lie with the Ministry of External Affairs as well as home Affairs to deal with the situation seriously which will definitely contribute in promoting the peace and tranquility in Northeast in general and Tripura in particular.

14

Genesis of Ethnic Conflict: A Study on Recent Ethnic Conflict and Internal Displacement of Population in the District of Karbi Anglong

Mousumi Choudhury

Ethnic conflict is a term quite familiar in relation to the post-colonial Northeast and it deeply influences the complex socio-political pattern of the society. In ethnic conflicts, ethnic identities constitute the principal basis of political contestation. Though such conflicts are understood in terms of conflicts among ethnic groups they do also involve conflict at the individual and intra-group levels. Sometimes ethnic cleavages co-exist with other important cleavages which forms the structure for political contestation, notably clan, religion race and regionalism. Ethnic conflict usually involves the mobilization of one or more of these cleavages depending on the situations and the issues of contestations. So ethnic conflict is fluid and situational. The class dimension of ethnicity is visible in the intra-group level where as an ideological-political counter point to the concept of class, ethnicity has emerged as the hub of the destruction of the economic system, of social set up and political formations. Sometimes ethnicity has been posited against abuse of state power and other types of oppressions. Being an undefined concept, ethnicity has also had a visceral gut-quality based on raw emotion rather than deliberate cogitation. (Das 2005: 4) This paper attempts to study the genesis of ethnic conflict in the context of Karbi Anglong District, various issues behind the internal strife and rivalry relating to some social and political issues culminating in frequent conflicts and focus would be on magnitude of displacement of population resultant from the recent conflict. This paper is based on field work, data collected from various

Government records and interactions with various persons related to relief work.

The district of Karbi Anglong was formed in 1976. Prior to that the present Karbi Anglong and North Cachar hill districts were two subdivisions, namely, Mikir Hills and North Cachar Hills, inaugurated on November 17, 1951 and was created by carving out certain portions of the erstwhile Nagaon and Sibsagar Districts and the United Khasi and Jaintia Hills Districts and the whole of the North Cachar subdivision of Cachar District. On Feb 2, 1970 North Cachar, the sub-division of United Mikir Hills and North Cachar Hill Districts were declared as a separate districts while the remaining portion, that is, Mikir Hills subdivision was constituted into Mikir Hills district which was again rechristened as Karbi Anglong vide Government Notification No.TAD/ R/ 115 /74/47 dt.14.10.76. Karbi Anglong consists of two hilly lobes of unequal size and they genetically belong to the Shillong plateau. The District has three civil subdivisions, Diphu, Hamren and Bokajan. There are four revenue circles and ten Development Blocks in the District. As per 1971 Census, Karbi Anglong had a total population of 379310 which had risen to 813311 by 2001 census. Of these, 7, 21, 381 were situated in the rural areas. The total S.T population in the district is 452, 963 and the percentage of literacy which was 45.57 per cent rose to 58.83 per cent by the turn of the 2001 census. (Census of India, 2001) In the absence of any remarkable subsidiary means of subsistence in the rural sector most of the people survive on shifting cultivation.

In the post-colonial era, when the civil society is supposed to be more responsive than before, when technological innovations and fast-paced development makes life different, the jagged edges of violence, the moment of rupture caused by ethnic violence of magnitude, still find a space within it and tarnish our civilization. Post-colonial Assam in general and the district of Karb Anglong in particular is not an exception to this. Modern civilization has been equated with a state of non-violence where mature adult human beings negotiate with one another and determine their rights and duties through rational argument. Elias' account of the civilizing process fits well with this view. Just as the civilizing progresses, Elias has suggested, the necessity to control impulses is increasingly transformed from an exterior prohibition imposed often by an external force to an almost unconscious self-restraint. However, the peculiar stability of the application of psychological self-restraint which emerges as a decisive trait built into the habitués of every civilized human being, stands in the closest relationship to the monopolization of physical force and the growing ability of the central organs of society. (Pandey 2001: 54)

To understand the gravity of the problem in the present Karbi Anglong district, one needs to trace back to history to discover the roots of the troubles and at the same time it is imperative to study society and polity formation, because a society when gripped by overwhelming crisis does not act in a sudden thrust but its action is a gradual manifestation of the rift interwoven in the system. If one turns the pages of history, one would confront with the fact that the hill districts of Assam were placed under the category of either excluded or partially excluded territory. The Hill areas of Northeast were uniformly administered until 1937 as a relatively backward tract, exclusively under the Chief Commissioner. However, in April 1937, there was a bifurcation in the administrative pattern .The Lusai hills, the Naga hills, North Cachar hills and North East Frontier tract were called excluded areas, excluded from ministerial jurisdiction. The Garo hills, British portion of the Kashi and and Jaintia hills and Mikir hills were partially excluded areas. The Excluded areas were guarded by the inner Line which restricted the entry of outsiders without permit. The hill districts thus developed a special kind of identity and this has remained as a crucial factor for its political development. Thus the hill areas of North East were not completely integrated with the political and economic system of the British Regime. The relative isolation from the main stream society paved the way for insurgency and unrest creating a volatile situation for which the common men are paying the prices.

The nature of the problem in Karbi Anglong cannot be constructed with the help of a single factor. Several factors would contribute significantly to understand the complex pattern of problems as it persists in the district today. The multi-ethnic society, though claimed to be peaceful at a certain point of time, is facing severe combination due to certain factors like cultural revivalism, territorial hegemony, havocs of unemployment, sluggish economic development and the like. The demand for Autonomous state has generated a number of armed groups competing with each other for supremacy and protection of culture and identity due to perceived threat from other communities. Such demand for exclusive homeland in a demographically mixed situation has produced similar conflicts with the attendant risk of ethnic violence and internal displacement of population. Even during the Colonial period, anticipations were expressed about the acknowledgement of the right of the aborigines to follow the traditional pursuit like the practice of shifting cultivation without making any provision to the needs of the general community. G. S. Ghurye in his "The Aborigines–so called and their future" (1943) wrote that the commissioners had not considered the impact on non-aborigines living in those areas and much less they gave their thought to the proportions of such people in various areas, unless we discover it in the distinction of the two categories of excluded and partially excluded areas made by them. The situation is further complicated over the issue of a Greater Nagaland for the Naga people and the Dimaraji for the Dimasas, which coincide with the competing legitimacy of the Karbis for territorial integrity of their homelands. In this connection, it is to be mentioned that the NSCM (I-M) has claimed almost half of Karbi Anglong district and almost the whole of North Cachar Hills district in its proposed Nagalim. Although the Nagas have not seriously claimed Diphu and Bokajan subdivisions, they are purchasing lands in Karbi Anglong district adjacent to Nagaland and it is likely that sooner or later they may occupy the wet cultivable land acquired by them in their proposed Nagalim. The Dimasas again demand the Dhansiri area in Eastern Karbi Anglong into its proposed Dimaraji, where the designated camp of the DHD has been set up with the signing of Ceasefire Agreement with the government of India since July 2003. The joint Coordination committee, a conglomerate of 25 civil organizations of the Karbis, ascribed the recent ethnic violence in the designated camp and submitted memorandum to the government for removal of the same.

According to one report the loss of land by tribals to non-tribals was the source of ethnic conflicts, rise of insurgent groups, counter-insurgency operations and violation of human rights (MASS). Due to the administration's patronage to convert areas under shifting cultivation to settled ones, lots of economic opportunities come to the new immigrants. Since the shifting cultivators are not well equipped to convert themselves into settled cultivators overnight, the immigrants due to their advantageous position of possessing cash, agricultural implements and with prior experience get a hold over the land very easily. Thus they integrate into the economy of the region in informal ways and acquire *de facto* property rights, which are likely to become the *de jure* rights in the future. In course of time, they demand the formal land title of those lands and can exert considerable influence due to their economic and political influence in the district. In recent times, several incidents of violence and even loss of lives took place due to this tribal-non-tribal dichotomy.

The economic backwardness of the district and the continuation of the feudal kind of society with very little of capital formation and commodity production and little exposure to the developed world, aggravates the situation. The outsiders do not want to invest capital due to threat perception and high extortion demand by the insurgents. This paves way for slow economic development. The political upgradation of the district from Karbi Anglong District Council to Karbi Anglong Autonomous Council on April 1, 1995, simply expanded the scope of executive and legislative functions. It does not provide job opportunities to the youths. The misled youths of the district take recourse to armed insurgency out of frustration and perverted patriotism adds more motivation to them. Subsequently insurgency becomes a cottage industry in such areas which provides adequate opportunities to the young generations to make a quick buck.

The failure of Constitutional provisions guaranteed to the ethnic minorities and the subsequent suppression by the imposition of various draconian acts by the government further escalates the situation. However, militarism remains the greatest impediment in fostering meaningful ties between different ethnic groups in Karbi Anglong. To use military force as a substitute for political settlement of concerns of civil society is a detrimental factor. The Armed Forces (Special Powers) Act 1958 as amended in 1972, which confers blanket powers to the various armed forces, who in order to crush the armed movement, indulge in oppression and repression over the civilian population. Mass raids on villages are carried out on the basis of mere suspicion that they may be harbouring armed insurgents without any hard actionable intelligence. Many innocent civilians have lost their lives in the arms of the forces under the pretext of interrogation. Thus instead of quelling the situation, the forces add more fuel for continuing armed struggle in Karbi Anglong district.

At present frequent ethnic conflicts rock the hill district of Karbi Anglong. In 2004 an ethnic conflict between the Kukis and Karbis took away hundreds of lives and thousands were forced to flee to the neighbouring states. Many had to languish in relief camps in a deplorable condition. Rehabilitation did not come at the time of need. Some of the poorest of the poor were not fortunate enough to avail themselves of the opportunities provided by the Government. The ethnic genesis of Karbi-Kuki clashes lies in economic and ethnic divide. In the 1960s and 70s, the Kukis migrated from Manipur to the Karbi Anglong district and settled in upper reaches of Singhasan hills and Khonbamon hills. They cultivates ginger and earned about Rs. 15 crore annually (*The Assam Tribune,* 10 Dec 2005) and the Karbis in the lower reaches collected commission of Rs. 5000 per truck load of ginger. The UPDS resented this and claimed that the Kukis are

Sl.No.	*Location of Relief Camp*	*Male*	*Female*	*Total*
1	Manja Cultural Bhavan	190	173	363
2	Manja Tinali L.P.School	13	10	23
3	Manja Mahila Samiti	102	116	218
4	Longnit Soil Conservation	148	146	294
5	Longnit Residental Camp	134	131	265
6	Borjan Community Hall	273	222	495
7	Borjan L.PSchool	183	169	352
8	Kindergarten English School	43	48	91
9	BaghmariKhongsai Community Hall, Diphu.	189	219	408
10	Paithe Community Hall, Diphu	54	44	98
11	Diphu community Hall	58	60	118
	TOTAL	1387	133338	2728

destroying the natural forests and that a part of the money from ginger cultivation went to Kuki Revolutionary army. The Kukis in order to defend themselves invited the Kuki Revolutionary Army from Manipur. This group had the backing of NSCM (I-M) of Dimapur. So the Kukis had to pay double taxation. The displaced population had to languish in several relief camps in Karbi Anglong district. The camp wise male and female breakup of Displaced persons during Kuki-Karbi ethnic clash can be traced from the following table: (Source: Deputy Commissioner's Office, Karbi Anglng)

The district of Karbi Anglong was once again rocked by ethnic violence on Sept 26, 2005. This time, violence occurred between the United Progressive Democratic Solidarity (UPDS), a militant organization of the Karbis and the Dima Halam Dougah, that of the Dimasas and both the organizations were under ceasefire agreement with the Government of India since 2002 and 2003 respectively. But this violence cannot be claimed as ethnic because the civil society of both the communities was not involved in the conflict. The immediate cause of the cauldron was the killing of three Dimasa auto drivers by unidentified miscreants and a spate of retaliatory killings followed. A three month baby was also not spared. People were robbed off their rationality and humanity just because the other side belonged to the rival community. As on 9 Nov 2005, 90 persons have been killed. The most gruesome of the killings occurred on 17 October 2005 when 34 Karbis were hacked to death and five were burnt alive at Churchim in West Karbi Anglong district. As on 30 October 2005 the number of internally displaced persons rose to 44,016 in Karbi Anglong, NC hills and Nagoan districts. Out of 57 relief camps set up in various places of Karbi Anglong district, 41 were set up in Diphu, 3 in Bokajan and 13 in Hamren. Six camps were set up in NC hills district: Dibarai, Diyungmukh, Maibang, Langting, Hatikhali, Manderdisa. As on 20 December 2005, the number of inmates in various relief camps rose to 1772. In the Karbi Anglong district, out of 32,871 displaced persons, 25,602 were Karbis, 5600 were Dimasas and 1669 were from other communities. The Director of the Asian Center of Human rights (ACHR), Mr. Subhas Chakma, undertook an on-the-spot field visit in Karbi Anglong District and reported the involvement of armed opposition groups intensifying such heinous killings. The ACHR firmly pointed out that repeated denials and hacking to death, instead of using fire arms to avoid violations of Ceasefire Ground Rules with the Government of India and the Government of Assam, do not exonerate the DHD and the UPDS from the charges of involvement in the killings. (Internet: Lesson not learnt by Assam)

The recent ethnic crisis in Karbi Anglong, as we are already aware, forced the civilian population to languish in relief camps in a most wretched condition. A survey of some of the relief camps and from various Government documents, the following facts are exposed.

A. *Over-crowded camps:* The displaced persons have to live in a most wretched condition. The Camps are extremely over-crowded and most inmates had to sleep in the open. When it rains, the conditions of the inmates become deplorable. There is no privacy for the women.

B. *Lack of adequate food and utensils:* The inmates are provided rice, dal, chirra, salt. There is no provision for any cash to procure vegetables, or other requisite materials. There was adequate shortage of firewood. In some of the camps the inmates could not eat for few days due to lack of firewood. With the initiative of some of the NGOs firewood was provided to the inmates.

C. *Lack of appropriate clothing:* The inmates have insufficient clothes on their bodies especially the minors and the women. Many children suffer extreme cold and some of them died due to severe cold .The State Government has provided only 6,964 blankets for 44,016 internally displaced persons. Women are unwilling to go out due to insufficient clothes over their bodies. The State Government provided only 5000 dhoti, pajamas for 13503 adult males, 4999 shawls for 12,452 adult women and 12,080 frocks, pant and shirts for 17,971 boys and girls. Many displaced persons did not have clothes to change their dress and had to lead an unhygienic life.

D. *Inadequate medical facilities:* There is lack of medical facilities. Diseases such as malaria, jaundice, dysentery, diarrhoea and influenza often pose serious threat. The Joint Director, Health informed the press that 14,327 inmates in the relief camps suffered from various ailments, 119 pregnant women, children and elderly suffer the highest health risk. An estimated 1,170 families have not been provided mosquito nets as on 3 Nov 2005. There are 6,349 families but the Government has provided mosquito nets to only 5,179 families. Lack of mosquito nets creates severe problem in almost all the camps. A number of cases of death are also reported from various camps.

E. *Closure of educational institutions:* There is total collapse of educational institutions in the district. All the schools and colleges remain closed. Most of the educational institutions have been converted into relief camps. Out of 53 camps in Karbi Anglong District, 32 are schools. The only Government colleges of the district remained closed for months together as about 2000 refugees were accommodated in the college. There was little scope for the encamped children. Hundreds of children are just whiling away their time for the lack of educational facilities during their encampment.

F. *Security question:* The inmates suffered from a sense of insecurity both inside and outside the camp. The trauma of witnessing the brutal killing and physical torture of their near and dear ones haunt them deeply. Within the camp, they feel insecure on account of their fellow campers and outside the camp they were at risk of being targets of further violence.

Considering the magnitude of displacement in the Hill district of Karbi Anglong, the Government, which is generally blind to such misery, should awake to the fact and frame a national policy on displacement so that problems related to displacement can be solved at the behest of the displaced. The following are some of the elements of such a policy.

- Recognizing that the application of appropriate confidence building measures, consistent with national security needs, the government should employ these measures in a spirit of mutual confidence and good faith. This is essential to reduce the likelihood of conflicts and enhance the prospects of peaceful settlement of disputes. The confidence building measures may also encompass training for the armed force personnel on how to deal with the conflict situation.

- The Legislature should come out with a white paper regarding the constitutional safeguards of the Sixth Schedule tribes as given in the constitution. The Armed Forces (Special Powers) Act 1958 as amended in 1972, should be reviewed, taking into consideration the complex situation prevailing in the region.
- To curb terrorism in Northeast India in general and the district of Karbi Anglong in particular, rapid economic reforms which can be achieved through rapid industrialization need to be initiated. This should happen by utilizing the natural resources available in the region without hampering the culture and tradition of the indigenous people.
- Human rights, peace and development are interdependent and interrelated, and the fostering of the one promotes the enhancement of the other. The absence of peace, or the achievement of development by a people, can never exempt a state from its obligation to ensure respect for human rights of the nationals and of the persons residing in its territory.
- The basic issues behind the conflict should be analysed and effective policy should be framed to resolve the misunderstanding between different tribes and communities.
- Karbi Anglong Autonomous Council must devote itself to regain the disordered social fabrication of the land by putting its best effort to build the basic infrastructure of the district. An Economic and Social renaissance would obviously boost the lost morale of the people.
- With the privatization of clan land, there emerged a poorer group of people eking out a living by working as agricultural workers or share croppers or by whatever other means possible. Most of them are local tribals, who, despite the protection given to them as members of scheduled tribes, lack social and political resources to benefit from privatization

of clan lands or to hold on to lands allocated to them. A large number of Denizens – Nepalis, Bharis and Bangladeshis – are also the claimants of these lands. Taking into consideration the fact that a tribal land owner finds it safer to informally lease out his land to a Denizen, land should be regulated and the defective revenue system of the Government should be regulated as well.

- An intra-group rivalry arising out of trading interest and resource sharing is a factor aggravating the situation. So this kind of situation should be eliminated with rational consensus and understanding.
- The ceasefire Ground rules should be implemented in letter and spirit. The loopholes included in the Ground rule should be plugged at the earliest. Measures should be taken to shun violence and to bring the ultras into the political main stream.
- Media should play a responsible role in mobilizing the masses for communal harmony. It should uphold journalistic ethics and utmost care to be taken so that publication of any news may not incite the masses.
- The Centre should not be a silent bystander any more. The leaders, politicians, other groups of people should be invited to the peace table and discussion should take place at the earliest so that another round of genocide can be averted.
- In a multi-ethnic society, there is nothing as grim as the wall of suspicion and hatred, which erupt in violence from time to time. Bitterness and suspicion exact a high toll on economic growth. Strikes and bandhs badly hit the Government, business and market. Due to high rate of extortion and threat the outsiders do not want to invest in the region. Obviously, the development scenario is sluggish.
- Planners and policy makers at the Central, state and regional level need to involve leaders of village and district rural groups in developing economic plans so that these reflect what people need and want and not what a handful of politicians and bureaucrats seek.

Conclusion

It is to be pointed out that the study mentioned above is relevant not only to those studying displacement but also to the state, international agencies and NGOs that are engaged in relief. The whole gamut of the problem emanates from a political understanding and the overall political solution and political goodwill are required in tackling the problem. In that direction, all the political parties should sit together and pursue a definite plan and program for containing the problem. The Government should take up conflict management programmes to resolve disputes and initiate dialogue where the victims should be involved and their experience counted. Awareness and sensibility of the society coupled with a transparent administration is the way to viable and sustainable solution of the conflict situation in the district.

References

Baruah, Sanjib, *Citizens and Denizens: Ethnicity, Homelands and the Crisis of Displacement in North East India.*

Chatterjee, Partha and Pradip Jeghanathan (2003) *Community, Gender and Violence: Subaltern Studies*, Permanent Black and Ravi Dayal Publisher, New Delhi.

Das, Arvind N. (2005) *India Invented*, Monohar, New Delhi.

Development Scenario of Karbi Anglong District, (2001) Directorate of Economics and Statistics, Assam, Dispur, Guwahati.

Gynendra, Pandey, (2001) *Remembering Partition*, Cambridge University Press, London.

Human Rights, (2001) *Non-violence and Conflict Resolution,* Indian Institute of Human Rights, New Delhi.

Internet (Lesson not Learnt by Assam)

Kumar, B.B. (1996) *Reorganization of North East India: Facts and Documents*, Omsons, New Delhi.

Misra, Udayan (1991) *Nation Building and Development in Northeast India*, Purbanchal Prakashan, New Delhi.

Nirmal, Nibedan (1981) *North East and Ethnic Explosion*, Lancers Publishers, New Delhi.

Pakem, B. (1989) *Insurgency in Northeast India*, Omson Publication, New Delhi.

Ratan, T. (2004) *Encyclopedia of North East India*, Vol.1, New Delhi.

Record, Deputy Commissioner's Office, Diphu, KarbiAnglong.

Singh, Sehgal B.P. (1996) *Human Rights in India – Problems and Prospects*, Deep & Deep Publications, New Delhi.

The Assam Tribune, 10 December 2005.

The Hills Times, October 5, 2005.

15

Development-Induced Displacement, Deprivation and Rehabilitation in Assam: A Critique of NPRR 2003

Gita Bharali

Development-induced displacement, resettlement and rehabilitation are controversial issues today. The displaced persons face many difficulties in adjusting their lives to a completely new environment. A large number of development projects such as dams, factories, mines etc., have been initiated and implemented in the last five and a half decades resulting in eviction of 50 to 60 million people, out of whom 40 per cent are tribals. Only about 33 per cent have had some sort of resettlement, the quality of which is far from satisfactory. The present paper will discuss the extent of land acquisition, displacement and deprivation caused by development projects in Assam and also will discuss the rehabilitation scenario in the State and make a critique of the rehabilitation policy from that point of view. It is based on a study being done by the North Eastern Social Research Center.

I. Details about NESRC Study

The main objective of the NESRC study was to establish a reliable data base on the extent of land acquisition, numbers of the displaced (DPs) or deprived of livelihood without physical relocation (PAPs) and the impacts on the people of such development projects. We have made the same initiatives in some other States. For example, such studies have been completed for 1951-1995 in Orissa, Jharkhand, Andhra Pradesh, Goa and Kerala, for 1947-2000 in West Bengal and Assam and are in progress in Gujarat and Maharashtra.

Like in the other States, in Assam also we did the study in three phases. The first step was to study the gazette notifications under the

LAQ 1947-2000 to get data on the total private land acquired through them. We classified the land thus acquired by year and type of projects. We have collected data from 13,000 such gazettes notifications. But gazettes give us only the records of private land acquired and give nothing on the people affected. That required another study to get land other than private and the number of DPs/PAPs of all the projects. In Phase 2, therefore, we studied the land records kept in the Deputy Commissioners' offices in the district land records rooms, visited some project sites to talk to their public relations officers and supplemented the information thus got, by looking at research done by others. At this stage we realised the paucity of research on this issue in the Northeast in general and in Assam in particular. We found some articles such as a collection of papers (Thomas 2002), some efforts at understanding the totality (Hussain 2006) and a few case studies (Nag 2002; Hussain 2006) but very little else unlike in AP, Orissa and Jharkhand, where research helped us to rectify the inadequate official database which is usually an underestimate.

To get over this constraint, we talked to knowledgeable persons in the locality in order to get an idea of the situation. Some of them are relatively old persons who had witnessed or had themselves experienced displacement or deprivation or were retired project or government officials or present and past workers of voluntary agencies who had inside knowledge of the situation. They could thus be insiders with information on the situation but remain outsiders without the pressure under which serving project staff work or the emotional component of being DPs/PAPs. That gave the data an objective content and made it possible for us to discuss the issue in depth with them. It was supplemented by the documentation preserved by others and in the library of North Eastern Social Research Centre, mostly from newspaper cuttings and articles written by scholars.

Phase Three was primary data based on interviews with the DPs/PAPs of a representative set of projects. Phases One and Two gave us quantitative data on the extent of land used and the number of DPs/PAPs. Phase Three was qualitative data on its impact on the DPs/PAPs. During the interviews, we were also able to get data on resettlement and compensation. We chose 12 projects according to their category, age and district. Phases One and Two were academic by their very nature. Data were collected from the Gazettes and the files, and that involved interaction mainly with the government officials. Phase Three required interaction with the DPs/PAPs.

We divided the projects into 17 categories viz., water resource, industry, mines, non-hydel power, defense and security, environment protection, transport and communications, human resource development, refugee resettlement, farms and fisheries, urban-development, housing, social welfare, tourism, health, education, administration and others (not known).

II. Major Findings of the Study

In our study, we have established a data base on the extent of land acquired and number of DPs and PAPs, and the impacts of such development projects. In this paper we will discuss first the extent of land used for all the development projects and the numbers of DPs and PAPs. We will not go into the details of the impacts.

A. *Extent of Land Acquisition*

The type of land acquired for development projects and the people deprived of their livelihood have implications for compensation and rehabilitation. For example, most land acquired in the Northeast is Common Property Resources (CPRs) while the Land Acquisition Act of 1894 (LAQ) accepts only individual ownership. Most displaced persons are tribals. These factors have implications for compensation and rehabilitation. We shall now look at the extent of land used and the people displaced and deprived of their livelihood. So, we have look at the official data on land acquisition and use for schemes under planned development and try to understand the legal status of various types of land used.

Table 1 shows that 3,91,772.9 acres have been acquired for development projects through Gazette notifications, 28.88 per cent of it in 1971-80 followed by 25.92 per cent in 1961-70. Of this total, 55.57 per cent are for projects meant for the administration, followed by 11.74 per cent for environment protection. The notifications refer only to private land and much more common land has been used and we got that information from other sources.

Table 1: Total Land Acquired for Different Projects under Gazettes

District	*1947-50*	*1951-60*	*1961-70*	*1971-80*	*1981-90*	*1991-00*	*NA*	*Total*
Water resources	104.21	716.44	2393.34	6814.86	5723.6	7722.19	3858.73	27333.37
Industry	105.15	2313.02	1284.32	904.11	506.06	1487.02	0	6316.57
Mines		3.47	11.15			0.9	2.91	18.43
Non- hydel power	0	8.89	583.89	93.92	234.2	2.16	38.97	962.03
Defence and security	6.69	790.63	5135.69	2009.37	678.56	289.06	181.4	9091.36
Environment and protection	240.34	5972.5	15989.8	13603.2	5204.02	2963.11	2031.28	46004.2
Transport and communication	3614.11	6025.07	8561.86	2760.84	4839.05	2344.92	471.32	28617.17
Human resource development	55.01	225.76	105.78	25.84	32.32	53.7	24.18	522.59
Refugee resettlement	3305.24	12068.82	531.73	379.81	2.15	4.76	5.39	16297.9
Farnms and fisheries	284.16	593.44	251.37	58.76	17.49	7.48	171.24	1383.94
Urban development	593.26	478.16	92.62	19.85	3.53	5.91	0	1193.33
Housing	1113.07	323.42	278.03	336.42	345.85	310.02	30.91	2737.72
Social welfare	48.86	5833.02	8875.6	2442.52	32.48	0.36	21.46	17254.3
Tourism		2.22	0.53				5.14	7.89
Heath	76.75	327.27	269.34	68.67	108.95	37.53	0	888.51
Education	301.89	695.77	1307.08	19.12	150.45	29.14	1125.96	3629.41
Administration	834.65	40285.72	54428.11	83026.75	40849.61	6094.03	43.79	225562.66
Others	4.94	1882.47	1443.42	574.97	45.32		0.39	3951.51
Total	10688.33	78546.09	101543.7	113139	58773.64	21352.29	8013.07	391772.9

Table 2 shows that the total thus comes to more than 14 lakhs

Category	Private	%	CPRs	%	NA	%	Total
Water resource	41835.34	21.87%	84938.42	44.4%	64534.39	33.79%	191304.15
Industry	11317.31	36.03	20092.88	63.97	00		31410.19
Mines	105.47	0.37	7894.53	28.05	20145	71.58	28215
Non-hydro	2187.17	19.94	8781.29	80.06	00	00	10968.46
Defence/Security	9483.03	35.91	1988.04	7.52	14933.44	56.56	26404.51
Environment protection	46002.2	55.91	36279.82	44.09	0	0	82284.02
Transport-Communication	7054.36	5%	11999.41	0.26%	96459.05	95%	115512.82
Farms/ Fisheries	1383.94	1%	227269.24	95%	10597.3	4%	239250.48
Refugees	16297	4.66	333703	95.34	0	0	350000
Social Welfare	17254.3	99.75	42.44	0.25	0	0	17296.74
HRD	647.77	35.68	1167.89	64.32	0	0	1815.66
Urban	1193.33	100.00	0	0	0	0	1193.33
Education	2464	10.66	500	2.16	20656	89.34	23120
Health	3400	56.12	2658	43.88	0	0	6058
Administration	225562.66	83.89	43307.96	16.11			268870.62
Others	7048.79	100.00	0	0	0	0	7048.79
Total	**393236.7**	**28.06**	**780622.9**	**55.71**	**227325.2**	**16.23**	**1401184.80**

We are also aware that Table 2 too is an underestimate made according to our principle of taking a conservative view of the matter. By this count, the total land used for development projects in Assam during 1947-2000 works out to 14,01,184.8 acres which is more than 8 per cent of the total geographical area of the State. In this total 55.71 per cent are CPRs and we do not know the category of 16.23 per cent. Only 28.06 per cent is private, which the State takes into consideration for compensation. Much of the CPRs are tribal land but is not recognized as such.

B. *Extent of Displacement and Deprivation*

From the extent of land acquisition, we can see the extent of deprivation and displacement of people by the development projects. We give at first the total number of persons affected by the projects. We have arrived at a total of 3,07,024 displaced and 16,02,341 persons affected otherwise without being displaced. Thus, the number of DPs/PAPs comes to 19,09,368. While giving this total, one cannot ignore certain discrepancies. The first of them is in the totals themselves. We know that much of the land is CPRs for which records are scanty. The number displaced by them is rarely given in official records. So, we tried to make an assessment through extrapolation but we know it remains an underestimate.

The second discrepancy is in the proportion of DPs/PAPs. The number of DPs should be higher than what we got. For example, in other States, around 60 per cent of the persons affected are DPs. In general there is one PAP for two DPs. Their proportion in Assam is a little over 50 per cent of the total. The reason may be that rehabilitation is weak in the State and because of it proper records are not kept.

We tried to rectify the proportion in some cases through studies done by scholars or by getting data from knowledgeable persons. For example, though official files referred to all the DPs/PAPs of IIT Guwahati as PAPs, research data showed that all or most of them are DPs. We modified our database accordingly. In some other cases we depended on knowledgeable persons. But neither source was available in most cases and we had to depend on official data and extrapolation. Thus, both the total and the number of DPs/PAPs are underestimates but we have kept to it according to our principle of making a conservative estimate.

Also the proportion of various categories is different in Assam from that of other States. For example, in Orissa around 60 per cent of the DPs/PAPs are of water resources while in Assam they are a little over 20 per cent. In most States that is followed by industry. The difference in Assam is also indicative of the type of investment in development. In Assam a big component has gone to transport, administration and defense and another big section in refugee rehabilitation. It is indicative of the type of its economy.

Table 3: Conservative Estimates of DPs/PAPs by Category (% to total)

Category	*DPs*	*%*	*PAPs*	*%*	*Total*	*Category %*
Water Resources	49977	11.14	398835	88.86	448812	23.51
Industry	14220	24.63	43512	75.37	57732	3.02
Mines	13680	33.20	27520	66.80	41200	2.16
Non-Hydel Power	1371	18.53	6029	81.47	7400	0.39
Defence and Security	3337	6.62	47083	93.38	50420	2.64
Environment Protection	51016	19.22	214393	80.78	265409	13.90
Transport-Communications	73232	43.38	95573	56.62	168805	8.84
Refugee Resettlement	10500	3.70	273000	96.3	283500	14.85
Farms and Fisheries	10671	9.37	103218	90.63	113889	5.96
Education	3097	3.60	82840	96.40	85937	4.50
Health	1008	4.33	22284	95.67	23292	1.22
Administration	64224	19.89	258679	80.11	322906	16.91
Social Welfare	6212	24.60	19041	75.4	25253	1.32
H R Development	4288	85.19	745	14.81	5033	0.26
Urban Development	191	15.39	1050	84.61	1241	0.06
Housing, Tourism etc.	0	0	18045	100.00	18045	0.95
Total	*307024*	*16.08*	*1602341*	*83.92*	*1909368*	*100*

C. *Type of DPs/PAPs*

As mentioned above we have not got the type of people affected by all the projects. In fact, information on this component is extremely scanty. Only for a few projects we have got the data. The main reason for this is what looks like the poor rehabilitation record of Assam. Rehabilitation requires an accurate record of the number of DPs and the type of persons. In the absence of rehabilitation, one does not need such a record. The second main reason seems to be the type of land. Around 80 per cent of the land used by development projects is CPRs. It is State property according to the present land laws. In Assam the State does not see any need to keep accurate records of land transfer for other purposes though it is an economic commodity. Much worse is the situation of the DPs and PAPs who are not an economic commodity and are not even counted in many cases.

Table 4: Conservative Estimates of Type of DPs/PAPs

Category	Tribals	%	Others	%	NA	%	Total
Water Resources	157786	35.16	271635	60.52	19391	4.32	448812
Industry	31661	54.84	23118	40.04	2963	5.12	57732
Mines	0	0	0	0	41200	100.00	41200
Non-Hydel Power	1696	22.92	311	4.20	5393	72.88	7400
Defence and Security	2962	5.87	29507	58.52	17951	35.60	50420
Environment Prot	9948	3.75	9874	3.72	245557	92.53	265409
Transport & Comm	554	0.33	4215	2.50	164036	97.17	168805
Refugee Resettlement	53865	19.00	192780	68.00	36855	13.00	283500
Farms and Fisheries	40000	35.12	60000	52.68	13889	12.20	113889
Education	30	0.03	60	0.07	85847	99.90	85937
Health	0	0	0	0	23292	100.00	23292
Administration	124926	38.69	16234	5.03	181746	56.28	322906
Social Welfare	0	0	0	0	25253	100.00	25253
H R Development	875	17.39	2775	55.14	1383	27.48	5033
Urban Development	0		0		1241	100.00	1241
Housing, Tourism etc.	0		0		18045	100.00	18045
Total	*416321*	*21.80*	*609015*	*31.90*	*884032*	*46.30*	*1909368*

Its net result is that the caste-tribe of a very big proportion of the DPs/PAPs is not known. The number that is known reflects the difference between the legal and social reality of land ownership. We know that much of the land used is tribal and other CPRs. That is reflected in the type of DPs/PAPs. Among those whose caste-tribe is known, more than 40 per cent are tribals who are only 12.9 per cent of the State's population. If we take the total number, they are around 28 per cent of the DPs/PAPs. There are many indications that most of those whose caste-tribe is not known are tribals, except in transport where most tend to be middle caste landowners. We believe that if their caste-tribe is identified, over 50 per cent of them will be tribals.

One should add that a large number of other DPs/PAPs are from among the plantation labourers who are tribals in their State of origin but are not recognised as such in Assam. If their number were to be added, the tribal proportion would go beyond 60 per cent. Another big proportion is of Dalits who are a little over 6 per cent of the State's population and of the OBCs. However, in the absence of definite indications, we remain at the data that could be got through the official records and extrapolation and stick to what is given in them.

Rehabilitation in Assam

In spite of the large number of affected persons by development projects in Assam, it does not have a rehabilitation policy. If it is private land, the State pays compensation to their original owners but does not resettle the displaced. We are aware of only a few cases like Cachar Paper Mill where the DPs were resettled but these projects too have not created conditions required for their rehabilitation. *Patta* holders get compensation but those who depend on the CPRs are ignored and are not even counted among the DPs/PAPs because the main requirement for being eligible for compensation is a written document of individual ownership which they lack. Since they cannot produce legal evidence of land ownership, they are excluded from the compensation package.

Government officials kept telling us that they pay a handsome amount as compensation to the people affected by the projects and they consider it rehabilitation. It is clear from studies in other States that compensation is inadequate to help the DPs/PAPs to begin a new life after they lose their livelihood to the project. On the other side, some irrigation officials told us off record that the project cannot be viable if a bigger amount than what they give is paid as compensation. They added that the people have to sacrifice something for national development. They use it as a justification for not rehabilitating people affected by the project. If that is practised, Assam too would reproduce the practice of other States in which one class pays the price for the development of another. That is what has made it a human rights issue.

The question of rehabilitation and the quantum of compensation have become important in the Northeast because a large number of projects are being planned. They include at least 48 dams to be built in the near future and more later. Other projects include the Gas Cracker Plant that is at the planning stage and the Bogi Beel Bridge that is being implemented. All of them require land. Some of them may be important for the development of the State but one needs to ask whether some classes should continue to pay its price when others get its benefits.

A few projects like the Pagladia dam in Nalbari district have rehabilitation packages but they are inadequate. The Pagladia package, for example, mentions about 20 per cent of the people to be affected by it because it is based on the same principle of individual ownership. Those excluded from the list of DPs/PAPs are primarily CPR dependants and are predominantly tribal. The same can happen to other projects, for example those being planned in Arunachal Pradesh where the communities whose sustenance is the land have the CPRs as the norm while the LAQ recognizes only individual ownership. (Menon 2003).

Even if the DPs are resettled, their number would be extremely limited. For example, according to its Environment Impact Assessment the proposed Lower Subansiri Project of Arunachal Pradesh will displace only 38 families or a little over 200 persons. Its detailed project report seems to say that only jhum and other land will be taken over. Neither document mentions that at least 5,000 persons will be affected by the wildlife sanctuary that the Supreme Court has asked the State to develop to compensate for what the dam will submerge. Besides, many more will lose their land though they may not be displaced. (Rina 2006). They will be neither compensated nor resettled and will be eventually impoverished and marginalised.

That shows the need to go beyond compensation to find other

alternatives. Studies in other States show that compensation is inadequate. The same is with the case of Assam. So, the problems of impoverishment and marginalisation are caused mainly because development is viewed primarily as economic growth and infrastructure development. This view of development ignores those who pay its price. The State needs growth-oriented development but if adequate compensation and proper rehabilitation are ignored, the poor may become victims of the development of another class.

NPRR 2003 and Its Implications for Assam

The rehabilitation policy promulgated in February 2004 (NPRR 2003) applies to projects that displace 500 families or more en masse in the plains and 250 families in hills or scheduled areas. The Madhya Pradesh and Maharashtra Acts promulgated in the 1980s make rehabilitation applicable to projects that displace 50 families but no other policy speaks of a lower limit. In Assam a large number of projects displace fewer families. People lose their livelihood but not their houses. For example, according to the official data, the Indian Institute of Technology, Guwahati displaced 350 families but in reality it is about 600 families, 250 CPR dependents were not counted. (Hussain 2002: 289). So most of those displaced from the CPRs are not eligible for rehabilitation. In other projects too people will lose their livelihood on a large scale. Among them is the Lower Subansiri project in Arunachal Pradesh. (Menon *et al.* 2003) In the Padladia dam only 2,371 families will come under the scheme and 18,000 families will be excluded. Only 35 families are on record as having been displaced by the Namrup Fertiliser Plant. But several hundred Naga and Cachari families living on the CPRs have not been counted. There are more examples on that. Thus the NPRR guideline of 500 families is not reasonable.

According to this policy, each project affected family will be given an amount of agricultural or cultivable wasteland to the extent of actual loss subject to a maximum of 1 ha of irrigated or 2 ha of unirrigated land, if enough government land is available in the concerned district. As mentioned in the policy 'availability of government land in the district', it seems to be a simple excuse. Besides, land is a major issue in Assam and the rest of the Northeast. Most ethnic conflicts are around land. Most Government land is already in possession of encroachers and it will not be available. So the State will not be able to make land available for rehabilitation without causing more conflicts. For example, the land earmarked for Pagladia rehabilitation dam has already been occupied by 1947 and later Hindu Bengali Refugees from Bangladesh. Displacing them from there will cause a conflict between these two groups. (Bharali 2004).

Though the policy states that it is unfortunate that the CPR dependants have not been compensated till now, in practice even after counting them among the project affected families, it gives them a few benefits but not rehabilitation or genuine compensation. Given that more than 75 per cent of the land acquired in Assam is CPRs and most of those deprived of their livelihood are tribals, the policy is not of much relevance to those who pay the price of development in Assam. For example, most of those deprived of their livelihood for the Lakhimpur airport and the proposed Gas Cracker project are Adivasis or other tea garden workers who are considered encroachers. They will not be entitled to any compensation or rehabilitation. Two districts of Assam come under the Sixth Schedule where community ownership is recognized. NPRR 2003 does not make any provision for the CPR dependants. How does one calculate compensation based on individual ownership within the community ownership system?

Conclusion

We have given in this paper a summary of the extent and type of land acquired and the number of persons displaced. We have got a total of 19,0,368 persons from a total of 14,01,184.80 acres of land. There is no rehabilitation policy in the State while the NPRR 2003 speaks of rehabilitation of people from projects that displace more than 500 families. In practice most projects can speak of a smaller number because only *patta* owners are counted. Based on that, one can say that the policy is not relevant to Assam and to the rest of the Northeast where many large dams are being planned mostly on the CPRs. The persons affected by them will not be counted. So it needs to overhaul completely.

References

Bharali, Gita (2004) "Dam Threat to Livelihood," *The Telegraph: North East*, November 29.

Hussain, Monirul (2002) "State Development and Population Displacement in Northeast India", In C J Thomas, ed., *Dimensions of Displaced People in North East India*, Regency Publications, New Delhi, pp 282-298.

Hussain, Monirul (2006) "Internally Displaced Persons in India's Northeast", In *Economic and Political Weekly*, Vol. XLI, No. 5 (Feb 4-10), pp. 391-393.

Menon, Manju (2003) *Large Dams for Hydropower in Northeast India: A Dossier*, Kalpavriksh, Pune.

Menon, Manju, Niraj Vagholikar, Kanchi Kohli and Ashish Fernandes (2003) "Large Dams in the Northeast: A Bright Future?", In the *Ecologist Asia*, Vol. 11, No. 1, pp 3-8.

Nag, Sajal (2002) "Whose Nation is it anyway: Nation Building and Displacement in Indian Sub-Continent", In C J Thomas, ed., *op.cit.* pp. 26-50.

Rina, Tongam (2006) "Dams and Development", Paper presented at a conference on *Tribal Land Alienation in the North East*, North Eastern Social Research Centre, Guwahati.

Thomas, C. Joshua, ed., (2002) *Dimension of Displaced People in North-East India*, Regency Publications, New Delhi.

16

IDPs in India's Northeast: Waiting for Elusive Resettlement and Rehabilitation

Monirul Hussain

The unprecedented and brutal ethnic violence that rocked Assam's Karbi-Anglong Hill District during the month of October-December 2005 has brought to the fore once again the question of the Internally Displaced Persons (henceforth IDPs) in North-East India. The IDPs and refugees are obviously highly marginalised and excluded of all social groups. Their status is very similar, except that to become a refugee one must cross an international border, whereas an IDP does not cross the border of his/her country. Technically an IDP is a citizen but empirically s/he is a refugee in his/her own country. Both the groups lack a voice of their own, and many a time they remain neglected and invisible. By and large, they remain outside the public "consciousness" or call it "imagination", experiencing a high degree of alienation, marginalisation, and exclusion from the larger society. Hence, they deserve attention from the state and civil society.

North-East India is a very distinct civilisational, geographical, socio-economic, cultural and political entity in India. As a result of distorted environmental and socio-economic and political transformation, the entire region has experienced massive internal displacement of population. Perhaps this region has generated the highest number of IDPs in India. The citizen-IDP ratio in Northeast India is indeed very high. It is, of course, very difficult to ascertain the exact number of IDPs in the region. However, we must point out explicitly that we find all the three categories of IDP, that is, environment, conflict and development-induced IDPs in all the seven States of Northeast India, that is, Assam, Arunachal Pradesh, Manipur, Meghalaya, Mizoram, Nagaland and Tripura. People of these States have suffered immensely from injured environment, brutality of state sponsored development and both actual and potential violence caused by the political conflict for exclusive ethnic territory, space and identity.

- As a result of continuous environmental degradation, flood' and river-bank erosion in the plains, and landslide in the hills have become endemic. This has caused innumerable deaths, destruction and population displacement. The intensity of flood, river-bank erosion and landslide has increased substantially over the years in terms of area and victims. It would be pertinent to point out that the plight of the river-bank erosion induced IDPs is much more severe than that of the victims of flood. The victims of flood at least can go back to their original land once the flood water recedes. However, the river-bank erosion induced ID peasants cannot go back to their land. Because, their land has become a part of river's new/extended bed. It is not only the mighty river Brahmaputra but also the innumerable small sized rivers that are causing havoc in the plains of Assam, that is, the Brahmaputra Valley and the Barak Valley.

- The Northeast has remained an economically blocked and underdeveloped region in India despite being rich in terms of natural resources. Whatever development that has taken place in Northeast India during the entire postcolonial period under the state initiatives has caused massive displacement of population, particularly the tribal. Even in a State like Assam wherein the tribals constitute no more than 12 per cent of the population, they have experienced the brunt of development induced displacement most.

- Northeast India has remained a politically sensitive and disturbed region since it entered the postcolonial phase of its history. Its perpetual vulnerability to ethnic conflicts and its resultant violence has caused innumerable deaths and massive displacement of population in the region. Unfortunately, the question of conflict induced IDPs do not find any place in the agenda for building peace and conflict resolution in the Northeast. Here, the benefits of any state sponsored rehabilitation package goes first to the insurgents/ex-insurgents and the criminals. Right to rehabilitation has only been granted to the ex-insurgents indeed. This precious right has been systematically denied to the actual IDPs.

Estimate of IDPs

It is difficult to ascertain the exact number of IDPs in the Northeast because even the States do not keep properly the data on IDPs. Of course, for the state it is cumbersome to acknowledge the existence of IDPs because it reflects 'state failure'. The state is not at all transparent in this regard. Besides, it is extremely difficult, if not impossible, for individual scholars or journalists to investigate the situation because of the inaccessibility of conflict zones and the people living therein.

- It is difficult to estimate the number of IDPs caused by environmental degradation, that is, food, river-bank erosion and landslide etc. However, it is possible to draw some reasonable conclusions about the enormity of the problem. The flood of 2004 alone affected more than ten million people in Assam valley, most of them are ordinary peasants. Excepting two hill districts, all the districts of the plains of Assam experienced devastating flood and river-bank erosion. In an unprecedented flash flood in October 2004 nearly one thousand people died in Goalpara district. The government provided some relief to some of these flood affected people which was far from adequate. The situation demands proper and scientific assessment, adequate relief and rehabilitation measures. It is not only that the floods pushed the people of Assam into an uncertain future, the river-bank erosion too has affected millions of people. Over the years environmental insecurity has increased substantially. According to an official report, the river Brahmaputra eroded 4,29,657 hectares of prime agricultural land. Roughly, seven per cent of the land in the plains has been eroded between 1951 and 2000. This has definitely displaced at least three million peasants. Today they constitute the most pauperized community in Assam's plains. In the absence of a proper resettlement and rehabilitation policy, most of them have experienced multiple displacements.

- In the absence of proper data base again, it is difficult to ascertain the number of development induced IDPs in North-east India. However, we can have a broad idea about the enormity of the problem from the following facts. The Dumber Hydroelectric Project in Tripura ejected 40,000 families from their prime agricultural land displacing about 200,000 tribal people. The Pagladiya Dam Project in Assam, if implemented, will displace about 105,000 people from their land. Besides, the Kaptai Hydroelectric Project in East Pakistan, now Bangladesh, displaced a large number of tribal Chakmas. It too had a severe spill-over affect in the North-East. About 40,000 of the Kaptai project affected people were shifted to the erstwhile North-East Frontier Agency (NEFA), now Arunachal Pradesh. Till now the Chakmas, numbering about 80,000, have remained stateless in India, still awaiting the ever elusive Indian citizenship.

The Government of India is now proposing to construct 145 dams of different varieties including mega dams in North-east India. This region is ecologically fragile and vulnerable to high intensity earthquakes. Hence, the people are questioning the very wisdom of mega dam projects in the Northeast. The Naga, Kuki and Hmar people, who are going to be affected by the ongoing Tipaimukh Hydroelectric Project, have vehemently opposed to construction of the dam on their sacred land/site. Similarly, the people of Lakhimpur and Dhemaji districts of Upper Assam are opposed to the construction of Lower Subansiri Hydroelectric Project being constructed at a site near the Assam Arunachal Pradesh border. This area was affected by a severe earthquake in 1950. People consider it to be a big threat to their lives and existence. The potential displaces of the Pagladiya Dam Project are resisting the construction of the dam. Dams have become a major source of displacement and threat for the future of the entire Northeast India. If we combine all the categories of development induced displacement together with the displacement of urbanisation, it is likely to be a massive three million plus IDPs in the Northeast. Significantly, most of the development-induced IDPs in the North-East like in the rest of India are the tribal people.

The Northeast has a large army of conflict-induced IDPs. Though we do not have exact data but with a fair degree of certainty we can talk about the number of IDPs in Kokrajhar district in lower Assam. Till April 2005, 1,26,263 inmates were living in 38 state sponsored relief camps in the district. Besides, there are also relief camps in Bongaigaon, Dhubri, Barpeta, Karbi-Anglong, North Cachar and Cachar districts in Assam. At one stage there were more than 200,000 IDPs living in the relief camps in Kokarajhar district alone. All these IDPs were the victims of the Bodoland movement. Some of these conflict-induced IDPs are living in the camps for more than a decade now. The government is providing only rice to the inmates of some of the camps for 10 days a month. The IDPs are living a dehumanised life in the camp. Significantly, the government has stopped rations for the inmates of many camps.

Besides, about 40,000 Reang/Bru IDPs are living in state sponsored relief camps in Assam and Tripura. They were displaced from Mizoram as a result of the ethnic conflict there. Besides, about 40,000 Chin refugees, who were working at the bottom level jobs in Mizoram for quite a long lime, were forced to go back to Myanmar from where they fled to Mizoram earlier. On the other hand, there are a huge number of conflict induced IDPs in Manipur because of the Naga-Kuki conflict there. The Hmar and Dimasa conflict also displaced several thousand people in the North Cachar Hill district in Assam. The Karbi and non-Karbi conflict too displaced thousands in the Karbi-Anglong Hill District in 2003 and 2004. Very recently the October 2005 ethnic violence in the Karbi-Anglong Hill District has displaced more than 60,000 tribal people belonging to the Karbi and Dimasa tribes. Hence, as of now Assam alone has more than two lakh IDPs in various relief camps both in the plains and the hills awaiting

> resettlement and rehabilitation. Additionally the "periodic' movements against the outsiders in Assam and Meghalaya have displaced a large number of people silently. They have gone virtually undocumented.

Most IDPs living in camps receive medical care and their children have neither access to formal educational nor to health services. Though some receive food aid, but it often arrives sporadically and is insufficient in quantity and nutrition. Within the IDP communities the children and the women suffer most. Throughout the North-East, conditions of the displaced are pathetic and no intergovernmental or international organisations are present. The displaced live in most degrading and dehumanised way in public buildings and makeshift shelters. They have lost their most precious possessions, that is, land, home and livelihood. If we look at the IDP issue from the impoverishment risk model developed by Micheal M. Cernea, we find that all the IDPs of the Northeast suffer from landlessness, joblessness, homelessness, marginalisation, food insecurity, increased morbidity and mortality, loss of access to common property rights, social disarticulation and disintegration.

We must point out that in postcolonial Northeast one cannot look into the problem of internal displacement of population through just one category of displacement alone. In many situations, one person may experience the same kind of displacement more than once. Similarly, one may become the victim of environmentally induced displacement repeatedly and at the same time the same person may experience conflict-induced displacement in his/her new place of residence or livelihood. For example, a person, displaced by flood or river bank erosion, may cross the boundaries of his district or region in search of livelihood, and s/he may become a victim of conflict-induced displacement. This very often happens in Assam. And the 'displaced', which is supposed to be a temporary/transitory status, becomes a permanently displaced person waiting and struggling to survive in an all encompassing situation of fear, vulnerability and uncertainty. It seems the displaced people in Assam in most cases experience displacement more than once in a lifetime; it is a serialised and multiplied experience. Displacement is being repeatedly reproduced in Northeast India in different shapes, sizes, situations and spaces as an inseparable part of the postcolonial political economy of India.

Are we in a position to stop or at least reduce the number of IDPs in Northeast India? This is a difficult question. Obviously the ongoing process of perilous environmental injuries, developmental brutalities and sharpening of exclusivist ethnicity and its resultant violence – all have together propelled massive internal displacement of population in the Northeast. And I guess this will continue with higher degree of intensity in future until and unless we look afresh at the whole gamut of environmental, developmental and political issue involved in the specific context of the Northeast. The issue of the Northeast IDPs deserves special attention and care of the larger civil society and the Indian state. The state needs to overcome its perennial governance deficit in the Northeast. Similarly the civil society needs to fight against the perennial human rights deficit in the region. To address the IDP issue one requires political will; we would maintain that this remains the real obstacle to stop avoidable displacement of population anywhere in India, including the Northeast. It would be of crucial importance to remove the environment, development and political conditions and processes that generated the IDPs in Northeast India. Besides, in the absence of a clear-cut IDP regime in India, one can look into the "UN Guiding Principles on Internal Displacement" in order to address the humanitarian and rights issues involved in the IDPs' question in the Northeast and India as a whole.

Section IV

Peace in Texts and Discourses

17

Bhakti as the Essence of Peace: Srimanta Sankaradeva's Aesthetics of Prayer

Krishna Barua

As early as the fifteenth century AD, when Assam was in the grip of political instability, Srimanta Sankaradeva's restructuring of indigenous and traditional aesthetics instilled a characteristic synthesis of refined taste and ethos and thereby peace to the Assamese life and society. In this paper I want to address the contextual features of the aesthetics of *Bhakti* as the essence and measure of Peace in Sankaradeva's mode of prayer. It will be an inquiry into the relevance of this aesthetic viewpoint, on the basis of the new aesthetic-ethical culture and the appreciation of traditional use of corporeal artifacts, which gave a transcending uplift to religion in Sankaradeva's times. For Sankaradeva (1449-1568), the appreciation of beauty involved experiential knowledge, and taking the external senses as reference, he attempted at a certain intuitive aesthetic pleasure in which the delight consisted in that which was seen and pleased. Thus, his ethics and religion might be regarded as a phase of aesthetics. That in engaging the aesthetic, the harmony that he found in the universe had an impact on his ethical and religious nature.

The aim of my paper would be to explore the role of aesthetic experience in Sankaradeva's perception and understanding of the holy, examined in relation to three principal dimensions of the aesthetic realm: feeling and imagination; beauty (or taste); and the arts. Herein theology itself can be imaginative or beautiful, concentrating on the theological significance of aesthetic data provided by each of the three major spheres of aesthetic perception and response. And further, as religious art strove to reflect the exemplar of the divine beauty itself, there were wonderful attempts to show that the beautiful was inexhaustible because the good and the true were inexhaustible.

For this, it is necessary to go back to the state of Assam around six centuries back, and how stupendous a task Sankaradeva faced in reorganizing and reforming the society. Assam in the fifteenth century comprised mostly of an Indo-mongoloid race, following individual tribal customs. The highly ritualistic and priest dominated religious rites of the Brahminical order were not suitable for the masses who had hardly any knowledge of Sanskrit in which the Hindu rites were conducted. Sankaradeva was deeply impressed by the neo-Vaishnavite movement in different parts of medieval India. The seeds of experimenting on novel procedures of social change were already sown. But he was aware of the hostile socio-economic conditions of ethnic warfare and political upheavals, where feudalism was gaining ground. Instead of radical changes in the structure, he evolved a condition that could bring an illusion of happiness to people. It was he who built a bridge of Assam's cultural exchange with the rest of India.

In the Vedic heritage, the ideal form of love has been named *Bhakti*, a usual and simple translation of which is "devotion." Sankaradeva worked on the meaning of *Bhakti* as a higher and purer form of *prema* or human love, rather than restricting it meaning to the usual "devotion". We can see that *Bhakti* penetrates art in a fundamental way and to describe it as one of the many sentiments (*rasas*) is to woefully belittle the impact of *Bhakti* as a pivotal concept of Sankaradeva's heritage. In other words, the dichotomy between the secular and the spiritual is overcome when *Bhakti* and love are taken as two sides of the same coin. The spirit of *Bhakti* imbibed the liberalism of the day, and its simple ceremonies consisted of *Nama-kirtana* – repeating the name of God (*Nama)* and singing His praise *(kirtana*) in community worship, fostering thereby community feeling. He gave the "regenerated Assamese people literature, drama, poetry, songs, dance and music, which have attained the status of a distinct school, and entwined the community with unity and oneness." (Barua 1961).

The underlying notion of aesthetics is perceiving, which is *to grasp by the senses.* Every broad notion makes art a *way* of making or experiencing things rather than a set of objects or genres. Hence, when pure consciousness identifies with the objects of experience, the knower could be said to be identified with the known – as unity of consciousness between humans and their environment. This state of consciousness is described by a famous verse from the Upanishads: "I am That, Thou art That, all this is That". As a logical extension of Sankaradeva's concept of Bhakti, Beauty is the living manifestation of God in Nature and Man. The ancient Indian aesthetician considered art as something woven into the very fabric of society with a clear conception of both Beauty and the significance of form. Since all aesthetic experience reaches the inmost depths of the soul, the pursuit of truth and goodness leads many to this artistry of life. "To equate the love of art with the love of fine sensations is to make of works of art a kind of aphrodisiac." (Coomaraswamy, 1974:34).

Sankaradeva thought that it was of utmost necessity to evolve a religion, which would not only be simpler in form but also easy to practice for all sections of people. He could well perceive that the world the masses lived in was a *seen* world, and he strove to refurbish *the seen* as a tool to transform the understanding and the experiences of the world as a visual domain of collective participation in a celebration of colour and sound. The social forces of the sixteenth century also craved for a non-instrumental understanding of the arts, realizing that the aesthetic and the civil society were somehow mutually interdependent, serving a still higher purpose of promoting peace and human harmony.

Herein lay the close links of the visual and the verbal as sites of identities, leading to the unity of Being through the personalization of emotive states of harmony. "A profound scholar, in Sanskrit as well, Sankaradeva translated into Assamese the great works of Indian thought and thus laid the foundations of the region's emotional and cultural links with the rest of India and while doing so, he used the local language and devised many media of popular articulation giving it the character of mass participation and boundless popular enthusiasm." (Barooah 1995: viii).

And so it was for Sankaradeva to necessitate the expression of the interdependence and correlation of the objective and subjective aspects of the splendour of the divine form in paintings, costumes, drapery, *bargeets* (devotional songs), makeup, masks, artifacts and architecture of *Namghars*, thus culminating in the aesthetic theory of unified experience of *rasa* and liberation. This interplay between the verbal and the visual has thus compelled us to rethink many of Sankaradeva's theoretical premises for reconstructing an authentic living dialogue with cultural encounters in festive or ceremonial contexts. Religion thus becomes a source of knowledge and experience through aesthetic functionalism. *Bhakti* did not merely define the religious quest but became the measure of all that was valuable in human life, all that was highest in the creative life of letters, music and art.

Sankaradeva thought that the best way to reform society and religion was not to attack what was evil in it but to strongly present what was good and to appeal to the believers' aesthetic sense. He remarked to one of his chief disciples, Govinda Ata, that religion was not for the king but for the common masses. He asked his disciples to "*seek* self realization not by an objective change of society through practical struggles, but by an attempt to change them, that is, by an attempt to change their subjective attitude towards life which caused so much pain." (Barman 1996: 185).

There had been a synthesis of indigenous and other forms that shaped the course of the arts in Assam, but most of it was derived partly from the Vedic tradition. The creation of pictorial representation was in itself a distinctive mode of aesthetic imaging, and in the early Assam of Srimanta Sankaradeva's time, most of the colours of various shades of red, green and orange, were derived from minerals. Art and religion and other forms of imagery that surrounded religion, were acknowledged as a distinct form of visual creativity in which visual artifacts could be historically and culturally conceptualized, and showed how the ornaments, the clothing, the arrangement of objects and so on performed that function. In Sankaradeva's view, the arts became a part of the culture and central to self-constructions and spiritual lives.

Culturally, Sankaradeva's genius was more in the sphere of drama. It was an appropriate medium where he could communicate his messages. He had an indepth understanding of the nature of performance practices, conventions and aesthetics of traditional performances, their context being an important factor. The first great step of attraction was enacting a drama with painted scenes of heavenly abodes at the backdrop, dances and songs. To his credit, he could democratize the monotheistic Vaishnavite faith, which was earlier, confined to Sanskrit scriptures that were inaccessible to the common person. Traditional performances, festivals, rites of passage, cycle of seasons, community celebrations etc., have a thick socio-cultural context. He saw that performers in associations with the spectators and the whole community resorted to what could be called context-building strategies, which greatly enriched the experience and the aesthetics of the performances. When the nuances of traditional Sanskrit drama had nearly been lost from the other parts of the country, it had been kept alive in Assam by Sankaradeva. These dramas are greatly evolved creations incorporating all the elements of drama, literature and even available technology of the time. While Sankaradeva used painted scenes for Assamese drama in the fifteenth century, the use of painted scenes in drama started in Europe only in the seventeenth century.

Sankaradeva used dance, drama and music to bring all sections of the society together through the *Bhaona* in the *Namghar*. The first *Bhaona* performance was staged in 1468 AD. In the *Bhaona,* a group of musicians called *Gayan-Bayan* accompanied by the *khols* (drums) and *tals* (cymbals) express different *ragas* (tunes) and *mudras* (gestures). Here's a passage on music from the ancient Confucian philosopher Hsun Tzu:

> When it is performed within the household, and father and sons, elder and younger brothers listen to it together, there are none who are not filled with a spirit of harmonious kinship. And when it is performed in the community, and old people and young people listen to it, there are none who are not filled with its spirit of harmonious obedience. Hence music brings about complete unity and induces harmony. (Hsun Tzu 1963: 113)

It is a journey from the sensuous to the super-sensuous for an aesthete and a reverse process from unity to multiplicity for an artist involved in creative expression. "The poet, dramatist as also the performing artist in Sankaradeva brought about a cultural birth, a rebirth for the Assamese people and instructed them in the arts of composite culture with its virtues of a tolerant society." (Barooah 1995: viii).

Bhaona plays paved the way for cultural development of other arts and crafts in Assam. Nearly all the elements necessary for *Bhakti* such as the sense of wonder, self-surrender, faith, repentance and confession could be gleaned from the dignity of involvement and joy of the masses. This is a sort of transpersonal theory, a participatory vision of human spirituality of knowledge, and in this vision, reality becomes a dialogue between instruction and delight which is basically universal.

This led to further development in customs, makeup, masks, screens, ornaments and other accessories. His *Chihnayatra* is regarded as the first Assamese drama where Sankaradeva is supposed to have painted scenes of the *"Sapta vaikuntha"* (seven vaikunthas) on "tula pat" (Neog 1965: 270), which does not exist today. As for ornaments, there were the bracelets, necklaces and lizard like jewels around the head. In the *cho ghar*, representations of animals and other animate objects were stacked together. The masks used in the performances were made of clay, wood, bamboo or cloth and painted with lime, vermillion, (*hengul, haital*, indigo and lamp-black. There used to be monks, even some *khanikars*, who painted on earthenware, who were responsible for the task.

The famous *Vrindavani Vastra* (parts of this work are preserved in London), meaning 'the attire of Vrindavan', which is a 120 cubits long and 60 cubits broad tapestry depicting the *lilas* of Lord Krishna at Vrindavan through richly woven and embroidered designs on silk. The *vastra*, commissioned by Chilarai, was woven by twelve master weavers in Barpeta under the supervision of Sankaradeva, probably between 1565 and 1568. It was housed in the Madhupur sattra but it disappeared at some point of time. (Crill 1992: p.92).

The manuscript paintings of Assam are an offshoot of this cultural upsurge. Few, even amongst scholars, are aware of these valuable relics though they belong to the pre-Mughal stream of miniature painting in India. Coloured by the similar religious fervour of the Bhakti cult, it has developed distinct features of its own. However, the painting of a later date gradually becomes more detailed and descriptive where an attempt at narrations is obvious. Excellence of form beheld is the root of aesthetic pleasure. And so it is apparent that religious practice ought to make use of artifacts because "the object of honour and reverence is something excellent". The use of artifacts which are beautiful in the practice of religion is not only because the excellence of the object leads to excellence in the reverence. It is also due to the fact that in divine worship, it is necessary to make use of corporeal things for arousing the human mind by their symbolism to the spiritual acts by means of which the devotee is united to God.

Sankaradeva took a very pragmatic approach, by establishing, within the confines of the society, the *Sattra*, which was a unique type of monastic or semi-monastic place of prayer and a safe haven where conditions of peace and equality could be preached. "The *Sattra* was the materialisation of Sankaradeva's dream of a perfect society, the fulfillment of his quest for tribal oneness and equality that has vanished not very long ago" (Kakati 1948: 87). These local *sattras* framed moral laws and controlled the activities of the society. A miniature replica of the *sattra* was the village *Namghar*, with combined functions of a village church, a village court and a village stage, which was also initiated by Sankaradeva himself. With the *namghar* many aspects of rural economy came to be promoted through the mass use of agricultural products like the pulses and the promotion of cottage industries like pottery, bamboo and cane craft and the use of bell metal, brass etc. The *namghars became* a popular institution in the everyday life of the Assamese people. What made them really vibrant was that there was no caste bar to enter the *namghars.*

The most unique aspect of the arts that are nurtured at the *sattras* is that they are part of a living cultural tradition. During the later centuries, the entire Brahmaputra valley, including some remote tribal areas, were more-or-less covered by a network of *Sattras*, nearly 600 in number, which propagated the ethnic and socio-cultural ideals of the new society. These *Sattras* are the treasure house of devotional songs like '*Borgeet*', and *Sattriya* dances, which give to the spectator a sense of heightened spiritual satisfaction.

Although the *Sattra* institutions were established for the propagation of Vaishnavite faith, with the passage of time these institutions gradually transformed themselves into open universities and socio-cultural centres dealing with a variety of subjects like education, music, dance, sculpture, drama, fine-arts, ivory-works etc. The principal purpose of art, in Indian philosophy, is to induce a unique state of transcendence or integration of all the levels at which awareness and experience occurs: physical, sensory, emotional, cognitive and reflective. What emerges from this study is that in Sankaradeva, beauty was not only perfection, but led to a distinct approach toward art as an attitude toward life. A wider understanding of Sankaradeva's *Bhakti* leads to a re-humanization and reconsideration of a deepened relationship between the graces of rhythm, proportion, balance and harmony that we find in nature.

It deserves to be acknowledged that Sankaradeva's concept of *Bhakti* involved all the levels of our own aesthetic ethos that causes absorption and bliss, a contemplation of the beautiful object. In his thought aesthetics is not the property of objects but an experience in everyday life, in the things he made, in the vessels he used, in the clothes he wore, in the prayer abodes and in the whole sociological design.

References

Barman, S. (1996) "The Quest for an Egalitarian Utopia: A Critique of Sankaradeva's Social Philosophy," *Essays on Sankaradeva*, Ranjit Dev Goswami, ed., Forum for Sankaradeva Studies, Lawyers Bookstall, Guwahati.

Barooah, Debo Prasad (1995) "Foreword", In *Sri Sankaradeva*, Sanjib Borkakati, ed., Bani Mandir, Guwahati.

Barua, Birinci Kumar (1961) *Sankaradeva, Vaishnava Saint of Assam*, Assam Academy for Cultural relations, Guwahati.

Coomaraswamy, Ananda (1973) "Ornament," *Traditional Art and Symbolism*, Bollingen Press, Princeton.

Crill Hali, Rosemary (1992) *Vrindavani Vastra: Figured Silks from Assam*, 62 : 14 (2): 1992. 76 -83.

Goswami, Keshavananda Dev (1999) *Life and Teachings of Mahapurusha Sankaradeva*, Forum for Sankaradeva Studies, Guwahati.

Hsun Tzu (1963) *Basic Writings*, trans. Burton Watson, Columbia University Press, New York.

Kakati, B. K. (1948) *Mother Goddess Kamakhya,* Guwahati.

Neog, Maheswar (1965) *Sankaradeva and His Times: Early History of the Vaishnava Faith and Movement in Assam*, Guwahati University, Guwahati.

Okakura, Kakuzo (1964) *The Book of Tea*, Dover, New York.

18

'Crossing the Border': Inter-religious Dialogue in Mediaeval Assam

Archana Barua

> '*We have learnt to fly in the air like birds and swim in the sea like fish, but we have not learnt the simple art of living together as brothers*'. (Martin Luther King Jr.)

Sankaradeva and the Bhakti Renaissance in Medieaval Assam

It is no wonder that in this conflict-torn historical situation, religion appears to act as a strong ally to the forces of divisiveness and violence, rather than a force for unity and peace. Although this politicization of a tradition or a text, including religious tradition, is a modern phenomenon, in pre-colonial Medieval India, the spiritual and cultural renaissance ushered in by the *Bhakti* movement paved way for meaningful dialogue between different religious communities, especially between the neo-Vaishnavism of Úankaradeva and the vernacularised, indigenous Islam influenced by one of the most revered preachers of Assam, Âjan Fakir. Both Úankaradeva and Âjan Fakir sought to restore the human face of religion drawing inspiration from the shared background and context of historically effected consciousnesses. Simplification of rituals and use of vernacular for translating the religious texts have played their roles in popularizing *Bhakti*. Both these religious reformers constructed a new kind of meaning as the horizon of the text or the tradition, which they sought to creatively reinterpret. This trend gave rise to new literary canons and poetics to legitimize the emergence of new literary genres. It is significant that the *Bhagavata*, the main source of inspiration for the Mediaeval *Bhakta* Saints, could open up new possibilities for creative interpretations. Both these diverse religious traditions placed special emphasis on bringing up those who are considered lower in the social strata, the Sudras, who form the most numerous component of the Indian population, and women, who are easily the half of any given chunk of population, into the forefront of religio-cultural practice through mass community participation. Until the British brought the communal factor into its colonial administrative ethos, *Bhakti* and Sufism flourished with benign influence on each other in the pre-colonial religious and yet secular Bharatvarsha. In this paper, I shall argue that a constant dialogue between the book-centered, that is, a scriptural, and a religious culture is possible so long as the authoritative texts are interpreted in terms of the horizons, which the texts open with the infinite potentiality of their content.

Inter-religious Dialogue in Medieaval Assam

The relation one has with the text is essential for the text to provide meaning. It is our longings, our fears, our hopes, etc., or it can be our very human desire for escaping from our ultimate solitude in an intimate dialogue with a personal 'thou', the relations we have with the text, or our experience, that colors our understandings. Dialogue invites us to come together as people, not as belief systems. "When one loves a person, one loves more than a person; one loves the secret that it hides and reveals, and which surpasses one. Love is connected to all and always, that is, to the infinite, the eternal, the absolute, to God. (Cadamer 1988: 270) If in the medieval ages we see "more religious tolerance than in the colonial and post-colonial society" (Gadamer 1988: 270) this is because the distinctive horizons of the political person differs from the wider horizon of a person of faith who is a *bhakta* at heart, one who knows the secret of true love that alone can transform the impersonal 'it' to a passionate 'Thou'.

In order to do this, the Vaishnavite saint Sankaradeva and the Sufi Saint "Ajan Fakir" or "Ajan Pir" (Saint) have opted for the Bhaktic interpretation of the text. "This process itself led to vastly downsizing, if not the total elimination of the need of an intermediary priesthood and softening the rigours of caste discrimination by reducing its role in religio-social observances". (Dutta) "*Sito candâlaka garistha mâni, Yâra jihbâgre thâke Hari vâni, Sehisé kulin Vedak bujé: Yâhara mukhé Hari Nâm sijé.*" "That outcaste and the untouchable is glorious who has the name of God in the tip of his tongue. He alone is pure and is versed in the Vedas in whose mouth God's name is fructified." (Neog

1965: page 15). The spiritual-cultural renaissance ushered in by the *Bhakti* movement in Medieval India acted as a cementing force that could spiritually bind Assam and its neighboring states to that cultural land of the Bharatas. Thus one can say it is politicization of religion, which is the real problem than religion per se. One, who is a *bhakta* at heart, could foster this sense of spiritual kinship across boundaries. "*Bhakatese mora hridi jâniba nichay, Bhakatajanara jâna âmisi hrday*". (Sankaradeva KIRTTAN) ("Know for certain that my *bhakta* is my soul and I his.") One of the most impressive examples of *Bhakti* doctrines preached by Ajan Fakir to express admiration for this sect of Hinduism is as follows: "*Sankardeur jiyari Madhavdeur buwari, Rahpur nagarat ghar, Rahpur nagarat rasak nami ani, Diya sakaloke bati*" ("She is the daughter of Sankardeva and daughter-in-law of Madhavadev; and she dwells in the city of 'Rahpur' or land of *rasa* (aesthetics); that is, the sentiment of love and devotion; bring down the *rasa* from the city of Rahpur and distribute it among us all".)

Socio-cultural and Linguistic Implications of the Bhakti Movement

Bhakti centric Medieval India kept room for constant dialogue between the book-centered, that is, scriptural culture (and religion) and the mediators who sought to re-interpret the authoritative texts, unveiling the infinite potentiality of the textual content in terms of the historical and cultural horizons. In its effort to safeguard the voices within the voice, the *Bhakti* movement made special effort to identify the following:

(a.) The right type of text

There is a relationship of fundamental unity among the authoritative texts like the *Gita* and the *Bhagavata*, but still they could open up new possibilities and could become the source of several religious movements each different from the other. There are numerous commentaries of these texts and Sankradeva himself used *Tattva Dipika*, *Bhagavata Bhabartha Dipika*, *Bhava Prakasika*, among many other commentaries. Œankaradeva rendered about eight books of the Bhagvata, including the last four, into Assamese. He also rendered the Ramayana *Uttara-Kânda* into Assamese, but it was never a mere literal translation. Ramananda, an early biographer of

Sankaradeva, makes a categorical statement: "*Tini skandha câi, bicariyâ pâi, ekaskandhe sehi kathâ: Bacaka-bania, dsadagare jena, eka thâi kari tahtâ*.' ("What is to be found by searching as many as three *skandhas* has been put in one *skandha* just as the most skillful merchant would gather [the select gems] together.") In this manner, this *bhakti* centric concrete dimension of meaning has added a distinct flavor to the notion of 'textual authority'.

(b.) *Meaning in dialogue through collaboration of the author and the readers*

The Gurus or the interpreters of the texts were sensitive to the types of devotees for whose sake the text needed specific re-interpretations time and again, taking into account their role in this whole meaning-discovering process. It is equally significant that Nanak, Tukaram, Namdev and Sankaradeva are all non-Brahmin by birth and could give new impetus to *bhasa*. The noted historian, H. K. Barpujari points out that the neo-Vaishnavite movement in Assam was backed by a strong literary upsurge which found expression in the translation of the epics and the *Puranas*, the adaptation of the *Puranic* episodes in the form of independent *Kavyas*, devotional works explaining the types and modes of devotion, lyrics (*bargeets*), dramas and biographies of Vaishnava saints". (Quoted in Borah 2006). In its practical sense, the text could now open up to a community of readers (or hearers), who have contributed their share in re-reception of the concrete dimension of meaning with sole emphasis on *sravana* and *kirttana*. The holy books in Sanskrit could be now easily accessible to the sudras and women, but it came to them in the medium of their own vernacular language that could safeguard the distinctive ethos of this composite society with its own distinctive identity.

(c.) *The right mediums*

At every instance in the process of understanding there is language. In a sense, reality lives in the linguistic medium itself, in the meanings, inspirations and illuminations which such languages tend to convey. To quote Iris Murdoch: "The language which constitutes reality here can open creative fringe where poets and critics take some part in inventing new concepts." (Murdoch 1987: 72-73) In a sense the story of Sankaradeva or of Ajan Pir is also "a story of the development of languages, a restructuring of the linguistic activity, giving centrality to the language of the people, to that of the of the power elite." (Dutta: 14-15). This needed new literary canons and poetics to legitimize the emergence of new literary genres. Sankaradeva created a literary language mixing the local vernacular with the North-Indian vernaculars for his dramas and his *Borgeet* (devotional songs) for the benefit of a larger section of the common masses. Brojabuli was never intended to be an elitist language. The spiritual and cultural Bharat got this linguistic vehicle for easy entry to and cultural commerce with the Assamese mind and this has now been transformed into a heritage.

The Assamese language has turned out to be a perfect medium for conveying this catholic spirit of *bhakti* that could provide a platform for fusion of horizons. Although developed from the *Magadhi Apabhransa* of Sanskrit origin, with infusion of many expressions of Tibeto-Burman stock of dialects, Assamese language could develop a distinct flavor of its own. The various tribal dialects and languages of the state such as Bodo, Karbi, Dimasa, Tiwa, Tai, Mishing, Rabha etc., have enriched this language. According to noted linguist Upendra Nath Goswami, since ancient times the dialects of the state have been enriching the Assamese language and have made it a synthetic one. "It was enriched in the past during the rule of Barahi-Kachari, Kamata, Koch and Ahom kings. Therefore, it is dear to everybody living in the hills and the plains". (Quoted in Neog 1965 p. No 62.). This could give new dignity to all communities (the Kiratas, Kacharis, the Khasis, Garos, the Miris, the Kankas) who remain outside the ambit of Hinduism to declare their dignified positions. Arabic and Persian words are another noteworthy addition to the Assamese language. Both Sankaradeva and Ajan Fakir were particularly sensitive to spreading the message of *bhakti* in the mediums of art, language, dance, drama and music.

Unlike in some other places, pre-colonial Assam has witnessed peaceful co-existence of different religions and religious fanaticism was unheard of. It is interesting that both Neo-Vaishnavism among the Hindus and vernacularised Islam influenced by Sufism stressed devotion to one God as the primary religious vehicle for the attainment of spiritual goal rather than elaborate practices and pursuit of scriptural knowledge. *Bhakti* and Sufism flourished with benign influence on each other. Although in our post-colonial reading of a text, the word "difference" is usually taken to mean 'absolute distance' or 'absolute otherness', in this very act of recognition of the limit, "we already have gone beyond it". The words 'Hindu' and 'Turk' or 'Musulman' which began to appear, as opposite pairs in the devotional literature, had a different meaning from that which is now commonly ascribed to them in the post-colonial reading of our tradition. The categories 'Hindu' and 'Muslim' emerged in the context of Medieval India simply because identities were predominately related to caste (*jati*), sect (*panth*) and regional traditions, but these were never identified as absolutely separate categories. There was possibility of caste mobility or *panth* mobility even within this hierarchy. In a new historical account, this dissent proposes that people themselves are agents of change and religion recovers its dignity as an essential aspect of the self-expression of ordinary people. Ajan Fakir's is a radical deviation from the model that has dominated the understanding of orthodox Islam, which destroys the image of people as passive beneficiaries of an elite religious order. All one can say at this point is that his is a voice of a dissident subaltern committed to telling a 'different' story.

Muslims have a history of more than seven centuries in Assam, which has the second largest concentration of Indian Muslims after Kashmir. However, in striking contrast to the stereotype understanding, Islam in Assam is open, accommodative, inclusive and adaptive in its local specificity. Here Islam is strikingly different from that in north and western India, the core areas of Islamic civilization in India, and actual social practices of the 'Asamiya Muslims' may be inconsistent with the laws of any Islamic school. Although Assam came into contact with Muslims as early as 1203, the systematic propagation of Islam as an organized religion started only in the early part of the seventeenth century by a wandering Muslim mystic Shah Milan – or as he was popularly known, 'Ajan Fakir' – who came to Assam in about 1630 A.D. Shah Milan and his brother Shah Nabi found that the Muslims of Assam did not follow any aspects of traditional Islam and assimilated into the medieval Assamese society and gained acceptance as one of its inseparable components. According to a legend, Hazrat Shah Miran received the name "Ajan Fakir" or Ajan Pir (Saint) because he was the one who taught the Assamese Muslim to recite "Azan" as its part of Muslim ritual. He introduced the Muslims of Assam to the Namaaz, the contents of Quran, the Hadiths and other Islamic literature, with which they were barely acquainted, through folk songs, instrumental music and dances.

The spiritually vibrant cultural context of the land and its tradition had cast its magical spell inspiring him to draw resources from his own tradition for strengthening the tolerant and loving spirit of *Bhakti* renaissance. Sankaradeva was the pioneer in this regard, taking courageous steps like opening doors of *bhakti* to one and all, including the Muslim devotees like Chand Sai, who later became one of the key religious figures during Sankaradeva's times local Muslims used to take part in the singing of *Kirtana*-songs for community prayer composed by Sankardeva, for the purpose of propagating Vaisnavism. The Muslim also took *mah-prasads* (uncooked eatables generally consisting of gram, sugarcane, coconut, ginger and fruits) distributed at the end of the community singing of *Kirtana.* These background beliefs formed the common horizon of meaning for both these distinct religious communities. Later Ajan Fakir introduced the custom of distribution of *sinni* (considered food prepared out of rice) at the end of the community singing. Chand Khan or "Chand Sai", disciple of Vaisnava Saint Sankardeva, composed spiritual lyrics more like *Borgits* of Sankardeva and Madhavadeva. (Deka 2006).

It is significant that Ajan Pir drew inspirations from the liberal spirit of Sufism that enabled him to give centrality to the human and the loving face of Alla. Like Sankaradeva, Ajan Fakir himself was a good singer and poet; and he alone composed one hundred and sixty Zikirs in Assamese. Ajan Fakir and his early disciples contributed significantly to educating the majority of local Muslims in the spirit and significance of Islam through un-orthodox methods, including those considered 'un-Islamic' by scriptural standards.

Although Islam does not promote music and dance for entertainment, from the religious perspective there is no restriction as such. At that time dance and music constituted a very popular way of praying to God among the Hindu and the Muslim communities of Assam. Ajan Fakir and his disciples, popularly known as "Bhakat" in Assamese performed Zikir, dancing and singing with hand clapping like folk performance such as *Diha nam*, *Husori*, etc. (Deka 2006).

The word Zikir comes from the Arabian root meaning 'to remember' or 'act of narrating or singing or proclaiming the good qualities of anyone'.

While spreading the religious principles of Islam, he had always been sensitive to the sentiments of the Assamese society. In the Zikir and Zari songs, he stressed respecting and praying to Allah whole-heartedly.

A man who came from the 'land of deserts' – Baghdad could easily mix with the Asomiya people. He learnt the Asomiya language and became an Asomiya to the core. His contribution towards the harmonious culture of Assam is remarkable. In his compositions he used earthy idioms and phrases that often came down in part to explaining the ideas and issues in terms of events and activities of daily life of the common people. It is worth mentioning here that language of Zikir, except for a few Arabic and Persian words is Colloquial Assamese." (Ahmed).

The chief objective of Ajan Fakir appears to have been the re-organization of Muslim society in Assam by regenerating Islam in such a way that there was no discord in the age-old harmonious relations between the Muslims and their Hindu and other non-Hindu neighbors. Through these songs, he tried to spread the religious principles of Islam among the common people. A sense of respect to all other castes, creeds and religions is present in Zikir and Zari songs. Due to the local influence, these songs could occupy an important place in the hearts of the common people of the State.

It is important to note here that the Zari songs are like elegies with their tragic tone. These songs, which are based on the stories of Karbala, Hasan and Hussain are usually sung in the month of Muharram. Generally, injustices prevalent in society are reflected in the Zari songs. Ajan Peer started writing these songs in folk form and as *tukari geets*, using the pure Asomiya language, so that the common people could understand them. He also maintained simplicity in expressing the tenets of Islam to the common people. He preserved the religious principles of Islam in the Zikir songs. (Borah 2006).

The Jari is also popularly known as "Jarigan", the songs concerned with the Karbala episodes of "Hasan-Hosein" and stories from Islamic history and legend. Jari is translated in Persian and Urdu dictionaries as "crying, groaning and wailing". Such demonstrative expressions of grief are an important part of Muharram celebrations. During the holy month of Muharram, these songs are sung by men accompanied by the musical instrument *dotara* (a two string instrument) and this has similarities with the tradition of *Oja Pali* (storytelling tradition with music and dance). "Greatly inspired by the regional music of Assam such as the tone and spirit of other Assamese folk genre like *Oja-paliand Deh bicarar geet*, Ajan Fakir adopted the practice of Vaisnavite lyrics. One often comes across lines "*Savaro ghate ghate Alla*" evidently borrowed from Vaisnavite poetry." (Deka 2006) These songs are sung in choral singing groups with a lead singer, *Oja* (leader), who intones the song and is later joined by members of the group like *palis* (group). As the group sings, they move in a circle, clapping and following rhythmic steps. Some of the Assamese Zaris were also composed as independent ballads depicting the stories of Haidar Ghazi. Usually the lyrics of these songs are an admixture of Arabic, Persian and colloquial Assamese words.

The meaning of the text is obtained through the interaction between the reader and the text. The present day historical situation and the modern way of looking at traditions and texts are colored by the current human situation of historical existence that is borne out by historical necessity. Today we find ourselves in a situation where there is large-scale consensus among scholars and practitioners that conflict has to be accepted as an integral part of life. Interestingly, people from two different communities could overcome human-made artificial barriers under the spiritual leadership of Sankaradeva and Ajan Fakir at a time when there was space for intimate and inter-personal dialogue across boundaries. The Assamese culture and literature witnessed a revolutionary change after the advent of these two great saints – Ajan Peer and Sankardeva. Ajan Peer had similar contribution towards the culture and literature of the State, like Sankardeva, who was not only a religious preacher but also a philosopher, litterateur, social mobiliser and a playwright. One can see that due to the influence of these two great saints, the culture and society of Assam got a momentum which helped transform the narrow-minded attitudes of people. Places like Bordoa, Poamakka of

Hajo, Bordoa and Saraguri Sapori are holy places to all the people living in Assam, belonging to different castes, creeds and religion.

Today, in the changed scenario where the 'political person' is valued only as a number in the political vote bank, people look for contracts and political accords that, they feel, should address the fears and apprehensions of the minorities or of majorities. At this moment, people who call themselves Assamese are facing a political question to define themselves, that is to say, to decide who they are. The Assamese people find themselves in a political situation in which they are required to propose a definition to mark their identity, although they are a part of the greater Indian nation and the nation-state accepts that they have a language, geographical location, a culture and a literature contributing to the multicultural ethos of the nation. Although the political person's dilemma of finding herself pulled between Indian nationalism and Assamese nationalism is a modern manifestation, it usually reflects the agony of a historically affected consciousness that looks for socio-political solutions to some of the existential problem.

If we have once succeeded in bringing our faith in all its fullness and integrity to the table of dialogue, that is a sign that people are not mere political and economic beings. We need to come together at the deepest level of our humanity. Religious experience, further, is that experience the significance of which refers to the whole. It can therefore never be understood from the standpoint merely of the moment, but only and always from that of eternity. Ajan Peer was a symbol of unity, social harmony and non-violence like Srimanta Sankardeva. Empathy, patience and greatness of human society were reflected in his writings. *Mor monot aan bhab nai o Allah, Mor monot bhin par nai o Allah, Hindu ki Musalman, Ekei Allahr farman, Mor monot eketi bhab.* ('In my mind, Oh dear Allah, I have no different thought, Hindus and Muslims are bounded by the same act of divine rules of Allah.') The religious person takes into account the whole context that provides meaning to the distinct horizons of political-social or economic person. Its meaning is an ultimate meaning and is conceived with the 'last things' in perspective. Its nature is eschatological, and transcends itself; while for a person it implies an ultimate, a boundary, a horizon of some sort. It touches humanity in its innermost core, in the mysteries of birth and death and in one's aspirations for transcending boundaries in an eternal lust for life and for meaning even within this realm of sheer meaninglessness. The truth is simple and bold: '*Gorethane kabar sari sari,Hinduk puribo Mominal garibo*' ('The act of cremating a Hindu and the entombing of a Muslim only signify one end – death for all.') (Borah 2006) This is the common lot of one and all, the same divine law is applicable to the living and the non-living: *'kukura gadarbha srigaloro atma Ram, Jania sabake Hari kariba parnam'* (Sankaradeva)'. Horizons might function as a limit at a particular time, but there are always also gateways to something beyond; it is the latter that Husserl emphasized in his 1913 *Ideas*: "the horizon is everything we are aware of in the perception of an object above and beyond what is given directly to our senses". (Quoted in Gadamer 1988: 270).

References

Ahmed, Sabi (1992) "Opinion", *Purbanchal: View point,* AXOM http://purbanchal.forumup.com/post-1861-purbanchal.html. (Accessed in November 2006).

Borah, Utpola (2006) "Zikir and Zari: Sufi songs of Assam", POSOOWA (accessed December 2006).

Deka, H.K. (2006) *Assamese Mind,* In www.assamnet.org/pipermail/assam_assamnet.org/2006-June/006689.html - 38k9.i (accessed in May 2006).

Dutta, Amaresh (1989) "Poetry, Religion and Culture", *The Indian Perspective and Sankaradeva*, Vol.1, p.10-16.

Gadamer, H. G. (1988) "The Principle of Effective History" In K. Mueller-Vollmer ed., *The Hermeneutics Reader: Texts of the German Tradition from the Enlightenment to the Present,* Continuum International Publishing Group, London, pp.267-273.

Malik, Syad Abdul (1966) *Ajan Fakir and His Melodious Jikir*, Student' Store, Guwahati.

Murdoch, Iris (1987) *The Bell*, Penguin, Harmondsworth.

Neog, Dimbeswar (1965) *New Light on the History of Asmiya Literature*, Lawyers Bookstall, Gauhati.

19

Negotiating Religious Discourses Towards Peace: A Philosophical Perspective

Akoijam Thoibisana & V. Prabhu

Peace has been the most crucial issue of human existence from the very beginning. And in this era of globalized, pluralistic social setup it has become all the more important. Out of the very many factors that instigate violence in this world, religion is one prominent factor. It is very evident that some of the conflicts in our society are primarily due to religion, more so in a country like India, where religion plays a major part in everybody's life. Religious practices and beliefs have often been at the center of conflicts throughout history. Take for example, the Ayodhya-Babri Masjid issue – the sectarian tensions in the north Indian town of Ayodhya have a history dating back to more than 400 years. In 1528 a mosque was built on the site where some Hindus say, Lord Rama, one of the most revered deities in Hinduism, was born. In 1992 that mosque was torn down by a mob of Hindu extremists, many using crowbars or just their bare hands. The demolition sparked religious riots across the country in which more than 2,000 people died. Dozens of temples and mosques were targeted in a series of revenge attacks by Hindu and Muslim mobs. The violence that emanated saw some of worst episodes of communal carnage since the bloody clashes that accompanied partition following independence in 1947. Again, India and Pakistan have been involved in conflict since the creation of their respective nations and religion was at the core of this conflict. After the end of British rule and the assassination of Mahatma Gandhi, the followers of Hinduism and

Islam turned upon one another. India, led by Jawaharlal Nehru could not satisfy its Muslim citizens concerning representation in government. Therefore, the Muslims of India broke away and formed the nation of Pakistan. Outside India, examples can be cited like the conflict for the "Holy land" of Jerusalem, with more then 50 years of fighting in a volatile and religiously sensitive region claimed by both Israel and Palestine. The conflict has grown more and more violent by the day with the Palestinian fundamentalists using suicide bombers, and the Israeli government fighting back with its nuclear army, creating one of the most volatile regions on earth. Further a series of wars were fought between the Jewish state of Israel and the various surrounding Islamic states. Religion was the core issue, while political and economic contentions made the wars to have a global significance. In all the cases we find conflict that is rooted in religion. In short, we see that people hold religion as something, which is worth fighting for. Religious beliefs are so deeply engrained in cultures that conflicts arise with change or when different religions come into contact with each other. However, possibly one of the greatest ironies is that religious conflict usually goes against the teachings of the religions. All religions teach promotion of faith that includes good will and peace. Nevertheless, religious sentiments take tremendous proportion in war and violence to justify and defend religious faith. Such a view is inconsistent.

As aspirants of philosophy, how we can look at this situation. Philosophy is not just one abstract subject preoccupied with some lofty thoughts. Philosophy, by the merit of its subject content is closely associated with religion. Religion and philosophy have always been interacting with each other throughout, for there is always a mutual influence of one domain over the other. Bertrand Russell remarks in his *A History of Western Philosophy*: "Philosophy, as I shall understand the word, is something intermediary between theology and science". (Russell 1961: xiii) Philosophers for centuries have been concerned about religion, for there is always a mutual influence of one domain over the other, since both talk about the same issues but appealing to different faculty. All theoretical concerns are the outcome of practical necessities. Religion and philosophy have always been interacting with each other throughout. We need suitable theories that promote peace in the practice of religion, either at personal level or at social levels and philosophers were trying to understand the foundations of such practices along with providing, sometimes norms on how to understand and practice religion. Here, we shall see how philosophers' views can give us a theoretical base to understand/practice religion much beyond the present paradigm, which invariably leads to religious conflicts.

Why there is religious conflict? Solution to this conflict is the paramount question for us. One of the major causes for such conflicts can be identified as the belief of the adherents of particular religions that religious events can be evidenced by scientific/ historical proofs. Our two examples of the Ayodhya-Babri Masjid issue and the Arab-Israeli conflict have their basis in such a belief. As long as the religious community is homogeneous, this issue may not be a problem. However, when the issue comes up in a heterogeneous society where pluralism is deep-rooted, we face conflicts arising on account of the aforesaid reason. Is it possible to be a religious believer without claiming that religious events can be evidenced by scientific or historical proofs? Can we have an alternative paradigm for a believer in a pluralistic context?

If we can get rid of the claim of evidence for religious events, and still ensure that one can lead a religious life, then, much of the problems could be resolved. In this paper, hence, an attempt is made to give a philosophical rationale, basing mainly on the views of Ludwig Wittgenstein. Our aim is to provide an alternative paradigm, within which religion could be practiced without claiming to have scientific or historical proofs for religious events.

Ludwig Wittgenstein (1889-1951)

Wittgenstein reminds us that a religious truth must not be confused with a historical one. Referring to Christianity he says:

> Christianity is not based on a historical truth; rather, it offers us a (historical) narrative and says; now believe! But not, believe this narrative with the belief appropriate to a historical narrative, rather: believe, through thick and thin, which you can do only as a result of a life. Here you have a narrative, don't take the same attitude to it as you take to other historical narratives! Make a quite different place in your life for it. There is nothing paradoxical about that! (Wittgenstein 1980: 32)

The point that Wittgenstein tries to drive home is that the (historical) narrative about the life of the Christ cannot be equated with the historical narrative about the life of Caesar or Napoleon. A historical narrative enhances one's knowledge of history. Thus it deals with a historical fact. On the contrary, a religious narrative enhances one's faith in his/her religion. A believer unlike a historian is not concerned with any concrete facts of existence, rather in the value of a given religious narrative as a parable. See the similarity of the Ayodhya-Babri Masjid issue here. Wittgenstein tries to show that belief in a religion goes beyond the historical aspects of it. As he further points out: "A believer's relation to these narratives is neither the relation to historical truth (probability), nor yet that to a theory consisting of 'truths of reason'." (Wittgenstein 1980: 32). What is important here is the difference it makes to one's life when one comes across the narrative about the life of Jesus as a saviour.

As a supplement to what Wittgenstein maintains, Phillips opines that religious truths are neither scientific nor metaphorical in nature. They belong altogether to a different category. According to him, it is an error to force religious belief into any one of the two standard alternatives, namely, empirical propositions or human attitudes. (Phillips 1970: 111-12).

Believers and nonbelievers cannot contradict one another because they do not share the same 'form of life.' For Wittgenstein a 'form of life' is the ground upon which actions prevail. It is the ultimate substratum that supports a particular way of acting or performing. A form of life is the final point and is beyond explanations and arguments. It is the ground upon which every argument is based. Forms of life form the common ground between two different individuals or communities who share the same mode of life. Here, in the case of religion, it is not the case that the believers and nonbelievers disagree with each other about some proposition within a given form of life. They appear to refute each other's claim because they express different opinions about the same thing from different forms of life. Such a refusal is different from contradicting one another. For instance, as an atheist or a nonbeliever one does not credit anything to God.

If someone says 'God is wise' we are entitled to presume that he thinks God exists; but, by the same token, if 'God is not wise' is intended as a contradiction, we are entitled to assume that the speaker also takes God to exist. The essential difference between believers and unbelievers is not that sort of difference. It is that the unbeliever refuses to participate in the believers' form of life at all. (Hudson 1975: 175).

Wittgenstein uses the word 'false science' to mean treating one's religious beliefs as science. Wittgenstein never tried to equate religious truths with scientific ones. And any such attempt to base one's religious foundations in terms of scientific understanding will only lead to religious superstitions. In other words, science cannot be used as a yardstick to justify a religious belief. Wittgenstein's contention is that since religion and science belong to two different forms of life they have their own rational justification. For Wittgenstein, religious activity and scientific activity are two different language-games and belong to different forms of life. For example, the terms 'evidence', 'certainty', 'proof' etc., do not have the same meanings when used in scientific parlance and in religious discourses. To explain one form of life (religion) in terms of another (science) is to lead to confusions, problems and loss of faith in that particular form of life. To treat one's religious beliefs as 'science' is neither convincing nor possible even. "In a religious discourse we use such expressions as: 'I believe that so and so will happen,' and use them differently to the way in which we use them in science." (Wittgenstein 1967: 57).

From the above position, what we try to show is that there is a scope for religious practices, beliefs and understanding that go beyond the paradigm formulated in our introduction. That paradigm is a constant stimulus for religious conflicts. If, as shown, religion could be practiced beyond this paradigm, then, it shall give us more scope for peace and harmony.

Peace is undeniably the highest value of our age and to promote peace in our pluralistic socio-religious setup is our duty. Religion should be accepted as way to the promotion of peace. Peace becomes possible only when we do not try to equal religious truths with scientific or historical truths. They are visibly of different domains. Rather, we should develop an empathetic interpretation of the rich complexity of the religious phenomena. Such an approach to religious study and religious practices may be profitably employed as a helpful tool in practicing religion in a harmonious way, particularly in a pluralistic society like ours.

References

Hudson, W. Donald (1975) *Wittgenstein and Religious Belief*, The MacMillan Press Ltd., London.

Phillips, D. Z. (1970) *Faith and Philosophical Enquiry*, Routledge and Kegan Paul, London.

Russell, Bertrand (1946/1961) *A History of Western Philosophy*, Allen and Unwin, London.

Wittgenstein, Ludwig (1967) *Lectures and Conversations on Aesthetics, Psychology and Religious Belief*, C. Barrett, ed., University of California Press, California.

Wittgenstein, Ludwig (1980) *Culture and Value*, G.H. Von Wright, ed., London.

Online Sources Used

Ayodhya

http://edition.cnn.com/2002/WORLD/asiapcf/south/12/06/ayodhya.background/

http://annalysis.blogspot.com/2006/12/petition-on-muslim-womens-dress.html

Religious Conflict

http://regentsprep.org/regents/global/themes/conflict/religious.cfm

Reverend Sun Myung Moon's Philosophy of Peace

http://www.unification.org/ucbooks/PhilofPeace/PhilosophyPeace.html

20

*Rissho Ankoku Ron**: Some Parallels between 13th Century Japan and the Present Crisis in Northeast India

Rahul Jain

The urge for peace has been one of the foremost, nay, the foremost urge of humankind, ever since the humans first came to be in the world. In fact, the hitherto understood primary urges – food, clothing and shelter – have all been there to secure peace to them from the pangs of hunger, from the onslaught of the winds and the sun, and the insecurity of an address called home. If we just take a cursory look at the period of recorded and orally-transmitted history, we find peace missing for all these millennia, save in patches. Naturally, the questions that arise are: What has gone wrong? Why has this most fundamental of desires not been accomplished all these years, despite tremendous surge wrought by human beings in all possible conceivable direction?

Though a sweeping conclusion is beyond the scope of this brief paper, it will suffice to say that humanity's mere semantic understanding of peace has got a lot to do with this impasse. Peace, more often than not, has been understood as an interlude between wars, and not as a dominant state of existence of a society or a country. It is not a static state but has to be understood as "the tension between a precarious equilibrium and the constant dynamic of its re-establishment". This means, we need to be constantly on our toe, so

* '*Rissho Ankoku Ron*' in Japanese means 'securing the peace of the land through the propagation of true Buddhism'.

as to ensure the continuance of this equilibrium. Sadly, history has paid scant regard to this, and hence the situation. However, this is not to say that peace is a permanent state; far from it, I would venture to say that peace is one of the life conditions of the society that we live in.

The Buddhism of Nichiren Daishonin, a thirteenth century Japanese sage and priest, states that a human being possesses ten life conditions in one single moment, the highest being Buddhahood, the lowest being Hell. We, as human beings, or our lives, continue to oscillate among these ten conditions. But through our continuous efforts (In a Buddhist's case, his prayers and action), we can, for a majority of the times, stay in the higher life conditions of Learning, Realization, Boddhisattvahood and Buddhahood. However, a drop in guard will bring us to the lower four worlds of Hell, Hunger, Animality and Anger. This is the same with the world in general. Actions on the part of a great majority have kept societies in the lower four worlds ever since human beings first made into this world, and it is here that Nichiren's Buddhism comes into play. If the world practices the true religion as suggested by the Daishonin, that is, respect to the fundamental laws of the universe by discarding shallow and incomplete philosophies of life, peace will be the most dominant condition. Yes, it will be interspersed with tensions and conflicts now and then.

Nichiren Daishonin, in his most important treatise, *Rissho Ankoku Ron* (On Establishing the Correct Teaching for the Peace of the Land), has highlighted the socio-political condition of Japan in the thirteenth century. The Japanese were facing the proverbial three great calamities and seven disasters, as had been predicted by Shakyamuni (Gautama Buddha) in his most profound work, *Lotus Sutra*, because of the fact that the 'True Law' was being violated there. What is quite remarkable is that the twenty-first century Northeast is almost facing similar threats. Of course, conditions vary.

Historical Background

Nominally under the rule of emperors since the end of twelfth century, Japan was being controlled by a set of de facto military rulers, the *shoguns*. Based in Kamakura, a city on the east coast of Japan near modern day Tokyo, the Shogunate was dominated by just one family, the Hojo, who exercised power by acting as regents to a succession of puppet emperors. Beginning from the thirteenth century, Japan suffered from a series of unprecedented disasters – earthquakes, epidemics, unseasoned typhoons, fires, flood, drought and famine. They all seemed to have robbed the Japanese of hope and security. People were of the opinion that Shakyamuni's prediction regarding the beginning of the evil Latter Day of the Law has come true. There were all-round conflict, confusion and suffering.

The Shogunate, feeling helpless, turned to the religious leaders for solution but in vain. The priesthood was racked with bitter, and sometimes, violent infighting which were not over doctrines but property rights and prestige. They had completely forgotten the basic spirit of compassion underpinning all Buddhist teachings. Rather than guarding the precepts, they took to violence for guarding their lands, and had, in fact, degenerated into wealthy elites.

Coincidentally, the papacy in Rome was also passing through a similar stage then. Even when Hojo Tokiyori retired as regent, early in his life in 1256 (age 30), and went to live as a lay priest at a Zen temple, he continued to wield enormous influence and was widely considered the de facto ruler of Japan, till his death in 1263 (37 years). Because the Hojo clan had founded a number of temples, the head priests were subject to the whims of their patron, irrespective of the teachings of their respective doctrines. All in all, the religious and secular authorities of the day proved incapable of offering wise leadership to the Japanese people during the period of their continual suffering.

Parallels between Thirteenth Century Japan and Twenty-first Century North-east

We can find many parallels as to what had prevailed in Japan then and what is going on in the North-east now. Successive governments in the north-eastern States continue to violate, with no remorse, the dignity of life of individuals. Though Japan had a de facto military rule in the thirteenth century compared to the democratic form of governance prevailing in the north-eastern States now, serious questions can and are being raised on the genuineness of the democracy in the region. The number of Acts authorizing free hand to the military and the Army in the name of bringing democracy to the people of the region, and the way in which a handful of ministers, bureaucrats and hawks at the Centre are running the show can put even the Orwellian definition of equality to shame. The infighting, which had characterized the priesthood in Japan, is now characterizing our body politic and civil society. This has given New Delhi enough opportunity to play a major role in the overall governance of the region, thereby resulting in weakened and powerless State Governments, which look up towards the north for all possible solutions. This has also resulted in in-fighting and sycophancy among the ruling class.

The parallel can also be extended to the role played by civil society groups and intellectuals. These groups, to corner a fair share for itself, have never been vociferous in its avowed mission. If the priesthood fought for land, property and honours, intellectuals, university professors, teachers, NGOs in the Northeast, barring exceptions, are no better. Allotment of land, desire for plum postings, honours and awards have all prevented these groups from playing their role effectively. For the priests in Japan, acquiescence to authority was a convenient way to escape persecution because it guaranteed their survival and prosperity at the cost of peace, justice and happiness of their followers. The actors are changed in the North-east, but sadly the script remains unchanged. The thirteenth century civil society (secular authority) in Japan failed to do anything to ameliorate the conditions of the masses, and that history is being repeated as tragedy in the Northeast.

What all these have done is to weaken the spirit of the people as was the case in Japan. A Buddhist sutra reads, "When a nation becomes disordered, it is the spirit that first shows signs of rampancy". Likewise, just as the Nembutsu sect's chant made matters worse for the Japanese, the hoarse cry for peace by political and social representatives, akin to a melancholic drone, is doing our region more harm. It is in the backdrop of these that we need to understand the *Rissho Ankoku Ron.*

And let us not miss the signs on the horizon after having witnessed an unprecedented drought-like situation in Assam and the extreme (by Northeast's standard) hot and cold weather during summer and the passing winter season.

Understanding *Rissho Ankoku Ron*

It is worthwhile to remember that *Rissho Ankoku Ron* was written in the form of a dialogue between the host (Nichiren) and his guest (Hojo Tokiyori) wherein the host answers nine questions put by his guest. It opens with the following opening lines, spoken in sorrow, by the guest:

> "In recent years, there are unusual disturbances in the heavens, strange occurrence on earth, famine and pestilence, all affecting every corner of the empire and spreading throughout the land. Oxens and horses lie dead in the streets, the bones of the stricken crowd the highways. Over half the population has already been carried off by death, and in every family, someone grieves."

He continues, "Despite the fact that the Buddhist temples are offering prayers, and the government is doing what it can do to help the people," the guest notes, "Famine and epidemics rage more fiercely than ever, beggars are everywhere in sight, and scenes of death fill our eyes. What is wrong? What error has been committed?"

Nichiren had studied the matter and other Buddhist scriptures for two years before drawing his conclusion and submitting the treatise to Hojo Tokiyori in 1260. He cited passages after passages to prove the veracity of his studies and that of his claim that erroneous and slanderous teachings in the realm of religion inevitably invite disasters in the external world. He forthrightly states, "The people of today all turn their backs on what is right; to a man, they give their allegiance to evil."

On the face of it, rationalists would be willing to brand this as mysticism or superstition. But it is important to pause and ponder as to what Nichiren seeks to convey through this statement of his.

The causality theory of Buddhism clearly states that the quickest way to create the karma, to experience suffering is to 'slander the True Law'. This is the cornerstone of Buddhist philosophy. However, among all other sutras, only the *Lotus Sutra*, explains clearly what it means by 'Slandering the True Law'. In strict doctrinal terms, it had then meant the failure of the priests and masses to recognize the *Lotus Sutra* as Shakyamuni's highest teaching and instead follow his earlier provisional and incomplete teachings. It is the only *sutra* that expounds the law that enables people to attain enlightenment. This is one reason why Nichiren was so critical of the various Buddhist sects of his day. One of the sects – Nembutsu – was particularly responsible in peddling escapism and encouraging apathy, while the need of the hour was the fortification of people's will to face and overcome their sufferings by reforming their own lives.

This is not doctrinal nitpicking but a clear enunciation of what Shakyamuni himself laid down in other sutras of his, wherein he describes in some detail the dire consequences of slandering the 'True Law'. They were the Three Calamities and Seven Disasters. The Three Calamities are high grain prices (inflation), warfare (low intensity conflict, insurgency) and pestilence (psychological or physical disruption), while the Seven Disasters are disease and pestilence, external invasion, plunder and internal revolts, strange heavenly occurrences among the stars and constellations, solar and lunar eclipses, unseasonable wind and rain, and unseasonable drought.

Nichiren explains in the *Rissho Ankoku Ron* that the impending catastrophes were not metaphoric in nature but were the result of the strict law of cause and effect. That is to say, when the true teachings of Buddhism are obscured or disregarded, resulting in the life force of the people being sapped through apathy and resignation to their fate (cause), the Three Calamities and Seven Disasters must appear (effect), since the people are no longer 'feeding' the protective force of the universe with the power of their positive impulses. He also argues that internal revolt and foreign invasion, which Japan had not seen till then, were bound to happen. Subsequent events showed that he was spot on.

In purely historical terms, the Daishonin was warning Hojo Tokiyori that unless the secular authorities stopped supporting sects based on teachings other than the Lotus Sutra, civil war and foreign invasion were on the horizon. Though Hojo Tokiyori never responded to this remonstration, but the submission of this treatise marked the beginning of a series of persecution for Nichiren Daishonin from vested interests.

Contemporary Relevance of *Rissho Ankoku Ron*

Now, how does *Rissho Ankoku Ron* apply to our times? Is not history a witness to all ups and downs of people, power and places occurring with relentless regularity? Even, calamities and disasters have occurred everywhere in all ages, regardless of the religion people practice. That is, how is one's belief related to the physical world? What about those who have not yet heard of the "True Law"? How are they related to it, even though we all know they are not Buddhist or are yet to encounter Buddhism? All these naturally invite the temptation of dismissing the above as irrational. However, we would do well to dig deep into the concept of Three Calamities and Seven Disasters discussed earlier.

The three calamities – inflation, civil war and insurgency and physical and psychological disruptions – are sufferings occurring in the three realms – natural environment, living beings and the five components that fuse temporarily in each individual's life. The five components are form, perception, conception, volition and consciousness. A life-form appears only when the five components come together harmoniously within the life entity. Any disharmony results in the disappearance of the life form. Form indicates life's physical aspect – the body. The other four components relate to life's spiritual aspect. In one sense, both the physical and spiritual aspects of life are inseparable. One cannot have a life form without these two aspects or the five components.

This is to say, Buddhism teaches that the three calamities are the result of disharmony in the realms of nature, human society and the self, and in effect, represent all the catastrophes that threaten the very basis of human survival. More simply put, if in the environment, grain becomes difficult to get due to any reason, we have the phenomenon of inflation; and when we have mutual antagonism among individuals and societies, there is this spectre of warfare; and when a sound body and mind cease to function in a harmonious way, the calamity of pestilence becomes visible.

This is no coincidence to find all the three occurring at the same time, and it needs no genius to find out that one is related to the other. In fact, very rarely we will find just one of these three calamities in an active state. The reason is simple: the three calamities represent the three poisons of greed, anger and stupidity arising from the worlds of Hunger, Anger and Animality (the lower worlds). All the three occur because of the fundamental darkness within human life. They are in fact its outward manifestation. We can relate higher grain price (Inflation) to greed. That is to say that a strong state of Hunger creates fundamental distortion in the economy. If the inherent greed is not satisfied, the cycle will continue. Similarly, warfare is caused by the state of Anger, where one side alone feels that it is right. Hunger leads to war and vice versa. The state of Anger is then manifested in war. However, it is the stupidity or ignorance of people associated with Animality that brings in the calamity of pestilence. It is because people do not know how to live a balanced life that they become 'ill'. It means absence of adequate physical and spiritual nourishment. Once this can be ensured, one will be able to exercise good judgment that will perpetuate one's general well-being. This idea is further related to the Buddhist principle of *shikishin funi*, or the inseparability of body and mind.

The three poisons of greed, anger and stupidity combine to form the world of Hell. Another question that begets an explanation is: How are human beings and natural disasters such as earthquakes related? The highest teaching of Buddhism perceives a connection between human activity and even these apparently random events. The principal of *Ichinen Sanzen* says that the environment possesses not only physical appearance but also unseen spiritual qualities (such as perceived by poets like Wordsworth, Hardy, et al), and so it is subject to the law of cause and effect. The implication of this is that even the inanimate objective world – the 'land' – possesses karma. The concept of *esho funi* – the inseparability of life and its environment – literally means that, at root, the karma of an individual life is identical to that of its physical environment. Buddhism also explains that our prior actions (karma) have a significant bearing on us, and our external circumstances. This explains why one is born into a particular circumstance; therefore, formation of one's environment coincides with one's emergence into the world.

In the light of this explanation, we can see that natural disasters are not punishments for sinful acts, but manifestation of one's karma. Whereas we create karma for suffering because of the three poisons of greed, anger and stupidity, we can also create karma to alleviate the effects of our bad karma, even from this very moment.

What Nichiren pointed out was that because the diagnosis of the sufferings of thirteenth century Japan was wrong, the treatment had to be naturally wrong, and therefore sufferings would exacerbate.

In the modern day, slander of the 'True Law' means using other provisional means to attain peace and security in this land, without the attempt to develop one's own life-condition (i.e. Buddhahood). Nichiren Daishonin teaches that valuing anything above the inherent dignity of all life, ultimately leads to unhappiness for individuals, injustices in society (usually emanating from bad government) and disharmony in nature.

Lessons from the *Rissho Ankoku Ron* with Special Focus on the Northeast

The fact that *Rissho Ankoku Ron* is written in the form of a dialogue makes it very pertinent for us to understand the significance of dialogue in resolving conflict, both within and without. Another feature that stands out in the *Rissho Ankoku Ron* is that both the guest and host were depicted in a one-to-one situation, thereby implying that for any conflict to be resolved, the conflicting parties must sit across each other to chart out a solution. There is a lesson for the ULFA leadership here. They are attempting to eke out a solution through third party mediation, which clearly is not working. It must do away with this approach and instead join the process of dialogue directly.

The other issue that draws our immediate attention is doubts and questions being placed or expressed in a free and forthright manner by the guest, and the Daishonin's willingness to answer them. The lesson is: Let the aggrieved party put forth all its doubts on the negotiating table and the government be willing to solve them for the sake of peace. In this context, the ULFA's demand for sovereignty should be put up for negotiation. The Centre must be in a position to convince the ULFA leadership to see the light behind its decision of not allowing sovereignty. But this can be done only after a genuine round of dialogue. There should not be any pre-condition, whatsoever, at least from the one who is more strongly placed. A change of heart during negotiation process is more likely than before it. The NSCN-Centre negotiation process is something worth following. All cards are on the table to be discussed. The result, however, is a different pair of shoes.

The other significant message from the treatise is the personality and honesty of Nichiren. He was a man who did his homework for two years, contemplated all issues and reached his conclusion only after brooding over all alternatives. Once he did that, he was fearless. He knew what was in store for him once he submitted his treatise, but never for a moment was he hesitant. This was because he had people's welfare foremost on his mind. His entire treatise was people-centric. Even the government of the day offered Nichiren with a temple, provided he prayed for the nation's protection and safety. Had he wanted to ingratiate himself with the political authorities, there would surely have been no better opportunity. However, Nichiren refused the offer point blank.

Do we have such persons or personalities amidst us? Are our peace-brokers men of integrity with people's welfare foremost on their minds? Are not they headline-and sound-byte-crazy? No wonder, negotiations are not making any headway in a majority of cases. Very recently, the Dalai Lama offered himself as a mediator to bring peace in the region. Can we not construe this as a sign that the revered leader was not at all confident of the ability of our negotiators to bring peace to this land?

The treatise also highlights the nexus between religious and secular authorities in Japan. It puts the blame of moral decay in society on this nexus. In Northeast India, the politician-bureaucratic-contractor complex is too well known to merit repetition. Hence, there is all-round decay in the social and moral fabric of the region, which is the root cause of all troubles afflicting us.

The Daishonin, in his treatise, clearly highlighted that the result visible in Japan then were because of the strict law of cause and effect. This means, events are not of their own creation, and they clearly are manifestation of an underlying cause or action. Those who are familiar with the Madhyamika (Middle Way) School of Buddhist Philosophy would realize this as part of the concept of Dependent Origination, which states that things and events come because of three different ways – principle of cause and effect, mutual dependence between parts and whole, and that any phenomena lack independent identity.

Finally, the Daishonin, in his treatise, urges Hojo Tokiyori to respect the true Buddhist teaching, the 'True Law'. He also states that because of false teachings, people's spirit has been sapped of all energy, and it has become rampant. The Daishonin cites a passage wherein Shakyamuni states that those monks and nuns, laymen or women, who speak carelessly and evil words, and slander the correct teaching, and who continue to do so without repentance are causing peace to disappear from the land. Almost towards the end of the treatise, when the guest is convinced of the host's explanation, the Daishonin assures him that if respect for the true law is established again, "the winds will blow gently, the waves will be calm, and in no time at all we will enjoy bountiful harvests." However, he suggests to his guest that he must quickly reform the tenets that he holds in his heart and embrace Lotus Sutra, and then his land will become the Buddha land.

Conclusion

In modern times, all these mean that we, human beings, must bring our own lives into a correct orbit. We must bring about our own human revolution, the development of our Buddhahood, which can lead to a lasting and secure happiness. Until we all learn to value the inherent dignity of life, peace will be a chimera.

As individuals, we must learn to live in rhythm with the ultimate truth of life, thus transforming the three poisons of greed, anger and stupidity in our lives into the great qualities of compassion, courage, wisdom and joy. As more and more people come to reveal their Buddha nature in this way, *ankoku* or peace of the land, will be secured.

However, the most important thing is to ensure that *ankoku* is secured first in our immediate environment – in our lives, in our families, and our work – and then it gradually moves out, like a series of small, overlapping ripples in a pond.

Glossary

Latter Day of the Law: Also, the Latter Day, the latter age, or the period of the Decadent Law. The last of the three periods following a Buddha's death, when Buddhism falls into confusion and his teachings lose the power to lead people to enlightenment. The Latter Day of the Law of Shakyamuni is said to last for ten thousand years or more. In

Japan, it was believed that the Latter Day had begun in 1052 A.D.

Lotus Sutra: A Mahayana sutra that reveals the true aspect of all phenomena and Shakyamuni's true identity as the Buddha who attained enlightenment numberless major world system dust particle *kalpa*s ago. One of the most popular Buddhist scriptures, it maintains that all people can attain Buddhahood.

Buddhahood: Also referred to by the word enlightenment. The supreme state of life in Buddhism, characterized by boundless wisdom and compassion. In this state, one is awakened to the eternal and ultimate truth that is the reality of all things. Buddhahood is regarded as the goal of Buddhist practice and the highest of the Ten Worlds.

Nembutsu Sect: A Japanese term generally meaning 'to meditate or invoke his name'. The practice of adherents of the Pure Land school. It was stressed as the means by which one could attain rebirth in the Pure Land of Amida Buddha. The term is also used to refer to the Pure Land school itself. It taught that it was impossible for people to change their unhappy state in this impure world but that, by calling on the legendary Amida Buddha, through his grace one could be reborn after death in a far-off 'pure land' of bliss — the Western paradise — over which Amida was sovereign.

Index